TONI MORRISON'S FICTION
Revised and Expanded Edition

UNDERSTANDING CONTEMPORARY AMERICAN LITERATURE
Matthew J. Bruccoli, Founding Editor
Linda Wagner-Martin, Series Editor

Volumes on

Edward Albee | Sherman Alexie | Nelson Algren | Paul Auster
Nicholson Baker | John Barth | Donald Barthelme | The Beats
Thomas Berger | The Black Mountain Poets | Robert Bly | T. C. Boyle
Truman Capote | Raymond Carver | Michael Chabon | Fred Chappell
Chicano Literature | Contemporary American Drama
Contemporary American Horror Fiction
Contemporary American Literary Theory
Contemporary American Science Fiction, 1926–1970
Contemporary American Science Fiction, 1970–2000
Contemporary Chicana Literature | Robert Coover | Philip K. Dick
James Dickey | E. L. Doctorow | Rita Dove | John Gardner | George Garrett
Tim Gautreaux | John Hawkes | Joseph Heller | Lillian Hellman | Beth Henley
James Leo Herlihy | David Henry Hwang | John Irving | Randall Jarrell
Charles Johnson | Diane Johnson | Adrienne Kennedy | William Kennedy
Jack Kerouac | Jamaica Kincaid | Etheridge Knight | Tony Kushner
Ursula K. Le Guin | Denise Levertov | Bernard Malamud | David Mamet
Bobbie Ann Mason | Colum McCann | Cormac McCarthy | Jill McCorkle
Carson McCullers | W. S. Merwin | Arthur Miller | Stephen Millhauser
Lorrie Moore | Toni Morrison's Fiction | Vladimir Nabokov | Gloria Naylor
Joyce Carol Oates | Tim O'Brien | Flannery O'Connor | Cynthia Ozick
Suzan-Lori Parks | Walker Percy | Katherine Anne Porter | Richard Powers
Reynolds Price | Annie Proulx | Thomas Pynchon | Theodore Roethke
Philip Roth | May Sarton | Hubert Selby, Jr. | Mary Lee Settle | Sam Shepard
Neil Simon | Isaac Bashevis Singer | Jane Smiley | Gary Snyder | William Stafford
Robert Stone | Anne Tyler | Gerald Vizenor | Kurt Vonnegut
David Foster Wallace | Robert Penn Warren | James Welch | Eudora Welty
Edmund White | Tennessee Williams | August Wilson | Charles Wright

TONI MORRISON'S FICTION

Revised and Expanded Edition

Jan Furman

The University of South Carolina Press

© 1996 University of South Carolina
New material © 2014 University of South Carolina

Published by the University of South Carolina Press
Columbia, South Carolina 29208

www.sc.edu/uscpress

Manufactured in the United States of America

23 22 21 20 19 18 17 16 15 14   10 9 8 7 6 5 4 3 2 1

Library of Congress Cataloging-in-Publication Data

Furman, Jan.
  Toni Morrison's fiction / Jan Furman. — Revised and expanded edition.
      pages cm. — (Understanding contemporary American literature)
  Includes bibliographical references and index.
      ISBN 978-1-61117-366-6 (pbk. : alk. paper) — ISBN 978-1-61117-367-3 (ebook)
  1. Morrison, Toni—Criticism and interpretation. 2. Women and literature—
United States—History—20th century. 3. African American women in literature.
4. African Americans in literature. I. Title.
  PS3563.O8749Z65 2014
  813'.54—dc23
                                                                    2013036703

For the girls

CONTENTS

SERIES EDITOR'S PREFACE

The Understanding Contemporary American Literature series was founded by the estimable Matthew J. Bruccoli (1931–2008), who envisioned these volumes as guides or companions for students as well as good nonacademic readers, a legacy that will continue as new volumes are developed to fill in gaps among the nearly one hundred series volumes published to date and to embrace a host of new writers only now making their marks on our literature.

As Professor Bruccoli explained in his preface to the volumes he edited, because much influential contemporary literature makes special demands, "the word understanding in the titles was chosen deliberately. Many willing readers lack an adequate understanding of how contemporary literature works; that is, of what the author is attempting to express and the means by which it is conveyed." Aimed at fostering this understanding of good literature and good writers, the criticism and analysis in the series provide instruction in how to read certain contemporary writers—explicating their material, language, structures, themes, and perspectives—and facilitate a more profitable experience of the works under discussion.

In the twenty-first century Professor Bruccoli's prescience gives us an avenue to publish expert critiques of significant contemporary American writing. The series continues to map the literary landscape and to provide both instruction and enjoyment. Future volumes will seek to introduce new voices alongside canonized favorites, to chronicle the changing literature of our times, and to remain, as Professor Bruccoli conceived, contemporary in the best sense of the word.

Linda Wagner-Martin, Series Editor

PREFACE

Since the publication of *Toni Morrison's Fiction* in 1996, Morrison has written four novels. These novels, primarily, are the focus of this revised commentary. Discussion of earlier books is largely unchanged, and four new chapters offer readings of the texts and multiple contexts. That is not to suggest that there is not a correspondence between the older and newer books. Eliot is correct in observing that

> what happens when a new work of art is created is something that happens simultaneously to all the works of art which preceded it. The existing monuments form an ideal order among themselves, which is modified by the introduction of the new (the really new) work of art among them. The existing order is complete before the new work arrives; for order to persist after the supervention of novelty, the *whole* existing order must be, if ever so slightly, altered; and so the relations, proportions, values of each work of art toward the whole are readjusted; and this is conformity between the old and the new.[1]

This matter of alteration of the whole by the new is addressed in a revised, although not substantially changed introduction, and the added chapters inevitably acknowledge conversation among the novels.

And yet the impetus for all the chapters here is exploring Morrison's aims for each book project as these relate to voice, narrative structure, historical context, thematic focus, and pedagogy. The novels are problem sets for Morrison, "a way of sustained problematizing."[2] As she says, "writing [each novel] for me is an enormous act of discovery. I have all these problems that are perhaps a little weary and general and well-worked-over that I want to domesticate and conquer. Then I can sort of figure out what I think about all this and get a little further along" (136).

CHAPTER 1

Understanding Toni Morrison

In a writing life that spans more than four decades, Toni Morrison has produced ten novels, a significant book of literary criticism, two plays, two edited essay volumes on sociopolitical themes, a libretto, lyrics for two productions of song cycles performed by the American operatic soprano Jessye Norman and another song collection performed by the American soprano Kathleen Battle. She has coauthored nine children's books, published numerous essays on literature and culture, and played an international role in supporting and encouraging art and artists. Morrison is also a poet and public intellectual.[1] Hers is the "dancing mind," a term Morrison uses to describe "the dance of an open mind when it engages another equally open mind . . . most often in the reading/writing world we live in."[2]

The metaphor of an enlightened mind in dance form is taken from Morrison's acceptance speech for the Medal of Distinguished Contribution to American Letters at the 1996 National Book Awards. In her talk, Morrison recalled an encounter with a writer in Strasbourg, Germany, where they were both attending a meeting of the Parliament of Writers. At the end of one symposium, the writer approached Morrison with an impassioned plea for help. "They are shooting us [women writers] down in the street," she said. "You must help. . . . There isn't anybody else."[3] Morrison offered the story as a cautionary note for her audience and to insist in that particularly relevant setting that the writing/reading space must be free, "that no encroachment of private wealth, government control, or cultural expediency . . . [should] interfere with what gets written or published."[4] Language is agency for Morrison, and she champions its role in shaping creative possibilities.

Morrison was born Chloe Ardelia Wofford on February 18, 1931. The name Toni and its origin are the subject of some conjecture.[5] Morrison has said she changed her name in college because people found Chloe difficult to pronounce; as a "nickname" she adopted a version of St. Anthony, her baptismal name. When her first book was published, Morrison notes that she "called the publisher to say I put the wrong name. But it was too late. [The book] had already gone to the Library of Congress."[6] She adds that "Chloe is my sister's sister. She is my niece's aunt. She is a girl I know and private. It pleases me to have these two names. . . . It's useful for me. Toni Morrison is a kind of invention. A nice invention."[7]

Morrison grew up in Lorain, Ohio, a Lake Erie town of about forty-five thousand people,[8] with her parents, George and Ramah Wofford, an older sister, and two younger brothers. She left Lorain in 1949 to attend Howard University but revisits community as she experienced it growing up by locating many of her stories in Ohio and other parts of the Midwest. In 1953 she earned a B.A. in English at Howard and two years later an M.A. from Cornell University. After Cornell, Morrison went to Houston, where for two years she taught English at Texas Southern University before returning to Howard as an instructor (1957–64). During this seven-year interim she married Harold Morrison, a Jamaican-born architect and fellow faculty member. They had two sons, Harold Ford and Kevin Slade, before the marriage ended in divorce, in 1964, and Morrison moved to New York.[9] She worked there for a year as an editor at the textbook subsidiary of Random House in Syracuse before going to its trade division in New York City, where she remained until 1983. As senior editor at Random House, Morrison nourished the careers of several writers, including Toni Cade Bambara, Gayle Jones, Angela Davis, and Henry Dumas.

Morrison's literary honors include both the National Book Critics Circle Award and the American Academy and Institute of Arts and Letters Award for *Song of Solomon* (1977). *Beloved* (1987) won a Pulitzer Prize for fiction and in 2006 was selected by the *New York Times Book Review* as the best novel of the preceding twenty-five years. For her collective achievements Morrison was awarded the Nobel Prize for literature in 1993. In its statement the Swedish Academy praised her as one who, "in novels characterized by visionary force and poetic import, gives life to an essential aspect of American reality."[10] In 2012 President Barack Obama, celebrating Morrison as having "had an amazing impact on the world through her talent for writing books that touch us to our core," awarded her the nation's highest civilian honor, the Presidential Medal of Freedom.

Morrison has taught part-time at Yale University; the State University of New York, Purchase; Rutgers University; and Bard College. In 1984 she was named the Albert Schweitzer Professor of the Humanities at the State

University of New York, Albany. And from 1989 to 2006 she was the Robert F. Goheen Professor of the Humanities at Princeton University. A 1980 appointment to President Jimmy Carter's National Council of the Arts was followed a year later by election to the American Academy and Institute of Arts and Letters. Morrison has served as the curator for art exhibitions in New York and Paris, and she has presented her ideas in a variety of lectureships, including the Robert C. Tanner Lecture series at the University of Michigan (1988); the Massey Lectures at Harvard University (1990); the Condorcet Lecture, College de France (1994); the National Endowment for the Humanities' Jefferson Lectureship (1996); the United Nations Secretary-General's Lecture Series (2002); and the Amnesty International Lecture series (2012).[11] In 1992 Morrison became a founding member (collaborating with nine other Nobel Prize winners in various categories from peace to medicine to literature) of the Académie Universelle des Cultures. Founded by François Mitterrand, then president of France, and chaired by Elie Wiesel, the academy was conceived as a continuing and highly visible colloquy on global matters of intellectual freedom.

These achievements notwithstanding, Morrison's work has not always been received well by critics and readers. *The Bluest Eye* (1970), her first novel, was out of print by 1974, four years after its publication. (It has since been reprinted.) And before it won the Pulitzer, *Beloved* failed to win the National Book Award in 1987 as many expected. In protest forty-eight black writers published a letter in a *New York Times* advertisement suggesting that Morrison had been treated unjustly. Although her work has garnered praise in academic quarters, that praise has been qualified by those critics who have called her prose florid and self-indulgent[12] and by some readers who disparage a challenging style of narrative.

Morrison admits that she reads reviews of her books, but she says they do not determine the direction of her work, which is informed only by her experience as a woman and African American and by the ancient stories of African American community. Unfavorable commentary on her novels often, Morrison asserts, "evolve[s] out of [a lack of understanding] of the culture, the world, the given quality out of which I write."[13] Morrison measures success not by the estimates of her critics but rather by how well her books evoke the rhythms and cosmology of her people. "If anything I do," she says, "in the way of writing novels (or whatever I write) isn't about the village or the community or about you, then it is not about anything."[14]

Most of Morrison's readers seem to agree; her book sales have been in the millions, aided, no doubt, by Oprah Winfrey's selection of *The Bluest Eye*, *Sula* (1975), *Song of Solomon*, and *Paradise* (1998) for her book club. In this

and other populist cultural formats, Morrison's historical narratives have
spawned a complex and, often, thoughtful national conversation about the
black experience of humanity in America. And, in a different, *haute* aesthetic
forum, her fiction and literary criticism have contributed to an expansion and
redefinition of the American literary canon. At work on her eleventh novel,
Toni Morrison lives in Grand View-on-Hudson in Rockland County, New
York.

Morrison's fiction is both historical and timeless: settings and plots evoke
periods of American history, collectively unfolding over decades as the
eloquent, coherent rendering of an African American epic. The ten novels,
although not consecutively, span three centuries, beginning with the back
story of seventeenth-century pre-Enlightenment colonization and settlement
and ending during the mid-1990s in postintegration America. In between,
Morrison examines the black experience during slavery and Reconstruction,
through modernity and the Jazz Age, at midcentury and in the Jim Crow
period, and the two decades of civil protest that followed. Individually,
however, Morrison's books derive their power and meaning from particular
stories of human obsession and survival. Characters, while contextualized
by historical settings and plots, develop from the perverse conditions of their
archetypal humanness. For these characters, Morrison is especially interested
in the life-defining journey, the coming-of-age enterprise as men and women
inhabit a conventional social space within community but also the outlaw
space beyond.

Morrison has said that she writes the kind of books she wants to read,
suggesting that she chooses subjects that interest her and not necessarily
subjects that are popular with readers and publishers. Sociology, polemics,
explanation, faddish themes do not concern Morrison, who is aiming to
express a cultural legacy. She wants her novels to have an oral, effortless
quality, evoking the tribal storytelling tradition of the African griot, who
recites the legendary events of generations. Her characters, too, should have
a special essence: they should be ancestral and enduring. In pursuing this personal, artistic vision, Morrison creates extraordinary tales of human experience that a less independent writer would perhaps not attempt. This is not
to suggest that the only impetus for Morrison's fiction is self-gratification.
Such an assertion would ignore a vital dimension of her accomplishment:
enlightening her readers about themselves. In this context, Morrison's novels
are not just art for art's sake; they are political as well. In fact, "the best art is
political," she says, not in the pejorative meaning of political as haranguing,
but as deliberately provocative.[15] Morrison rejects the dichotomy between

art and politics, insisting that art can be "unquestionably political and ir-
revocably beautiful at the same time."[16] She is careful to say that "I am not
interested in indulging myself in some private, closed exercise of my imagination that fulfills only the obligation of my personal dreams."[17] Instead,
her novels are instruments for transmitting cultural knowledge, filling a void
once occupied by storytelling. They replace "those classical, mythological,
archetypal stories that we heard years ago."[18] She believes in the artist's
measure of responsibility for engendering cultural coherence and cohesion
by retrieving and interpreting the past—what she calls "bear[ing] witness."[19]
That responsibility largely informs her literary aesthetic.

Morrison's chief strategy for achieving this goal is to integrate life and
art by anchoring her fiction in the folkways that echo the rhythms of African
American communal life. Her women get together in kitchens to talk about
husbands and children. They do each other's hair, and they exorcise each
other's demons. Her men walk the streets of Michigan and New York, congregate in pool halls, argue in barber shops, hunt possum in rural Virginia.
Her stories encode myths about flying Africans and tales of tar babies. As
Trudier Harris demonstrates in a classic study, Morrison thoroughly inte-
grates folk patterns into her fiction. "Instead of simply including isolated
items of folklore, she manages to simulate the ethos of folk communities, to
saturate her novels with a folk aura intrinsic to the texturing of the whole."[20]
This pervasive incorporation of folk materials explains why Morrison strums
such deeply satisfying chords of familiarity for many readers. Indeed, Morrison's work is "genuinely" representative of the folk. She shuns what she
labels "the separate, isolated ivory tower voice" of the artist.[21] The (black)
artist, for Morrison, "is not a solitary person who has no responsibility to the
community."[22]

Morrison identifies with her readers and labors to achieve intimacy with
them. She invites readers to share in the creative process, to work with her
in constructing meaning in her books. She is the black preacher who, as she
puts it, "requires his congregation to speak, to join him in the sermon, to behave in a certain way, to stand up and to weep and to cry and to accede or to
change and to modify."[23] And, like black music her stories should, Morrison
continues, solicit a dynamic response. By avoiding defining adverbs and by
allowing the reader to interpret character and incident, Morrison encourages
participatory reading. There are, for example, no explicitly detailed sexual
scenes in her work. As she says, she aims "to describe sexual scenes in such
a way that they are not clinical, not even explicit—so that the reader brings
his own sexuality to the scene and thereby participates in it in a very personal
way. And owns it."[24]

This approach, of course, reflects any good writer's understanding of the necessary subtlety of imaginative writing and the reader's work of interpreting meaning. But Morrison's studied effort to elicit the reader's participation suggests a not-so-subtle emphasis upon the special relationship she shares with her audience. As storyteller she is bound to authentically represent experience as readers know it and to encourage their confirmation of and involvement in that representation.

As satisfying as this collaboration may be for the reader, it is just as challenging, because Morrison's work is not predictable. While her language, metaphors, settings, and themes evoke the familiar and the timeless, her characters seldom reinforce the reader's expectations—not because they are unrealistic but because they often depict a reality that is too distressing to consider. Morrison's characters (and her readers with them) are brought to the edge of endurance and then asked to endure more; sometimes they crack. Under these conditions Morrison shows what extraordinary and unspeakable acts ordinary people are capable of committing. Cholly, in *The Bluest Eye*, rapes his twelve-year-old daughter because he is overcome with pity and love for her; Pauline, the girl's mother, refuses to love her and loves instead the little white girl whose family employs her. As a child, Sula watches with mild curiosity as her mother burns to death. Sula's grandmother Eva Peace sets fire to her drug-addicted son and walks away, with tears on her face, from his burning body. Milkman, in *Song of Solomon*, abandons his cousin after a nineteen-year affair; she grieves to death. Son, in *Tar Baby*, drives his car through the bed in which his wife and her lover are sleeping. The quiet and passive Margaret Street systematically tortures her young son, Michael, with pinpricks. Sethe slits her baby's throat to keep the child from death in slavery. Fifty-five-year-old Joe Trace, in *Jazz* (1992), shoots the eighteen-year-old woman he loves. Old men take aim to kill young women in *Paradise*. In *Love* (2003), Bill Cosey marries his granddaughter's eleven-year-old friend; for two hundred dollars her family agrees. Frank Money murders a Korean child in *Home* (2012) when the little girl tempts him to sexual arousal; killing her protects his ideal of manhood.

Although these and other characters are never absolved of their guilt (they suffer the consequences of their criminality in one way or another), their crimes are mediated by the characters' humanity, by their desperate love and compassion. Bound by this paradox of human behavior—good people commit horrific acts—Morrison's people often embrace their transgressions, and then transcend them. Not always, but sometimes, they may even be redeemed by the crime. Terry Otten, in his analysis of criminality in Morrison's work, perceives innocence to be worse than guilt. Otten correctly points out that in many of Morrison's novels "the fall from innocence becomes a necessary gesture of freedom and a profound act of self awareness."[25] Characters must make choices and suffer the outcome of those choices. Failing to choose is never an option for those who would be free. Sethe (*Beloved*) objectifies this dilemma when she asks why her brain refuses to shield her from the pain of knowing: "Why was there nothing it refused? No misery, no regret, no hateful picture too rotten to accept? Like a greedy child it snatched up everything. Just once, could it say, No thank you? I just ate and can't hold another bite?"[26] But Sethe's brain does consume much more, and when the pain spills over and erupts in violence against others, her tragic life elicits both sympathy and blame. Morrison's "moral vision," Otten surmises, "allows for few single-minded villains and heroes."[27]

It has been suggested that this generous judgment of moral exigencies reflects a premeditated revision of the black male literary tradition in which the world is divided into black/white, good/evil, virgin/whore, self/other, male/female paradigms. Most black women writers avoid such simplistic dichotomies; they avoid what the critic Deborah McDowell calls "false choices."[28] *Sula*, McDowell points out, "is rife with liberating possibilities in that it transgresses all deterministic structures of opposition."[29] The shifting boundaries between good and evil in the novel are intentionally methodical, and this signals not Morrison's "abdication of moral consciousness"[30] but a revision of it—one that is truer to the complexity and indeterminacy of real life. In echoing this estimate of her work, Morrison says that she (like other black women) is writing to "repossess, rename, renown." She (and they) "look[s] at things in an unforgiving/loving way,"[31] a paradigm that is remarkable in its parallel to real life. This view accommodates contradictory responses and refuses simplistic, polarizing representations. Black women's texts, in America and the diaspora, Morrison notes, project a wide gaze. "It's not narrow, it's very probing and it does not flinch."[32]

Although Morrison flatly rejects a black feminist model of criticism or evaluation, she just as decisively asserts that she and other authors write for black women: "We are not addressing the men as some white female writers do. We are not attacking each other, as both black and white men do."[33] In fact, she recalls that when she began writing in the 1960s and 1970s there was a paucity of books about the black woman. There was no fiction representing her experience: "this person, this female, this black did not exist centre-self."[34]

The black woman, then, is a consistent and evolving presence in Morrison's work. Her first novel examines the consequences for black womanhood of an oppressive standard of white beauty. The reader is called to witness the psychological disintegration of Pecola Breedlove, an adolescent girl whose blackness is an affront to a society in which blue eyes are valued above all others. In *Sula* Morrison moves from adolescence to womanhood, recording the community's response to one who dares defy all narrowly conceived ideologies of woman. Only in defiance is freedom possible, the author suggests. Even in *Song of Solomon,* which is "driven by male characters,"[35] it is the presence of a woman, Pilate, that imparts the spiritual dimension for which the novel has been praised. Pilate, too, is in kinship with the authentic women who haunt Jadine's dreams and challenge her choices in *Tar Baby.* Womanhood, motherhood, selfhood come together in *Beloved,* Morrison's novel about slavery's unspeakable crimes against a woman and a people. Sethe, like Pilate and Sula, refuses defeat even if triumph means violating conventional standards of moral behavior. In *Jazz,* Morrison asks what happens when women's dreams are deferred. Four subsequent novels return to earlier themes with different outcomes. In *Paradise,* Consolata—magical, divine, mythic—reaches the essence of selfhood and harmonizes the partisan divides of race, gender, religion, and class. She accomplishes what Pilate could not in her time and place. *Love* revisits Nel and Sula's breakup, but, unlike them, Heed and Christine make up and learn to speak the language of love. In *A Mercy* (2008), Florens's mother saves her child in a way less brutal than Sethe's choice. Frank Money, the subject of Morrison's latest novel, *Home,* comes of age, like Milkman, in the presence of his sister (first cousins, Pilate insists, are like siblings) and tough-minded women (or a woman in Milkman's case). But, unlike Milkman, Frank keeps his familial relations unsullied, and, unlike Hagar, whom Pilate could not save, Cee survives her trauma, aided by the Lotus women.

Woman's experience, of course, is not Morrison's sole concern. Her novels examine aspects of male life as well. She writes about the ways men dominate, sometimes ruthlessly, the ways some pursue freedom from responsibility to women and children, the ways others nurture family. Hers are certain kinds of men who, like all her characters, transcend sociological stereotypes and trample convention as they walk outside societal norms. These, the author asserts, are the kind of "lawless" characters who interest her because they resist controls. "They make up their lives, or they find out who they are."[36] Morrison calls this spirit of adventure a masculine trait, but it is not found in men only; some women have it as well. Sula, according to Morrison, is "a masculine character in that sense. . . . She really behaves like a man. . . . She's adventuresome and will leave and try anything.[37]

Men and women, then, in Morrison's novels speculate; they take risks, and they seek. Her characters are often in motion. Sometimes the movement follows the historical migration of blacks out of slavery, out of the postwar South to the industrial North; sometimes the movement is in reverse, from the North to the South. They walk, drive, take buses and trains, fly, always in search of something—money, happiness, love, themselves. Yet seldom is the object of their quest realized. More often than not, the journey ends in isolation and alienation. They may find material success but not often happiness. Only when the physical journey mirrors a psychological passage is the course even worthwhile. Morrison aims her characters "toward knowledge at the expense of happiness perhaps."[38] In *Song of Solomon,* Milkman Dead leaves his home in Michigan and travels to Pennsylvania in search of a cave with hidden gold. The gold, he thinks, will liberate him from any responsibility to family and community. He does not find gold, but he gains much more than wealth or financial independence. In Pennsylvania and later in Virginia, he hears stories about his ancestors, stories about sacrifice and rebellion. This knowledge of the suffering and courage of those who came before empowers Milkman and propels him toward spiritual ascendance.

The right knowledge is important to Morrison's characters. They may be liberated by it. The things Milkman learns from his father in Michigan about proprietary control of money and people are useless, but the stories about his grandfather's and great grandfather's resistance and defiance give him strength. These lessons in survival should not have to be learned late in life as they are by Milkman. They should come in childhood from "a chorus of mamas, grandmamas, aunts, cousins, sisters, neighbors, Sunday school teachers."[39] These are the people who constitute the community, which is central to Morrison's epistemology. Perhaps taking a cue from her own childhood experience in Lorain, Ohio, where the entire village assumed responsibility for a child's life, Morrison often calculates the psychological distance her characters have traveled by estimating their proximity to the community. The closer they are, the better. As the repository of self-affirming cultural traditions and beliefs, the community shapes character and gives a measure of protection from external assaults upon the psyche. Those who leave the village, Morrison says, must take it with them. "There is no need for the community if you have a sense of it inside."[40] Not internalizing it, however, invites tragedy. Hagar (*Song of Solomon*) remains uninitiated and beyond the boundaries of community fellowship. She therefore knows too little to save herself from insanity and death when she is abandoned by her lover. As one character asks, "Had anyone told her the things she ought to know . . . to give her the strength life demanded of her—and the humor with which to live it?"[41]

Some characters disdainfully reject the village and choose a different form of knowledge, and they, too, pay a price. Jadine (*Tar Baby*) is such a victim. She is orphaned in childhood and raised by an aunt and uncle in the household of their white employers. In this island of whiteness Jadine is far from any knowledge of village culture. Becoming a successful fashion model in Paris only widens this distance. Consequently, Jadine never feels authentic and complete. As an uninitiated black woman, she will always be vulnerable to recriminations such as the accusing stare of an African woman she encounters in a Paris supermarket.

Morrison's novels have a vital role to play in this process of acculturation. They cannot replace the village, but they can summon its spirit. Folk culture, as revealed in maxims, beliefs, attitudes, and ways of speaking, walking, and thinking, permeates Morrison's fiction and inspires its identifiably lyrical style. In her work mythic truths are revived, examined, and passed on, keeping the individual in touch with black American and African traditions. "I want to point out the dangers," Morrison writes, "to show that nice things don't always happen to the totally self-reliant if there is no conscious historical connection. To say, see this is what will happen."[42] The future is threatening without knowledge and acceptance of the past.

As culturally specific as Morrison's novels are, they are not restrictive. They appeal to an eclectic audience, one that is not limited by race and gender. Hers are the themes of humanity: the quest for buried treasure, the fall from innocence, disconnection and alienation, the struggle for self-actualization. "We know thousands of these [clichés] in literature,"[43] Morrison points out. A bicultural reading of her novels by Karla Holloway and Stephanie Demetrakopoulos is a testimony to this universality in Morrison's work. Each of these critics reads Morrison from a different perspective, and each finds in Morrison a rich response to her academic cultural experience. Demetrakopoulos explains:

> As a Black woman in a white society and institution (the university), Holloway brings many insights to the novels that I had not seen. Her studies of West African cultures as well as Black American culture also enlarge her critical approach so that her linguistic approach is philosophical, political, and anthropological.
>
> My academic background has been in Jungian and Women's Studies, so I am always looking for what is archetypically feminine, what is universal in feminine individuation. I also look for the spiritual in the female psyche. My use of Greek or Indian goddesses as a frame on characters in women's novels is for me a frame of universality that transcends my

Judeo-Christian world. I am also interested in men's patterns of individuation and transitions from middle to old age, that I found plentifully in Morrison's generations of characters.[44]

Indeed, Morrison's fiction is a tour de force of American folk culture, but within its layers of mythic patterns, as Demetrakopoulos demonstrates, is the archetypal experience of mankind and womankind. And within the exigent stories of ethical dilemma and tragic choice is a pedagogy of moral knowledge for all human life.

CHAPTER 2

Black Girlhood and Black Womanhood
The Bluest Eye and *Sula*

From the beginning of her writing career Morrison has exercised a keen scrutiny of women's lives. *The Bluest Eye* and *Sula,* Morrison's first and second novels, are to varying extents about black girlhood and black womanhood, about women's connections to their families, to their communities, to the larger social networks outside the community, to men, and to each other. Lending themselves to a reading as companion works, the novels complement each other thematically and may, in several ways, be viewed sequentially.[1] (Morrison calls her first four novels "evolutionary. One comes out of the other."[2] In *The Bluest Eye* she was "interested in talking about black girlhood," and in *Sula* she "wanted to move to the other part of their life." She wanted to ask, "what . . . do those feisty little girls grow up to be?").[3] *The Bluest Eye* directs a critical gaze at the process and symbols of imprinting the self during childhood and at what happens to the self when the process is askew and the symbols are defective. In *Sula,* Morrison builds on the knowledge gained in the first novel, revisits childhood, and then moves her characters and readers a step forward into women's struggles to change delimiting symbols and take control of their lives. But excavating an identity that has been long buried beneath stereotype and convention is a wrenching endeavor, and Morrison demonstrates in *Sula* that although recasting one's role in the community is possible, there is a price to be paid for change.

The Bluest Eye (1970)

The opening lines of *The Bluest Eye* incorporate two signifying aspects of Morrison's fiction.[4] The first sentence, "Quiet as it's kept, there were no marigolds in the fall of 1941," emanates from African American community, capturing the milieu of "black women conversing with one another; telling a story, an anecdote; gossip[ing] about someone or event within the circle, the family, the neighborhood."[5] The line also demonstrates Morrison's urge to connect with her reader by choosing "speakerly" phrasing that has a "back fence connotation." Morrison explains: "The intimacy I was aiming for, the intimacy between the reader and the page, could start up immediately because the secret is being shared at best, and eavesdropped upon, at the least. Sudden familiarity or instant intimacy seemed crucial to me then, writing my first novel. I did not want the reader to have time to wonder 'what do I have to do, to give up, in order to read this? What defense do I need, what distance maintain?' Because I know (and the reader does not—he or she has to wait for the second sentence) that this is a terrible story about things one would rather not know anything about."[6]

The line's foreboding aura charitably prepares the reader for powerful truths soon to be revealed. The pervading absence of flowers in 1941 sets that year off from all others and produces a prophetic and ominous quality which unfolds in the second line: "We thought, at the time, that it was because Pecola was having her father's baby that the marigolds did not grow" (3). Exploiting the child speaker's naïve but poignant logic, Morrison requires the reader, during this first encounter, to be accountable, to acknowledge a dreadful deed and respond to its dreadful consequences. "If the conspiracy that the opening words announce is entered into by the reader," Morrison explains, "then the book can be seen to open with its close: a speculation on the disruption of 'nature' as being a social disruption with tragic individual consequences in which the reader, as part of the population of the text, is implicated."[7] This three-way collaboration among author, speaker, and reader is the effect for which Morrison strives in all her novels.

From this profoundly stirring beginning Morrison advances to an equally moving examination of Pecola's life—her unloving childhood, her repudiation by nearly everyone she encounters, and finally the complete disintegration of self. Through it all Morrison exposes and indicts those who promulgate standards of beauty and behavior that devalue Pecola's sensitivities and contribute to her marginalized existence.

The search for culprits is not arduous. The storekeeper who sells Mary Jane candies to Pecola avoids touching her hand when she pays and barely disguises his contempt for her: "She looks up at him and sees the vacuum where curiosity ought to lodge. . . . The total absence of human recognition—the glazed separateness. . . . It has an edge; somewhere in the bottom lid is the distaste. . . . The distaste must be for her, her blackness . . . and it

is the blackness that accounts for, that creates, the vacuum edged with distance in white eyes" (36–37). The white Yacobowski is condemned for his
cultural blindness, but he is not the only one responsible for Pecola's pain.
Responsibility must be shared by blacks who assuage their own insults from
society by oppressing those like Pecola who are vulnerable. Little black boys
jeer and taunt her with "Black e mo. Black e mo. Yadaddsleepsnekked" (50),
defensively ignoring the color of their own skins. But "it was their contempt
for their own blackness that gave the first insult its teeth. They seem to have
taken all of their smoothly cultivated ignorance, their exquisitely learned
self-hatred, their elaborately designed hopelessness and sucked it all up into
a fiery cone of scorn that had burned for ages in the hollows of their minds"
(50).

Teachers ignore Pecola in the classroom, giving their attention instead
to a "high-yellow dream child with long brown hair" (47) and "sloe green
eyes" (48). And when this same high-yellow Maureen Peal declares to Pecola
and the MacTeer sisters "I *am* cute! And you ugly! Black and ugly black e
mos" (56), she is dangerously affirming intraracial acceptance of the world's
denigration of blackness. "Respectable," "milk-brown" women like Geraldine see Pecola's torn dress and uncombed hair and are confronted with the
blackness they have spent lifetimes rejecting. For Morrison these women are
antithetical to the village culture she respects. They attend to the "careful
development of thrift, patience, high morals and good manners" (64) as these
are defined by white society. And they fear "the dreadful funkiness of passion,
the funkiness of nature, the funkiness of the wide range of human emotions"
(64) because these qualities are defined by black society. They are shamed
by the "laugh that is too loud, the enunciation a little too round; the gesture
a little too generous. They hold their behind in for fear of a sway too free;
when they wear lipstick, they never cover the entire mouth for fear of lips too
thick, and they worry, worry, worry about the edges of their hair" (64). As
one of these women, Geraldine executes the tyranny of standardized beauty
that enthralls some in the black community and terrorizes too many others.

When Pecola stands in Geraldine's house—tricked into going there by
Geraldine's hateful son—she transgresses a line demarking "colored people"
from "niggers," light-skinned from dark, hand-me-down whiteness from
genuine culture. In her innocence Pecola does not perceive the transgression
or its consequences. To her, Geraldine's world and house are beautiful. The
house's ordered prettiness contrasts sharply with the shabby make-do appearance of the Breedloves' storefront. Geraldine, however, does perceive
Pecola's outrageous breach, and the hurting child that Pecola is becomes a
"nasty little black bitch" (72) in Geraldine's mouth. Geraldine sets her teeth

against any recognition of some part of who she is in Pecola. To Pecola, Geraldine is "the pretty milk-brown lady in the pretty gold and green house" (72). To Morrison, she is a shadow image of the Dick-and-Jane life, a sadistic approximation of the storybook people. Through her Morrison demonstrates that a life such as Geraldine's is validated only by the exclusion of others.

Michael Awkward discusses this "purgative abuse" of Pecola in terms of the black community's guilt about its own inability to measure up to some external ideal of beauty and behavior. Pecola objectifies this failure (which results in self-hatred) and must be purged. She becomes the black community's shadow of evil (even as the black community is the white community's evil). "In combating the shadow . . . the group is able to rid itself ceremonially of the veil that exists within both the individual member and the community at large. To be fully successful, such exorcism requires a visibly imperfect, shadow-consumed scapegoat" like Pecola.[8]

Even her parents, Cholly and Pauline Breedlove, relate to Pecola in this way. Ironically named since they breed not love but violence and misery, Cholly and Pauline eventually destroy their daughter, whose victimization is a bold symbol of their own despair and frustrations. In the pathos of their defeated lives, Morrison demonstrates the process by which self-hatred becomes scapegoating.

Pauline's lame foot makes her pitiable and invisible until she marries Cholly. But pleasure in marriage lasts only until she moves from Kentucky to Ohio and confronts northern standards of physical beauty and style. She is despised by snooty black women who snicker at her lameness, her unstraightened hair, and her provincial speech. In the movie theaters she seeks relief from these shortcomings through daydreams of Clark Gable and Jean Harlow. But even in high heels, makeup, and a Harlow hairstyle, Pauline is a failure. "In equating physical beauty with virtue, she stripped her mind, bound it, and collected self-contempt by the heap" (95); she then deposits her own self-contempt on her husband and children, who fail by "the scale of absolute beauty . . . she absorbed in full from the silver screen" (95). Eventually, Pauline gives up on her own family and takes refuge in the soft beauty surrounding her in the Fisher home, where she works—the crisp linens, white towels, the little Fisher girl's yellow hair. She cannot afford such beauty and style. In the Fisher house, however, she has dominion over creditors and service people "who humiliated her when she went to them on her own behalf [but] respected her, were even intimidated by her, when she spoke for the Fishers" (101). With the Fishers she has what she cannot have at home—"power, praise, and luxury" (99). By the time Pecola finds herself awkwardly standing in the Fishers' kitchen, responsible for the spilled remains of a freshly baked pie at her feet, Pauline is incapable of a mother's love and forgiveness. Her best response is to knock Pecola to the floor and to run to console the crying Fisher child.

In substituting fierce intolerance of her family for love, Pauline refuses what she cannot transform. Her husband is an irresponsible drunk; the son and daughter are sloven. Only she has order and beauty and only in the Fisher house. Under these conditions Pauline is reborn as self-righteous martyr with no time for movies, unfulfilled dreams, and foolish notions of romantic love. "All the meaningfulness of her life was in her work. . . . She was an active church woman . . . defended herself mightily against Cholly . . . and felt she was fulfilling a mother's role conscientiously when she pointed out their father's faults to keep them from having them, or punished them when they showed any slovenliness, no matter how slight, when she worked twelve to sixteen hours a day to support them" (100).

Like Pauline, Cholly too is driven by personal demons, which he attempts to purge in violence against his family. Pauline does not see or understand Cholly's hurts, but Morrison represents them as remarkably egregious. Callously abandoned on a garbage dump by his mother, years later Cholly searches for his father, who also discards him. His response to his father's angry denunciation—crying and soiling his pants—eclipses any opportunity for emotional maturity and returns him, in a sense, to the helplessness of his abandonment in infancy. After the rejection, he seeks relief, even rebirth, in a nearby river, curled for hours in the fetal position with fists in eyes. For a while he finds consolation in "the dark, the warmth, the quiet . . . [engulfing him] like the skin and flesh of an elderberry protecting its own seed" (124). Protection is short lived, however. There is no prelapsarian innocence available to Cholly.

In marrying Pauline, Cholly seems fully recovered from these earlier traumas. Initially, he is kind, compassionate, protective, but these feelings too are fleeting. He retreats from her emotional dependence, he is humiliated by economic powerlessness, and he mitigates his frustrations in drink and abuse. In turning on Pauline, Cholly fights whom he can and not whom he should. This is the lesson of childhood learned when he is forced by armed white men who discover him with Darlene in the woods to continue his first act of sexual intimacy while they watch and ridicule. When the men leave in search of other prey, Cholly realizes that hating them is futile, and he decides instead to hate Darlene for witnessing his degradation. He could not protect her, so he settles for despising her. Later Pauline comes to stand for Darlene in Cholly's mind: "He poured out on her the sum of all his inarticulate fury and aborted desires" (37). Cholly, then, needs Pauline to objectify his failure.

His treatment of Pecola may also be seen in terms of scapegoating, but not entirely. While Pecola's ugliness is an affront to Pauline's surreptitious creation of beauty in the Fisher house, it is a sad reminder to Cholly of not only his unhappiness but Pecola's as well. Such concern makes him a somewhat sympathetic character. He is one of Morrison's traveling men, one whose freedom to do as he pleases is jeopardized by dependent, possessive women. He has roamed around dangerously, carelessly, irresponsibly, lovingly. The appealing contradiction of his life can find expression only in black music. "Only a musician would sense, know, without even knowing that he knew, that Cholly was free. Dangerously free" (125). After his mother's abandonment and his father's rejection, Cholly has little to lose, and his behavior is disdainful of consequences. "It was in this godlike state that he met Pauline Williams" (126), and marriage to her threatens to conquer him.

In romanticizing Cholly, Morrison defies the unflattering orthodoxy of black maleness and makes peace with the conflict between responsibility to family and freedom to leave. Morrison respects the freedom even as she embraces the responsibility. In the freedom she sees "tremendous possibility for masculinity among black men."[9] Sometimes such men are unemployed or in prison, but they have a spirit of adventure and a deep complexity that interests Morrison. No doubt she views their freedom as a residue of the "incredible . . . magic and feistiness in black men that nobody has been able to wipe out."[10] Cholly exercises his freedom, but not before he commits a heinous crime against Pecola. Even his crime, however, is tempered by the author's compassion for Cholly. Coming home drunk and full of self-pity, Cholly sees Pecola and is overcome with love and regret that he has nothing to relieve her hopelessness. "Guilt and impotence rose in a bilious duct. What could he do for her—ever? What give her? What say to her? What could a burned-out black man say to the hunched back of his eleven-year-old daughter?" (127). His answer is rape—in spite of himself. In rendering this incomprehensible instance, Morrison captures the curious mixture of hate and tenderness that consumes Cholly. "The hatred would not let him pick her up" when the violation is over; "the tenderness forced him to cover her" (129). The awful irony of his position is overwhelming. In the end Cholly's complexity dominates the moment. Having never been parented, "he could not even comprehend what such a relationship should be" (126). And, being dangerously free, he has no restraints.

Morrison does have sympathy for Cholly (she admits that she connects "Cholly's 'rape' by the white men to his own of his daughter"),[11] but he is not absolved; he dies soon after in a workhouse. And Morrison does not minimize his crime against his daughter. Pecola's childlike "stunned silence," "the tightness of her vagina," the painfully "gigantic thrust," her "fingers clinching," her "shocked body," and finally her unconsciousness bear witness to Morrison's aim in the novel to represent Pecola's perspective, to translate her heartbreak. "This most masculine act of aggression becomes feminized in my language," Morrison says. It is "passive," she continues, "and, I think, more accurately repellent when deprived of the male 'glamour of shame' rape is (or once was) routinely given."[12]

Feminizing language does not lead Morrison to comfortable binary oppositions of good and evil, feminine and masculine. Rather, it leads to a sensitive treatment of the complex emotions that determine character, male and female. In Morrison's writing there are no easy villains to hate; there are no predictable behaviors.

Just as Cholly is not as reprehensible as he might be, Pauline is not as sympathetic as she might be if she were stereotypically portrayed as an abused wife and as a mother. In fact, Pauline in some sense is as culpable as Cholly for Pecola's suffering. Cholly's love is corrupt and tainted, but Pauline is unloving. After the rape, Morrison subtly alludes to the difference: "So when the child regained consciousness, she was lying on the kitchen floor under a heavy quilt, trying to connect the pain between her legs with the face of her mother looming over her" (129). Is Pauline associated with the pain? She did not physically rape Pecola, but she has ravaged the child's self-worth and left her vulnerable to assaults of various proportions.

With single-minded determination, Pauline survives, but Pecola withdraws into the refuge of insanity. Like the dandelions whose familiar yellow heads she thinks are pretty, Pecola is poisoned by rejection. But, unlike the dandelions, she does not have the strength to persist, and in madness she simply substitutes a better reality for her inchoate one: she has blue eyes, which everyone admires and envies. In pathetic conversations with an imaginary friend, Pecola repeatedly elicits confirmation that hers are "the bluest eyes in the whole world" (161), that they are "much prettier than the sky. Prettier than Alice-and-Jerry Storybook eyes" (159).

Pecola's sad fantasy expresses Morrison's strongest criticism of a white standard of beauty that excludes most black women and that destroys those who strive to measure up but cannot. Everywhere there are reminders of this failure: the coveted blond-haired, blue-eyed dolls that arrive at Christmas, Shirley Temple movies, high-yellow dream children like Maureen Peal—and, for Pecola, the smiling white face of little Mary Jane on the candy wrapper, "blond hair in gentle disarray, blue eyes looking at her out of a world of clean comfort" (38). In desperation, Pecola believes that nothing bad could be viewed by such eyes. Cholly and Mrs. Breedlove (Pecola's name for her mother) would not fight; her teachers and classmates would not despise her; she would be safe. And, ironically, perhaps Pecola is right. With the blue eyes of her distorted reality comes the awful safety of oblivion.

Pecola's tragedy exposes the fallacy of happily-ever-after storybook life. Morrison repeatedly calls attention to this falseness. In the prologue and chapter headings are recounted the elementary story of Dick and Jane, mother and father:

> Here is the house. It is green and white. It has a red door. It is very pretty. Here is the family. Mother, Father, Dick, and Jane live in the green-and-white house. They are very happy. See Jane. She has a red dress. She wants to play. Who will play with Jane? See the cat. It goes meow-meow. Come and play. Come play with Jane. The kitten will not play. See Mother. Mother is very nice. Mother, will you play with Jane? Mother laughs. Laugh, Mother, laugh. See Father. He is big and strong. Father, will you play with Jane? Father is smiling. Smile, Father, smile. See the dog. Bowwow goes the dog. Do you want to play with Jane? See the dog run. Run, dog, run. Look, look. Here comes a friend. The friend will play with Jane. They will play a good game. Play, Jane, play. (1)

In two subsequent versions Morrison distorts the Dick-and-Jane text. In bold print with no spacing between words, these latter passages take on a frenetic tone that signals perversion of communal perfection for Morrison's characters, who do not blithely run and play and live happily ever after. In removing standard grammatical codes, symbols of Western culture, Morrison expurgates the white text as she constructs the black. Timothy Powell aptly points out that "Morrison is literally deconstructing the essential white text, removing capitalizations, punctuation, and finally the spacing until the white text is nothing more than a fragmentation of its former self at the beginning of the chapter."[13] Home for Pecola is not the green and white picture-perfect house of white myth. Home is a storefront where mother and father curse and fight, brother runs away from home, and sister wishes with all her soul for blue eyes. Pecola appropriates the storybook version of life because her own is too gruesome. In her life she is subject to other people's cruel whims, against which she can offer no voice of protest.

Indeed, she has no voice in this text at all, a condition that loudly echoes her entire existence. She has no control over the events in her life and no authority over the narrative of those events. That authority goes to twelve-year-old Claudia, who narrates major portions of Pecola's story with compassion and understanding. Claudia and her older sister Frieda are the "we" of the opening paragraph. They witness Pecola's despair and try to save her.

"Her pain agonized me," Claudia says, "I wanted to open her up, crisp her edges, ram a stick down that hunched and curving spine, force her to stand erect and spit the misery out on the streets" (61). But the sisters fail. They do not save Pecola from her breakup. As the girls mourn their failure, Morrison chronicles the loss of their innocence. But, unlike Pecola's short-circuited innocence, their loss is part of a natural ritual of growing up.

Morrison proffers Claudia and Frieda as foils to Pecola. They are strong and sturdy; Pecola is not. Claudia's independence and confidence especially throw Pecola's helplessness into stark relief. For Claudia, blue-eyed dolls at Christmas and Shirley Temple dancing with Bojangles Robinson are unappealing and even insulting. With youthful but penetrating insight, she declares her exemption from "the universal love of white dolls, Shirley Temples, and Maureen Peals" (148).

Claudia and her sister traverse Morrison's landscape of black girlhood. Bound by a social environment that is hostile to their kind, they have "become headstrong, devious and arrogant" (150) enough to dismiss limitations and believe that they can "change the course of events and alter a human life" (150). With ingenious faith in themselves, Claudia and Frieda attempt to rescue Pecola and her baby. They would make beauty where only ugliness resided by planting marigolds deep in the earth and receiving the magic of their beauty as a sign of Pecola's salvation. When neither marigolds nor Pecola survives, the girls blame a community that is seduced by a white standard of beauty and that makes Pecola its scapegoat: "All of us—all who knew her—felt so wholesome after we cleaned ourselves on her. We were beautiful when we stood astride her ugliness. . . . We honed our egos on her, padded our characters with her frailty, and yawned in the fantasy of our strength" (160).

For the most part, their parents, Mr. and Mrs. MacTeer, save Claudia and Frieda from this sort of persecution. Mr. MacTeer (unlike Cholly) acts as a father should in protecting his daughter from a lecherous boarder. Mrs. MacTeer's place is not in a white family's kitchen but in her own, where familiar smells hold sway and where her singing about "hard times, bad times and somebody-done-gone-and-left-me times" (28) proclaims that pain is endurable, even sweet. To her daughters she bequeaths a legacy of compassion for others and defiance in the face of opposition. Her love for them was "thick and dark as Alaga syrup" (7). The MacTeers embody the communal resiliency at the heart of black culture.

Mrs. MacTeer is not one of Morrison's ancestors—a person wise in the ways of life who transmits that wisdom and knowledge of self to the uninitiated. She is, however, one of Morrison's nurturers. Claudia remembers the feel of her mother's hands on her forehead and chest when she is sick: "I think," she says, "of somebody with hands who does not want me to die" (7). Mrs. MacTeer takes Pecola in when Cholly burns his family out. She presides over Pecola's first menses, hugging her reassuringly (the only hug the adolescent Pecola ever receives; Mrs. Breedlove's hugs and assurances are reserved for the little Fisher girl). But Mrs. MacTeer's influence in Pecola's life is short in duration. With no one else available, Pecola turns to the whores who live upstairs over the storefront for instruction given lovingly. China, Marie, and Poland stand in opposition to the Geraldines in the community. They are not pretentious heirs to false puritanical values, and Morrison respects their unvarnished natures. "Three merry gargoyles. Three merry harridans," they are quick to laugh or sing. Defying all stereotypes of pitiable women gone wrong, they make no apologies for themselves and seek no sympathy. "They were not young girls in whores' clothing, or whores regretting their loss of innocence. They were whores in whores' clothes, whores who had never been young and had no word for innocence" (43). Pecola loves these women, and they are more than willing to share the lessons they've learned, but their lessons are wrong for Pecola. They can tell her stories that are breezy and rough about lawless men and audacious women. But they cannot teach her what she wants most to know: how to be loved by a mother and father, by a community, and by a society.

For that she turns in the end to Soaphead Church, the itinerant spiritualist and flawed human being. A pedophile and con man, Soaphead has not transcended the pain of life's humiliations and is deeply scarred. Morrison describes him as "that kind of black"[14] for whom blackness is a burden to be borne with self-righteous indignation. Of West Indian and colonial English ancestry that has long been in social decline, Soaphead, existing at the bottom of the descent, is "wholly convinced that if black people were more like white people they would be better off."[15] He, therefore, appreciates Pecola's yearning for blue eyes. But Soaphead's powers are fraudulent, as are his claims to have helped Pecola by "giving" her blue eyes; he does little more than use her in his own schemes of revenge against God and man. With no one to help her counteract the love of white dolls with blue eyes, Pecola cannot help herself, and she is obliged to be the victim—always.

Indeed, the effects of Pecola's devastation are unrelenting as measured in the passing of time in the novel—season after season: Morrison names each of the novel's sections after a season of the year, beginning with autumn and ending with summer. The headings are ironically prophetic preludes to the story segments. They stand out as perverse contradictions of Pecola's experiences: thematic progression is not from dormancy to rebirth as the autumn to spring movement would suggest. There is no renewal for Pecola. In spring she is violated; by summer she is annihilated. Morrison uses this disruption of nature to signal the cosmic proportion of Pecola's injury.

Sula (1973)

The Bluest Eye was not commercially successful at the time of its publication (its popularity has risen in tandem with Morrison's reputation). Yet, it did inaugurate its author's public literary life. After writing it, Morrison became a frequent reviewer for the *New York Times* and an authoritative commentator on black culture and women's concerns. Three years later, *Sula* was both a commercial and critical triumph. It was excerpted in *Redbook* and widely reviewed. The Book-of-the-Month Club selected it as an alternate, and in 1975 it was nominated for the National Book Award.

If *The Bluest Eye* chronicles to some extent an annihilation of self, *Sula,* in contrast, validates resiliency in the human spirit and celebrates the self. In *Sula* Morrison returns to the concerns of girlhood explored in her first novel, but this time she approaches her subject in celebration, as if to see what miracles love and friendship may accomplish for Sula and Nel that they could not for Pecola, Claudia, and Frieda.

Sula Peace and Nel Wright are each the only daughter of mothers whose distance leaves the young girls alone with dreams of someone to erase the solitude. When they first met, "they felt the ease and comfort of old friends."[16] Indeed, "their meeting was fortunate, for it let them use each other to grow on" (44). Sula's spontaneous intensity is relieved by Nel's passive reserve. Sula loves the ordered neatness of Nel's home and her life, and Nel likes Sula's "household of throbbing disorder constantly awry with things, people, voices and the slamming of doors" (44). Over the years "they found relief in each other's personality" (45).

In examining their friendship, Morrison tests its endurance. As she says, not much had been done with women as friends; men's relationships are often the subject of fiction, but what about women's strongest bonds? As perfect complements, one incomplete without the other, Sula and Nel together face life, death, and marriage, and eventually they also must face separation. Throughout, Morrison affirms the necessity of their collaboration.

Adolescence for Nel and Sula is marked not by individuation but by merger, as a single, provocative play scene illustrates. In the summer of their twelfth year, with thoughts of boys and with "their small breasts just now beginning to create some pleasant discomfort when they were lying on their stomachs" (49), the girls escape to the park. In silence and without looking at each other, they begin to play in the grass, stroking the blades. "Nel found a thick twig and, with her thumbnail, pulled away its bark until it was stripped to a smooth, creamy innocence" (49). Sula does the same. Soon they begin poking "rhythmically and intensely into the earth," making small neat holes. "Nel began a more strenuous digging and, rising to her knee, was careful to scoop out the dirt as she made her hole deeper. Together they worked until the two holes were one and the same" (50). In their symbolic sexual play, Nel and Sula, unlike Pecola, have absolute control in this necessary rite of passage (without the intrusion of a masculine presence) that conjoins them until, like the holes, they are one and the same.

Two other significant moments define their intimacy as well. The first is Sula's cutting off the tip of her finger in response to a threat by a group of white boys whose menacing bodies block the girl's route home. If she could do that to herself, what would she do to them, Sula asks the shocked boys. The second is the death of Chicken Little, the little boy whose body Sula swings around and around in play until her hands slip and he flies out over the river and drowns. Nel watches, and no one discovers their culpability. At the graveside they hold hands. "At first, as they stood there, their hands were clenched together. They relaxed slowly until during the walk back home their fingers were laced in as gentle a clasp as that of any two young girlfriends trotting up the road on a summer day wondering what happened to butterflies in the winter" (56–57).

Not even Nel's marriage dissolves their "friendship [that] was so close, they themselves had difficulty distinguishing one's thoughts from the other's" (72). They are both happy; Nel becomes a wife, and Sula goes to college. Ten years later, Sula's return imparts a magic to Nel's days that marriage had not. "Her old friend had come home. . . . Sula, whose past she had lived through and with whom the present was a constant sharing of perceptions. Talking to Sula had always been a conversation with herself" (82). Their lives resume an easy rhythm until Nel walks into her bedroom and finds her husband and Sula naked. Not surprisingly, this episode supersedes the women's friendship. Jude leaves town, Nel, and their children, and Nel blames Sula. Three years later, when Nel visits a dying Sula, she asks, "Why you didn't love me enough to leave him alone. To let him love me. You had to take him away" (125). Sula replies, "What you mean take him away? . . . If we were such good friends, how come you couldn't get over it?" (125).

With Sula's question Morrison calls into doubt the primacy of Nel's marriage over the women's friendship, intimating that their friendship may even supplant the marriage. Years after Sula's death, Nel comes to this realization at her friend's grave. "All that time, all that time, I thought I was missing Jude. . . . We was girls together Lord, Sula . . . girl, girl, girlgirlgirl" (149).

Nel and Sula's estrangement offers Morrison an opportunity to examine women's lives in and out of marriage. As girls Nel and Sula had cunningly authored the dimensions of their own existence without the permission or approval of their families or the community. "Because each had discovered years before that they were neither white nor male and that all freedom and triumph was forbidden to them, they had set about creating something else to be" (44). Morrison does not elaborate further on the specific nature of their creation, but clearly each positions herself just outside the village perspective, thinking and behaving with a certain independence. "In the safe harbor of each other's company they could afford to abandon the ways of other people and concentrate on their own perceptions of things" (47).

The experience that determines Nel's perspective is a train ride with her mother. The two travel for days from Ohio to New Orleans for Nel's great grandmother's funeral. Her mother's shuffling acquiescence in the face of the white conductor's hostility during the trip, the sullen black male passengers whose refusal to help her mother reflects their own helpless humiliation, the indignity of squatting to relieve themselves in the brush in full view of the train, her mother's stiff shame at her own Creole mother's life as a prostitute—all these experiences teach Nel lessons about other people's vulnerabilities. Back home in the safety of her bedroom, she resolves to develop her strengths. Looking in the mirror, she whispers to herself, "I'm me. . . . I'm me. I'm not their daughter. I'm not Nel. I'm me. Me . . ." (24). Adopting me-ness as her mantra, Nel gathers power and joy and the "strength to cultivate a friend [Sula] in spite of her mother" (25). Nel's daring is eclipsed, however, by her marriage to Jude. For Helene Wright, Nel's mother, marriage is one of the neat conditions of living that defines a woman's place, and Nel accepts a similar arrangement for herself. Nel does not choose Jude; she accepts his choosing her as a way of completing himself. Without Nel, Jude is an enraged "waiter hanging around a kitchen like a woman" (71) because bigotry keeps him from doing better. "With her he was head of a household pinned to an unsatisfactory job out of necessity. The two of them together would make one Jude" (71). In marrying Jude, Nel gives up her youthful dreams (conceived before she met Sula) of being "wonderful" and of "trips she would take, alone . . . to faraway places" (25). In marrying Jude, she gives up her me-ness.

Predictably, when Jude leaves, after his betrayal with Sula, Nel suffers psychic disintegration, and later, after a necessary recovery, she endures shrinkage of the self. She considers the release that may come with death but that will have to wait because she has three children to raise. In this condition Nel wraps herself in the conventional mantle of sacrifice and martyrdom and takes her place with the rest of the women in the community. Although Nel does not discover it until after Sula's death and she is old, the real loss in her life is that of Sula, not Jude. And the real tragedy is that she has allowed herself to become less than she was.

Sula is different from Nel. It is Sula's rebellious spirit that fuels the intermittent moments of originality that Nel manages to have. In Sula's presence Nel has "sparkle or sputter" (618). Sula resists any authority or controls, and Morrison offers her as one of the lawless individuals whose lives she is so fond of examining. From Sula's days in childhood when she retreats to the attic, she rebels against conventionality. She is surprised and saddened by Nel's rejection of her over Jude. She had not expected Nel to behave "the way the others would have" (635). But nothing, not even her closest and only friend's censures, will force Sula to abridge herself.

Even near death, Sula will have none of Nel's limitations. To the end she proclaims, "I sure did live in this world. . . . I got my mind. And what goes on in it. Which is to say, I got me" (645). Sula's me-ness remains intact; she has not betrayed herself as Nel has, and any loneliness she feels is a price she is willing to pay for freedom.

By and large, Sula's assessment of her past is credible. Only once has she come close to subsuming herself to some other, a man named Ajax. Shortly after Ajax shows up at her door with a quart of milk tucked under each arm, Sula begins to think of settling down with him. All of the men in her past had, over the years, "merged into one large personality" (104) of sameness. "She had been looking . . . for a friend, and it took her a while to discover that a lover was not a comrade and could never be—for a woman" (104). But those thoughts exist before she meets Ajax; he is different in some ways. He brings her beautiful and impractical gifts: "clusters of black berries still on their branches, four meal-fried porgies wrapped in a salmon-colored sheet of the Pittsburgh *Courier*, a handful of jacks, two boxes of lime Jell-Well, a hunk of ice-wagon ice" (104). Sula is most interested in him, however, because he talks to her and is never condescending in conversation. "His refusal to baby or protect her, his assumption that she was both tough and wise—all that coupled with a wide generosity of spirit . . . sustained Sula's interest and enthusiasm" (110).

Their interlude ends when Ajax discovers Sula's possessiveness. For the first time Sula wants to be responsible for a man and to protect him from the dangers of life. Giving in to a nesting instinct that is new for her, she is on the verge of making his life her own. But before that happens, Ajax leaves, and Sula has only his driver's license as proof of his ever having been there. Sula's sorrow is intense but short lived, unlike Nel's enduring suffering for

Jude. In the end, when Nel accuses her of never being able to keep a man, Sula counters that she would never waste life trying to keep a man: "They ain't worth more than me. And besides, I never loved no man because he was worth it. Worth didn't have nothing to do with it. . . . My mind did. That's all" (124). Sula needed Nel, but she never needed a man to extend herself. Even in lovemaking she had manufactured her own satisfaction, "in the postcoital privateness in which she met herself, welcomed herself, and joined herself in matchless harmony" (107). With Ajax those private moments were not necessary, but without him Sula abides. The self, Morrison instructs, should not be liable in its own betrayal.

Sula is, without doubt, a manifesto of freedom, and that fact in large part accounts for its popularity with readers and critics who champion its triumphant chronicle of a black woman's heroism. That does not mean, however, that the novel approximates the ideal or that Sula's character is not flawed. Morrison describes her as an artist without a medium. "Her strangeness . . . was the consequence of an idle imagination. Had she paints, or clay, or knew the discipline of the dance, or strings; had she anything to engage her tremendous curiosity and her gift for metaphor, she might have exchanged the restlessness and preoccupation with whim for an activity that provided her with all she yearned for" (105). An art form augments life by giving it purpose; perhaps it teaches the individual compassion, but without it someone like Sula is, as Morrison describes her, strange, naïve, and dangerous.

In this view Sula is without an essential quality of humanity. She has taken little from others, but, more important, she has *given* little.[17] She does not mean others harm: "She had not thought at all of causing Nel pain when she bedded down with Jude" (103), but, without the moderating and mediating influence of her own humanity, Sula is unthinking and childlike. It is as if some crucial element of consciousness had been arrested in childhood when she overheard her mother say to a friend that she loved Sula but did not like her or when "her major feeling of responsibility [for Chicken Little's death] had been exorcised" (102). After that, "she had no center, no speck around which to grow" (103). The most bizarre episodes of her conduct may be understood in this context: feeling no emotion but curiosity while watching her mother burn to death, putting her grandmother in a nursing home for no good reason, and, of course, having sex with her best friend's husband.

Imperfect as she is, however, Sula does escape the falseness and emptiness of Nel's life. As Nel takes her place beside the other women in the community, she and they are identified with spiders, whose limitations keep them dangling "in the dark dry places . . . terrified of the free fall" (104). And if they do fall, they envision themselves as victims of someone else's evil. Sula, on the other hand, is one of Morrison's characters who is associated with flight and freedom. Sula does not fear a full wingspan, of "surrender[ing] to the downward flight" (104). She is unafraid of the free fall.

Flight in Morrison's design is most persuasively linked with men and not with women, who are more often than not nurturers. Of course, Morrison offers neither quality by itself as the archetypal model; in the best scenarios the individual is capable of both nurturance and flight. Indeed, Nel and Sula are incomplete without each other. As Morrison says, "Nel knows and believes in all the laws of that community. She *is* the community. She believes in its values. Sula does not. She does not believe in any of those laws and breaks them all. Or ignores them."[18] But both positions are problematic, Morrison continues: "Nel does not make that 'leap'—she doesn't know about herself [she does not discover until too late, for example that she had watched Chicken Little's drowning with excitement]. . . . Sula, on the other hand, knows all there is to know about herself. . . . But she has trouble making a connection with other people and just feeling that lovely sense of accomplishment of being close in a very strong way."[19] Nurturance without invention and imagination is analogous to flight without responsibility. Ajax is the only other character in the novel who is identified with flying. He loves airplanes, and he thinks often of airplanes, pilots, "and the deep sky that held them both" (109). When he takes long trips to big cities, other people imagine him pursuing some exotic fun that is unavailable to them; in truth, he is indulging his obsession with flying by standing around airports watching planes take off.

Metaphorically, Ajax is always in flight—from conventionality. Without work but willing to be responsible for himself, Ajax does not take cover in domesticity. Unlike Jude, who is only half a man without Nel as his refuge from life's injustices, Ajax does not need Sula to kiss his hurts and make them better. Unlike Jude, Ajax has self-esteem that is not diminished by white men's refusal of work, and, unlike Jude, he does not run away and leave behind a wife and children. Ajax does leave Sula, but his action is not a betrayal. Ajax and Sula had come together, not as fractional individuals in need of the other to be complete but as whole people, and when that equation is threatened by Sula's possessiveness, Ajax leaves for Dayton and airplanes. Of men like Ajax Morrison writes,

> They are the misunderstood people in the world. There's a wildness that they have, a nice wildness. It has bad effects in a society such as the one in which we live. It's pre-Christ in the best sense. It's Eve. When I see this wildness gone in a person, it's sad. This special lack of restraint, which is a part of human life and is best typified in certain black males, is of

particular interest to me. . . . Everybody knows who "that man" is, and they may give him bad names and call him a "street nigger"; but when you take away the vocabulary of denigration, what you have is somebody who is fearless and who is comfortable with that fearlessness. It's not about meanness. It's a kind of self-flagellant resistance to certain kinds of control, which is fascinating. Opposed to accepted notions of progress, the lock step life, they live in the world unreconstructed and that's it.[20]

As characters in flight, both Ajax and Sula stand in opposition to the community that is firmly rooted in ritual and tradition. As the devoted son of "an evil conjure woman" (109) whom most regarded as a neglectful mother, Ajax is accustomed to rebuffing public opinion, and as a man he is given a license to do so. As a woman Sula must *take* that license, and in the fray she alienates the community. Sula returns to town after ten years and refuses to honor the town's ceremonies: "She came to their church suppers without underwear, bought their steaming platters of food and merely picked at it—relishing nothing, exclaiming over no one's ribs or cobbler. They believed that she was laughing at their God" (99). Soon the town names her a devil and prepares to live with its discovery. In fact, Morrison says, the town's toleration of Sula is in some way a measure of its generosity: "She would have been destroyed by any other place; she was permitted to 'be' only in that context, and no one stoned her or killed her or threw her out."[21]

Clearly, however, the town needs Sula as much as or perhaps more than she needs it. In giving the novel an extraordinary sense of place,[22] Morrison builds the community's character around its defense against this internal threat. Sula is not the only danger, but for a time she is the most compelling. Her defiance unifies the community by objectifying its danger. Women protected their husbands; husbands embraced their wives and children. "In general [everyone] band[ed] together against the devil in their midst" (102). No one considered destroying Sula or running her out of town. They had lived with evil and misfortune all of their lives; it "was something to be first recognized, then dealt with, survived, outwitted, triumphed over" (102).

The predominant evil in their lives, more pervasive and enduring than Sula, is the external force of oppression. Morrison's characteristic treatment of bigotry is not to delineate the defining episodes of white hatred but instead to direct attention to the black community's ingenious methods for coping: using humor, garnering strength from folk traditions, and perversely refusing to be surprised or defeated by experience. Residents of the Bottom waste little time complaining and get on with the business of their lives. Morrison captures here, as she does elsewhere, the rhythms of the black community: men on the street corner, in pool halls; women shelling peas, cooking dinner, at the beauty parlor, in church, interpreting dreams and playing the numbers, working roots.

Yet, Morrison says, the music and dance belie the pain of men without work and of families living on the frayed edges of the prosperous white town below. Each contact with life beyond the borders of the Bottom recalls the isolating constraints of race prejudice: the train conductor's brutal reminder to Helene that her place is in the car with the other blacks; Sula and Nel's encounter with the four white teenagers who determine the physical boundaries of the girls' world by forcing them to walk in roundabout circuitous routes home from school; Shadrack's arrest by police who find him "wandering" in the white part of town. Even dead Chicken Little's space is designated by the bargeman who drays the child's body from the river, dumps it into a burlap sack, and tosses it in a corner. The sheriff's reports that "they didn't have no niggers in their country" but that some lived in those hills "cross the river, up above Medallion" (54) underscores the expectation that black life will not spill out of the hills. Morrison acknowledges the destructiveness of this enforced separation, but she also treats the isolation ironically by converting its negative meaning into a positive one. Cordoned off as they are, the people are self-sufficient; they create a neighborhood in the hills "which they could not break"[23] because it gives continuity to their past and present.

In assigning character to the Bottom, Morrison establishes worth in terms of human relationships. As she says, "there was this life-giving very, very strong sustenance that people got from the neighborhood. . . . All the responsibilities that agencies now have were the responsibilities of the neighborhood. So that people were taken care of, or locked up or whatever. If they were sick, other people took care of them; if they were old, other people took care of them; if they needed something to eat, other people took care of them; if they were mad, other people provided a small space for them, or related to their madness or tried to find out the limits of their madness."[24]

Shadrack's presence in the Bottom is evidence of the community's willingness to absorb the most bizarre of its own. When Shadrack returns from World War I and does not know "who or what he was . . . with no past, no language, no tribe" (10), he struggles "to order and focus experience" (12) and to conquer his fear of death. The result is National Suicide Day, which Shadrack establishes as the third of January, believing "that if one day a year were devoted to it [death] everybody could get it out of the way and the rest of the year would be safe and free" (586). At first frightened of him, in time people embrace him and his day. Once they "understood the boundaries and nature of his madness, they could fit him, so to speak, into the scheme of things" (13). That is, according to Morrison, the black community's way.

Sula's mother, Hannah, and grandmother Eva had borne their share of these community responsibilities in the big house where youth, old age, disease, and insanity kept company. (Eva takes the life of her son, Plum, but Morrison treats it as an act of compassion, not of selfishness.) Sula is different, however. In refusing to become a part of the community, she refuses a part of her cultural and her personal history. Her determination to define herself and to redefine a woman's role places her at odds with the community. And yet the community makes room for her in a way perhaps no other place would. There are both variety and cohesiveness in the Bottom, where characters as unlike as Sula, Nel, Ajax, and Shadrack coexist. "There are hundreds of small towns" like Medallion, Morrison explains, "and that's where most black people live. . . . And that's where the juices came from and that's where we *made it,* not made it in terms of success but made who we are."[25]

Morrison suggests that this quality of neighborhood life is endangered. As the buildings and trees are leveled in the Bottom to make room for a new golf course and as blacks leave the hills to occupy spaces vacated by whites in the valley below, Morrison wonders whether economic and social gains are worth the sacrifice of community, because without community the cultural traditions that inform character are lost to future generations.

CHAPTER 3

Male Consciousness
Song of Solomon

When asked during an interview whether she thinks her novels are evolutionary, Morrison responded that she believes they are: "from a book that focused on a pair of very young black girls . . . to a pair of adult black women,
and then to a black man . . . is evolutionary."[1] The black man Morrison
speaks about is the subject of her third novel, *Song of Solomon* (1977). (*Song
of Solomon* greatly enhanced Morrison's literary reputation and broadened
her reading audience. It was a Book-of-the-Month Club selection—the first,
it has been widely noted, by a black writer since Richard Wright's *Native
Son* in 1940—and a year after its publication 570,000 copies were in print.)
Ajax and Cholly, the men who took shape in previous novels, were drawn in
outline and may be viewed as previews of the more detailed male characters
in *Song of Solomon* and in later novels. In *Song of Solomon*, Morrison scru-
tinizes friendship, marriage, family, and relationship to community, primarily
(but not exclusively) from men's points of view. Such scrutiny is driven by
Morrison's belief that a man's experience of life is different from a woman's.
Maleness "tends to be inherent," she believes, in spite of "eighty percent of
the literature" to the contrary.[2] Morrison realizes that her comments may be
"astonishing" to some and that male and female roles may be learned, but
she still holds to an idea of masculinity. Relying on her observations of two
brothers, a father, and sons, she concludes that men have "different spatial
requirements than girls"; they relate "to architecture and space differently."
Her sons "were attracted to danger and risk" in a way she was not, and on
the "question of dominion" men, she says, have "a definite need to exercise

dominion over place and people." They "desire to control" in a way that women do not.[3]

Milkman Dead's major conflict of values in the novel exemplifies, to some extent, gender-determined perspectives: as a son he feels immense pressure to embrace his father's affection for things. But Morrison, as an artist concerned with dimensions of spirituality, offers Milkman an alternative to the pursuit of material success: spiritual fulfillment. Milkman, as one would expect, chooses spirituality, and in explicating his judgment Morrison retraces her precise boundaries of freedom and responsibility for the individual. Like other Morrison characters who would be spiritually free, Milkman must be willing to resist all narrow definitions of the self and take responsibility for the tough choices he makes.

Macon Dead, Milkman's father, has lost this essential freedom; he has traded it for wealth under the mistaken belief that "money is freedom. . . . The only real freedom there is."[4] Macon advises his son to "own things. And let the things you own own other things. Then you'll own yourself and other people too" (55). But, despite his thinking so, property does not elevate Macon above other blacks or earn him respect from whites. In truth, blacks do not hold him in high esteem; they merely fear his ruthless exercise of power, and corrupt whites respect not him but his money. A lifetime of acquiring property, collecting rents, and making deals has rendered Macon a greedy, self-absorbed, unforgiving (and unforgiven) man who is incapable of showing love or receiving it. Hating his wife, Ruth, ignoring his daughters, Lena and First Corinthians, and disowning his sister, Pilate, are the sum of Macon's family connections. Even the one relationship—with Milkman—that promises to humanize him is contaminated by their scheme to steal the gold that he thinks his sister possesses. Family for Macon is just another category of personal wealth. His Sunday drives in the new Packard with Ruth and Milkman in the front seat and Corinthians and Lena in the back are merely parades of assets. The lifeless metallic form of the Packard, which the people in the community dub "Macon Dead's hearse," is a looming symbol of the dead relationships and feelings of the people inside.

At age thirty-two, Milkman is his father's son. The macho rebellion of adolescence has been replaced by a self-indulgent callousness and a tacit acceptance of his father's ways. Collecting Macon's rents, partying with bourgeois blacks who spend silly hours imitating the leisure of whites—these anchor Milkman's life, "which was pointless, aimless, and it was true that he didn't concern himself an awful lot about other people. There was nothing he wanted bad enough to risk anything for, inconvenience himself for" (107). As it is with his father, family for Milkman is a burdensome afterthought. His interactions with them—all women—are mostly an exercise in male prerogative. In fact, he had never really "been able to distinguish them [his sisters] from his mother" (68). Once he had knocked his father into a wall for hitting his mother, but that was less a display of regard for his mother's welfare than a startling instance of arrogance. The younger man had bested the older and, in doing so, felt a "snorting, horse-galloping glee as old as desire" (68). Coming to his mother's defense is a singular instance for Milkman. More typical of his filial tie to her is the unresponsiveness revealed in a "dream" that he relates to his friend Guitar. In Milkman's vision Ruth is in the backyard garden planting tulip bulbs, which immediately sprout "bloody red heads" that grow tall and menacing. Eventually, as Milkman watches from the kitchen window, the smothering plants suffocate his mother, who "was kicking to the last" (105). When Guitar asks, "Why didn't you go help her?" Milkman's uncomprehending retort is "what?" Attending to others has never seemed necessary or beneficial to Milkman. As his sister Lena observes, Milkman's has been a thoughtless life of self-gratification: "You have yet to wash your underwear, spread a bed, wipe the ring from your tub, or move a fleck of your dirt from one place to another. And to this day, you have never asked one of us if we were tired, or sad, or wanted a cup of coffee. . . . You are a sad, pitiful, stupid, selfish, hateful man. I hope your little hog's gut stands you in good stead, and that you take good care of it, because you don't have anything else" (217–18). Lena's accusations shock Milkman into a necessary but unfortunately shallow self-examination, and the conclusions he reaches illustrate his profound shortsightedness: he will find the gold his father thinks Pilate stole from a cave in Pennsylvania and declare his independence. With enough money he would be free of all human obligations. Such thinking reveals Milkman's incredible conceit. His soul, like his mirror image, lacks "coherence, a coming together of the features into a total" (70).

In many ways Milkman's journey from his home in Michigan to Pennsylvania to Virginia and back home conforms to the classical male monomyth of the heroic quest. In this structure the hero's adventure takes him on a journey beset with mortal danger but one that, in the end, brings him nobility and great honor among his people. Of course, Morrison does not faithfully, or with a straight face, appropriate the monomyth paradigm to her story and character. She admits that Song of Solomon is her "own giggle (in Afro-American terms) of the proto-myth of the journey to manhood."[5] She feels that "whenever characters are cloaked in Western fable, they are in deep trouble."[6] One kind of trouble is the customary designation of male narrative as more imperative than female narrative. Morrison would no doubt decline to identify her novel with a narrative tradition so antithetical to her aesthetic, which makes her consistently attentive to women's narratives even in a text like *Song of Solomon*, which is primarily devoted to men's experiences. Instead, then, of blithely conceiving Milkman's journey in terms of the traditional hero's, Morrison satirically calls attention to limitations of the traditional quest by making Milkman less heroic and more human.[7] Not a classical hero, Milkman is a contemporary black man lost to his community and family and, most important, lost to himself. His true quest is not for fortune or honor but for his humanity.

Every phase of his search for gold brings Milkman closer to these truths. In Danville, Pennsylvania, Fred Garnett, a passing motorist, teaches Milkman that not everyone is motivated by financial gain. When Milkman offers him money to pay for a Coke and a ride from the country into town, Garnett shakes his head in disgust and disbelief. Milkman learns that one man can give another "a Coke and a lift now and then" (257) without expecting payment. Reverend Cooper's stories about "old Macon Dead," Milkman's grandfather, about Lincoln's Heaven, the farm that he worked and loved, about the old man's son, Macon Dead Jr., who worked "right alongside" his father, reveal for the first time to Milkman the powerful balm in the phrase "I know your people!" (231). As he listens to the old men's recollections of the past, "he glittered in the light of their adoration and grew fierce with pride" (238). These experiences in Danville begin to unravel Milkman's webbing of indifference just as the difficult country terrain where he searches for the gold spoils the superficial finery of his clothes. By the time he returns to town, Milkman has experienced, in the river stream where he loses his balance and falls in, the first baptismal into a new life. His three-piece suit and Florsheim shoes are soiled and torn, his "heavy over-designed" (240) watch is splintered, the minute hand broken as if to signal an eruption. In the country he comes face to face with his limitations. "He had no idea that simply walking through trees, bushes, on untrammeled ground could be so hard. Woods always brought to his mind city parks, the tended woods on Honore Island where he went for outings as a child and where tiny convenient paths led you through" (252). But here Milkman is alone, far from a town, in a place where his father's money is irrelevant. Here he must chart his own course. And that course must be one that takes him away from old paths of indolence, greed, and vanity toward new paths of spiritual enlightenment. Milkman still has far to travel. The journey so far has brought him to an appreciation of family and hard work that he did not have before, but buried treasure continues to make a slave of him. He does not yet know that money cannot buy the kind of freedom he needs.

This insight is not available to Milkman until the second phase of his journey, in Shalimar, Virginia. Pilate may have gone there, he thinks, and buried the gold. In this small southern community with no commerce or industry, what is left of Milkman's flashy affluence appears insolent to the people who live there: his casual willingness simply to buy a car to replace the broken one he bought the day before, the insult of his locking his car against the men he has asked for help, his calling them "them" and not bothering to give his name or ask theirs. "He was telling them that they weren't men . . . that thin shoes and suits with vests . . . were the measure" (269). The possum hunt, however, that Milkman is goaded into joining changes all of that. Finally, stripped of everything except his watch (and he will soon lose that), dressed in brogans, army fatigues, and a knit cap, Milkman, like the other hunters, must take his measure against the laws of nature. Survival depends upon penetrating the darkness, traversing the rocky terrain, interpreting the dogs' barks, anticipating his prey, sending wordless messages to his companions.

Milkman is not up to this work, and he is nearly conquered by fatigue and fear. But with these trials come flashes of genuine insight (not the shallow self-examination of a few weeks earlier). He now realizes that the black men of Shalimar are more than the sum of money they might earn in city factories or from rent collections. Their primordial link to the earth, to animals, and to one another inspires Milkman's respect. For "if they could talk to animals, and the animals could talk to them, what didn't they know about human beings? Or the earth itself, for that matter" (280). Since he can do none of these, Milkman must acknowledge his own glaring limitations in this place:

> There was nothing here to help him—not his money, his car, his father's reputation, his suit, or his shoes. In fact they hampered him. Except for his broken watch, and his wallet with about two hundred dollars, all he had started out with on his journey was gone: his suitcase with the scotch, the shirts, and the space for bags of gold; his snap-brim hat, his tie, his shirt, his three-piece suit, his socks, and his shoes. His watch and his two hundred dollars would be of no help out here, where all a man had was what he was born with, or had learned to use. And endurance. Eyes, ears, nose, taste, touch—and some other sense that he knew he did not have. (280)

Milkman's reveries have a domino effect, toppling one illusion after another: money is not freedom but enslavement; independence means submitting himself to people in his life, not escaping them. He confesses and repents of his shameful retreat from relationships—refusing any involvement in his parent's problems, using Hagar's love and then throwing it "away like a wad of chewing gum after the flavor was gone" (280), betraying Pilate, the one who had saved his life and then loved him unconditionally. He is alone, without the accoutrement of his vanity, and the old personality gives way to make space for a new spirituality so expansive that only "the whole entire complete deep blue sea!" (330) will contain its volume.

In Shalimar, after the hunt, a transformed Milkman engages a woman's generosity with his—for the first time in his life and without hesitation. Sweet, "a nice lady up the road a ways" (288), takes Milkman in, bathes his sore body, and tends his hurts. In return Milkman gives her a cool bath, rubbing and soaping her "until her skin squeaked and glistened like onyx" (288). He washes her hair, massages her back, makes her bed, washes her dishes, and scours her tub. His unselfish attentions to Sweet are a striking contrast to his inattention to the other women in his life, especially his cousin, Hagar, and a lock of Hagar's hair in his wallet will be a persistent reminder that she died forlorn, with the sound of his spiteful words resonating in his wake. When he was a little boy making the obligatory Sunday drives with his father, mother, and sisters, Milkman had disliked kneeling on the front seat and looking out the back windows in order to see anything. "Riding backwards made him uneasy. It was like flying blind and not knowing where he was going—just where he had been" (31–32). Yet, now he must do just that. In order to move forward with his life, he must review where he has been.

That is the heroic journey for Morrison's characters: to press toward knowledge for its own sake. Morrison holds Milkman responsible for his transgressions, but she also forgives him. "He was not in a position to do anything about [them] . . . because he was stupid," she says. In the future he can "do better, and don't do *that* again."[8] It is important to Morrison that her characters "have revelations, large or small."[9]

The new Milkman is a striking contrast to the other male characters in the novel, who are not transcendent. Macon Dead and Guitar Bains are shaped by ugly circumstances over which they have no control. Each (over) reacts to his helplessness with a compulsive and unremarkable will to conquer. Macon's greedy obsession with owning things and people is a mutated version of his love, as a child, of the land and his family. Belonging to the earth, working with his father, caring for his sister, and earning respect and admiration from the black community define Macon's childhood. His father's violent death at the hands of powerful white men who take the land changes love to obsession. "Owning, building, acquiring—that was his life, his future, his present, and all the history he knew. That he distorted life, bent it, for the sake of gain, was a measure of his loss at his father's death" (304).

Proprietorship consumes Macon and alienates him from family and community, leaving no room for spiritual virtues like love, compassion, kindness, tolerance. He loves only the keys to buildings that he carries in his pocket and that he fondles often and reassuringly. Morrison offers them as a symbol of his empty victory.

Similarly, when Guitar's anger over white brutality against blacks impels him to join the Seven Days as their Sunday man, the anger inside implodes, and he becomes what he hates—a murderer. Like Macon, Guitar is a victim of his experience. Although he is a self-declared avenger of his people, the love of black life is eventually twisted into a love of power. That power gives him, he thinks, authority, which he uses to kill indiscriminately—white and black.

Guitar and Milkman are opposite sides of a single fabric, and Morrison constructs their friendship from the threads of male life—street fights, barbershop talk, pool hall banter, sexual conquest, adventure—just as she constructs Nel and Sula's friendship from the threads of women's lives. Guitar's wild courage excites the sheltered Milkman. Guitar is older than Milkman and street-smart. He protects Milkman, he initiates him to street life, and he does not blame the son for the sins of his father. As Guitar reminds a friend who refuses to serve beer to the underage Milkman for fear of Macon's retaliation, "You can't blame him for who his daddy is."

As the easy laughter of their adolescent intimacy gives way to conflict that throws their differences into stark relief, Morrison uses the space to examine black militancy, not in the service of advocacy but as a way of characterizing the spectrum of black response to white violence in the 1960s. Some, like Milkman, convinced themselves that white oppression of blacks did not concern them. Others, like Macon Dead, turned white hatred into self-hatred and in turn directed that hatred toward their own people. Diametrically, Guitar and the Seven Days, enraged by the lynchings, the burnings, the murder, respond in kind. For them white hatred precipitates acts of black love. "What I'm doing ain't about hating white people," Guitar tells his friend. "It's about loving us. About loving you. My whole life is love" (160). In pledging his "whole life" to the universal love of all black people, Guitar cannot claim a more personal love of wife, children, friends. The secrecy of his work isolates him and precludes intimacy. Eventually, the appealing interplay of street wisdom and hard-edged generosity that defines Guitar gives way to brooding paranoia.

The complementing differences in Guitar's and Milkman's personalities that make each part of a whole are not the differences that eventually divide them. They become competing personalities, unrecognizable to each other.

As Milkman journeys toward self-discovery and cultural identification, Guitar travels a parallel road toward psychic disintegration and cultural alienation. The belonging and understanding that Milkman recovers on the hunt in Shalimar are lost to Guitar, who as a child shared the camaraderie of the hunt. But now in the woods he feels not brotherhood but murderous hostility. He is diseased with "white madness"—the bizarre executions of total strangers. Black crimes are not freakish in that way, according to Morrison. Blacks commit crimes "in the heat of passion: anger, jealousy, loss of face, and so on" (109). (Even the Seven Days, though their crimes are deliberate and premeditated, fall within some broad boundary of legitimacy since their work is a response to aggression.) But stalking Milkman and killing Pilate, whose healing, ancestral guidance he rejects in favor of street justice, place Guitar outside all boundaries of rationality and morality. There can be no moral authority in killing for gold or for pleasure.

In a role reversal, as their journeys come to an end, it is Milkman who draws closest to achieving genuine universal love. His final leap from the rock is not the theatrical miscalculation of a disillusioned man wearing blue silk wings that opens *Song of Solomon* but a hard-earned conviction that, like Pilate, he has courage enough to face any episode of life—even death. When Milkman first gleans these truths, he longs to share them with Guitar, but he can only mourn Guitar's loss. Like Nel and Sula's, Milkman and Guitar's breakup is irreparable.

To his credit, Milkman empathizes with his friend and with his father and is able to forgive their transgressions. Indications are that he even forgives Pilate's murder. "You want my life?" Milkman calls out to Guitar in the aftermath of the shooting. "You want it? Here" (341). Milkman's tearful offer of himself, even in the service of Guitar's corrupt need, seems to suggest that Milkman has evolved to the point that he values love more than he values the physical world. Many readers decry what they believe is the deliberate ambiguity of Morrison's conclusion, which does not explore Guitar's guilt and/or remorse and does not resolve Milkman's feelings: does he leap toward Guitar in anger or in love? But understanding what may appear ambiguous requires remembering Morrison's commitment to readers' participation in making meaning by leaving "spaces" in the text. She explains that "into these spaces should fall the rumination of the reader and his or her invented or recollected or misunderstood knowingness."[10] Each reader interprets text in terms that reflect her experiences. Even with that stipulation to readers, however, Morrison does explain that in the final scenes Guitar recognizes Milkman's transformation "and recalls enough of how lost he himself is . . . to put his weapon down"[11] and perhaps rises up to meet Milkman's gesture of love with a comparable one. Ultimately, however, there is always something more "interesting at stake than a clear resolution in a novel"[12] for Morrison. She is more occupied with her character's survival and with the "complexity of how people behave under duress— . . . the qualities they show at the end of an event when their backs are up against the wall."[13] Milkman's response under duress is to accept what Pilate already knew—that there is no reason to fear death if the spirit is freed in life.

Milkman's unfettered spirit is marked by a dream about flying, Morrison's metaphor for the unconventional life of spiritual freedom. In Sweet's bed he dreams "about sailing high over the earth. . . . Part of his flight was over the dark sea, but it didn't frighten him because he knew he could not fall" (302). As a child Milkman had longed for physical flight, and his discovery at age four that "only birds and airplanes could fly" had made him lose "all interest in himself" (9). The result is a dull, unimaginative childhood that stretches into a pointless, indifferent adulthood. Flying remains a literal conception, impossible to achieve except on his first airplane ride, where "in the air, away from real life, he felt free" (222). Freedom in an airplane "away from real life" is illusory, however. Milkman does not yet know that it is the spirit that must soar. As the insurance agent Robert Smith discovers, in modern times, believing in literal flight is a mental aberration that leads to certain death on the street below. In Michigan, Milkman is wedded to the streets where he estimates his worth in the marketplace in terms of money and commodities. Milkman is like the peacock he chases at the car lot, moored by the weight of his own finery. Guitar could just as easily be describing Milkman when he observes that the peacock has "too much tail. All that jewelry weighs it down. Like vanity. Can't nobody fly with all that shit. Wanna fly. You got to give up the shit that weighs you down" (179–80). In Virginia, Milkman "gives up" the vanity acquired on Not Doctor Street when he accepts the timeless rhythms of men and animals in the woods.

Flight, the free fall, consistently means freedom, independence, unconventionality, self-knowledge for Morrison. In *Song of Solomon* flight also evokes the American folk tradition.[14] Solomon's song is Morrison's version of the flying African myth about enslaved Africans who escaped slavery in the South by rising up and flying back to Africa and to freedom. In adopting and adapting the myth, Morrison becomes the modern griot, reciting stories from the past to a new generation. And her novel serves an essential function as cultural artifact. Myths are forgotten or misunderstood, Morrison thinks, because people in transit move away from the places where they were born and from the culture bearers who remain in those places. The flying myth is her example of one that is misunderstood by those who can relate to it in Western classical terms only. But Morrison wishes to restore its tutorial power for black people. As she says, "If it means Icarus to some readers, fine; I want to take credit for that. But my meaning is specific: it is about black people who could fly. That was always part of the folklore of my life; flying was one of our gifts. I don't care how silly it may seem. It is everywhere— people used to talk about it, it's in the spirituals and gospels. Perhaps it was wishful thinking—escape, death, and all that. But suppose it wasn't. What might it mean? I tried to find out in *Song of Solomon*."[15]

When Milkman realizes that the children's song "Solomon done fly Solomon done gone / Solomon cut across the sky Solomon gone home" is about his great grandfather Solomon, who had such powers, he rejoices: "Solomon didn't need no airplane. He just took off; got fed up. All the way up! No more cotton! No more bales! No more orders! No more shit! He flew, baby. Lifted his beautiful black ass up in the sky and flew on home" (332). Milkman is exhilarated, but Morrison is cautious. African myth is not less vulnerable to contamination than Western fable. Solomon flew off, and Morrison asks, "Who'd he leave behind?" (332). What about the wife and twenty-one children that he left here on the ground?

With that question, Morrison's novel about male consciousness signals her ongoing delineation of women's concerns. Solomon flies off, and Ryna, his wife, is left to take care of the children. Her cries of protest and anguish are still carried on the wind more than a century later for Milkman to hear. In the third generation Milkman and Hagar reenact this tragedy of abandonment. When Milkman leaves, Hagar loses all capacity to think rationally, and she dies, as the euphemism goes, of a broken heart. Milkman dreams of flying as Hagar is dying (336). As always, however, Morrison intimates that matters of freedom and responsibility are not so easily settled. Milkman is, without a doubt, culpable. He has been callous and careless. But does Hagar's love for him give her the right to demand his love in return? Morrison answers no. Guitar reminds Hagar that "love shouldn't be like that" (309). Love is not possession. "You can't own a human being" (310). And, most important, you cannot love someone more than you love yourself. Hagar, who "wanted to kill for love, die for love," (310) has not learned these lessons. Guitar calls her one of those "doormat women" whose "pride and conceit" amaze him (310). Hagar will not or cannot save her own life because she does not value herself outside the narrow limits of Milkman's love. Her frantic efforts to make herself over to fit the popular image of female beauty continue Morrison's recurring invective against the tyranny of such an image. Morrison's description of the carnival of smells, colors, and textures at the cosmetics counter in the department store where Hagar goes is a tour de force of the seductive influences of commercial marketing stratagems:

> The cosmetics department enfolded her in perfume, and she read hungrily the labels and the promise. Myrurgia for primeval woman who created for him a world of tender privacy where the only occupant is you, mixed with Nina Ricci's L'Air duTemps. Yardley's Flair with Tuvache's Nectaroma and D'Orsay's Intoxication. Robert Piquet's Fracas, and Calypso and Visa and Bandit. Houbigant's Chantilly. Caron's Fleurs de Rocaille and Bellodgia. Hagar breathed deeply the sweet air that hung over the glass counters. Like a smiling sleepwalker she circled. Round and round the diamond-clear counters covered with bottled, wafer-thin disks, round boxes, tubes, and phials. Lipsticks in soft white hands darted out of their sheaths like the shiny red penises of puppies. Peachy powders and milky lotions were grouped in front of poster after cardboard poster of gorgeous grinning faces. Faces in ecstasy. Faces somber with achieved seduction. Hagar believed she could spend her life there among the cut glass, shimmering in peaches and cream, in satin. In opulence. In luxe. In love. (315)

Hagar is bound for disappointment as the promises of cosmetic beauty are washed away with the scents and powders in a pouring rain on the street outside the department store. Morrison's work is a warning shot for those, like Hagar and like Pauline Breedlove before her, who would be victim to a false standard of beauty. Morrison's heroic characters must resist; they must be transformed, not cosmetically but internally by their own humanity, and, like Milkman, they must take responsibility for their own lives. Milkman's journey shapes his metamorphosis so that by the novel's conclusion he has achieved freedom and accountability. Intuitive, compassionate, forgiving, generous, he knows that "if you surrendered to the air, you could *ride* it" (341).

Pilate is the other heroic character in *Song of Solomon*. Her journey to self-knowledge having been completed, she knows, from the beginning of the text, what Milkman discovers in the end, and, as her name suggests, Pilate is Milkman's spiritual guide throughout his passage. During Milkman's infancy and even before, she shields him from Macon's angry attacks, and later, during Milkman's adolescence, she catalyzes his course of self-discovery. In her presence, at age twelve, he discovers a woman, who, without property and social position, is taller and wiser than his father. That "was the first time in his life that [he] remembered being completely happy" (47). Pilate's stories about her life on the farm, about her father's bravery, about her brother's love,

and her refusal to adopt the meaningless rituals that occupy most people—
these counter Macon's stories about conquest, ownership, and dominion.
Macon's declaration to his son that "Pilate can't teach you a thing you can
use in the world" (55) proves false, for Pilate alone teaches him the true
meaning of flying without ever leaving the ground (340). Pilate's is not the
selfish flight of Solomon, who leaves everyone behind. Pilate teaches Milkman that "you can't fly on off and leave a body" (336). When Milkman
leaves Hagar, it is Pilate who locks him in her cellar upon his return, forcing
his dawning realization that Hagar is dead, that "it was his fault and Pilate
knew it" (336). His punishment by Pilate's reckoning is to carry with him
"something that remained of the life he had taken" (336). That evening
Milkman returns home with a box of Hagar's hair as a healing reminder that
with freedom comes responsibility.

Pilate, of course, is one of Morrison's ancestors, one of the timeless people who dispatch their wisdom to others, who consciously or unconsciously
initiate others to the ways of African American culture that give life continuity and intent. Out of place in "the big northern city" (266), Pilate embraces
more natural rhythms, like those of the women of Shalimar who walk the
road without purses, "bare-legged, their unstraightened hair braided or
pulled straight back into a ball" (266). Pilate has little need for the creature
comforts of "elaborately socialized society" (150). In deciding early in her
life whom she wanted to love and what was important to her, Pilate has given
up interest in manners and money but has "acquired a deep concern for and
about human relationships" (150).

Ancestral, mythic, free, Pilate embodies memorable traits of character
that give form to the major theme of Morrison's work: spiritual transcen-
dence. Born without a navel, which evidences the common birth of one human from another, Pilate seems ageless, immortal. As a natural healer whose
"compassion for troubled people" and "respect for other people's privacy"
(150) are her passport, she has no fear of life. Neither does she have the
familiar terror of death: "she spoke often to the dead [and] . . . knew there
was nothing to fear" (149). At the end of her life, Milkman wonders if there
is another like Pilate. "There's got to be at least one more woman like you,"
he whispers (340). As ancestor, Pilate bears a major share of the novel's work
in passing on cultural knowledge to Milkman and to the reader.

All of Morrison's novels mirror the characters, language, folklore, my-
thology of African America. In *Song of Solomon*, Morrison nudges cultural
memory by examining the importance in the black community of names and
naming. Names of places and people are routinely appended, denoting some

exploit or episode or special skill or talent or notoriety. Names have meaning; names tell stories: Ryna's Gulch, Solomon's Leap, Not Doctor Street— once called Doctor Street (its official name is Mains Avenue) by blacks in honor of the first black man to practice medicine in the city, who lived and died on Doctor Street. When the white city legislators posted notices in businesses on the street reminding residents of the avenue's official name, Southside residents deliberately and unceremoniously took up Not Doctor Street, a name that signaled their inventive resistance to any oppression. Milkman (whose name is one old man's idea of humor) considers the import of black men and women knowing their names:

> Names they got from yearnings, gestures, flaws, events, mistakes, weaknesses. Names that bore witness. Macon Dead, Sing Byrd, Crowell Byrd, Pilate, Reba, Hagar, Magdalene, First Corinthians, Milkman, Guitar, Railroad Tommy, Hospital Tommy, Empire State (he just stood around and swayed), Small Boy, Sweet, Circe, Moon, Nero, Humpty-Dumpty, Blue Boy, Scandinavia, Quack-Quack, Jericho, Spoonbread, Ice Man, Dough Belly, Rocky River, Gray Eye, Cock-a-Doodle Doo, Cool Breeze, Muddy Waters, Pinetop, Jelly Roll, Fats, Lead-Belly, Bo Diddley, Cat-Iron, Peg-Leg, Son, Shortstuff, Smoky Babe, Funny Papa, Bukka, Pink, Bull Moose, B.B., T-Bone, Black Ace, Lemon, Washboard, Gatemouth, Cleanhead, Tampa Red, Juke Boy, Shine, Staggerlee, Jim the Devil, Puck-up, and *Dat* Nigger. (333–34)

To know one's name is to own it, to insist upon claiming its history. Milkman learns to accept his name as a testimony to the loneliness that kept his mother nursing him until he was old enough to dangle his legs to the floor. Jake keeps and owns the unfortunate name given him by an illiterate white man and passes that name on to his son, who passes it on to his son. Pilate keeps "her own name and everybody else's," Guitar thinks (89), in a brass box attached to her ear. Perhaps she understands, as Milkman does, that "when you know your name you should hang on to it, for unless it is noted down and remembered, it will die when you do" (333). As Morrison explains it, the gold of Milkman's search "is really Pilate's yellow orange and the glittering metal of the box in her ear" (29) containing her name. In the opening epigraph of *Song of Solomon*, Morrison reminds that "the fathers may soar / And the children may know their names." Each generation is obliged to remember and pass its knowledge on to the next.

CHAPTER 4

Community and Cultural Identity
Tar Baby

Song of Solomon, in part because of its popular appeal, gave dramatic momentum to Morrison's writing career. By 1981, the year of her fourth book, *Tar Baby,* that career was soaring. As one reviewer observed, "The promotion of *Tar Baby* was a stunning show," choreographed by "the Madison Avenue machinery [which] spun into highest gear."[1] Morrison was, the reviewer continued, "the toast of the literary world," appearing at parties and on television, giving readings, and (arguably the most remarkable of these unveilings) appearing on the March 30, 1981, cover of *Newsweek.* Morrison's by now familiar and unsentimental response to the magazine's coverage was "I can't believe *Newsweek* will have a middle-aged colored woman on its cover."

In *Tar Baby,* Morrison continues to expand the range of her subjects and characters. For the first time in her work she gives white characters significant roles. Here they figure prominently in her examination of the intricacies of inter- and intraracial relationships. Valerian Street, a wealthy candy manufacturer, and his wife, Margaret, both come under scrutiny as employers, as husband and wife, as parents, and both perform poorly in every category. Morrison finds much to condemn and little to redeem in either. And yet she does not withhold the hope of redemption. With Morrison few crimes are beyond human understanding, and few of her characters are unworthy of her compassion. She wants readers to see not just a character's "façade" but the "point of view inside."[2] *Tar Baby* is not a protest novel; Morrison is not looking for someone to blame for white oppression of blacks. Certainly Valerian and Margaret are reflections of their social, economic, and racial backgrounds (and Morrison explores these), but she renders them more interesting as individuals, each with his or her own crimes quite apart from those of the rest of their race.

Valerian's complications of character demonstrate well Morrison's unwillingness to take the easy path of stereotype. Valerian is indulgently world weary. His cynical, unromanticized view of his own orphaned youth as a candy heir surrounded by doting uncles and maiden aunts is easily applicable to his view of all social relations. His wife, Margaret, is tolerated as an incapable, middle-aged beauty twenty years his junior. Their son, Michael, is an irrelevant thirty-year-old social activist always in search of the next cause. And all that can be said of Sidney and Ondine is that, after thirty years as Valerian's butler and cook, they are at least as familiar to him as his wife and son.

It is partly this cynicism that prompts Valerian to leave Philadelphia for L'Arbe de la Croix, his residence on a remote Caribbean island, to live as a quasi hermit tending hothouse plants. On the island, unlike in the city, Valerian is shielded from people and places that have become increasingly unfamiliar. On the island he can avoid a public review of his imminent dotage. The ordered greenhouse is proof of these effects. Valerian spends days tending the plants and playing the music of European classical composers, oblivious to the natural rhythms of the island that play outside. The measured growth of the greenhouse plants is a symbol of his control. But such order amid wildness is unnatural, just as Valerian's presence on Isle des Chevaliers is unnatural. Morrison personifies all of nature in protest of Valerian's intrusion. When the rain forests are destroyed to make space for opulent winter playhouses like Valerian's, "clouds of fish were convinced that the world was over" and "wild parrots . . . agreed."[3] The river, too, understood that the balance was destroyed, that "never again would the rain be equal," (7) and the two-thousand-year-old forest that had been "scheduled for eternity" was instead bound for extinction. When Valerian's dotage finally arrives, he can no longer keep the life of the island in check. Ants eat their way through the copper wires of his stereo and promise to invade the greenhouse itself, and trees are poised to overrun the house. "Things grew or died where and how they pleased. Isle des Chevaliers filled in the spaces that had been the island's to begin with" (208). Indeed, Morrison envisions nature's revenge: "After thirty years of shame," the champion daisy trees, which had remained serene during man's assault, "were marshaling for war" (236).

Beyond cynicism, Valerian suffers from the arrogance afflicting the majority of his social and economic class: the arrogance that makes rearranging the wild, beautiful island landscape to install his foreign presence possible, the arrogance that allows him "to dismiss with a flutter of the fingers the people [of the Caribbean] whose sugar and cocoa had allowed him to grow old in regal comfort" (174).

Valerian, however, does not sink completely beneath the white man's burden of responsibility for the planet's sorrow. He is in part borne up by his acts of decency: giving stocks to Sidney and Ondine; paying for the education of their niece, Jadine; paying Social Security taxes to prevent Sidney and Ondine from ending up like many domestic workers who spend their lives tending other people's children and kitchens with no retirement income to sustain them in old age.

Valerian is not malevolent, nor is he an ordinary bigot. To accuse him of these failings would be a sure way for Morrison to develop her theme, but such a reductive characterization would not represent Valerian's "point of view inside." In Morrison's estimation Valerian is more complex and more interesting: he is innocent. For all his worldly cynicism, Valerian is essentially unaware of the harm that he has caused and that he has allowed others to cause. He does not know that his presence in the Caribbean is an extension of Western colonialism or that firing Gideon and Therese for stealing apples is immoral since he has stolen much more from them: a place in the continuing history of their island. And, worst of all, he does not know that his wife is a child abuser, that Margaret systematically burned, pricked, and cut their son, Michael, throughout his childhood. Valerian does not know these things "because he had not taken the trouble to know. . . . He was guilty, therefore, of innocence" (209). When it is too late to make a difference, Valerian wonders if there is anything "so loathsome as a willfully innocent man?" He realizes that "an innocent man is a sin before God." Sin is human; innocence is "inhuman and therefore unworthy. No man should live without absorbing the sins of his kind" (209). This realization pushes Valerian into sudden old age, and he must finally admit the arrogance and cynicism that have defended him against knowing. As Terry Otten demonstrates, in Morrison's fiction "those who sin against the flawed order become the agents of experience and so run the risk of freedom. Those who do not are often doomed to spiritual stasis and moral entropy."[4] In the end, only those with knowledge survive.

That includes Margaret, whose point of view renders her larger than her crime. Her offense—horrible though it is—links her to the rest of humanity. In comparing himself to her, Valerian muses that "Margaret knew the bottomlessness—she had looked at it, dived in it and pulled herself out obviously tougher than he" (209). Suffering all those years with the secret of what she has done earns Margaret the right to judge herself and Valerian. She can also forgive herself and ultimately feels tranquility and contentment. Morrison comes close to empathizing with Margaret as a woman like other women victimized by a society that overvalues physical beauty. Born beautiful into a family of plain parents and ordinary siblings, Margaret is ignored, despised, and finally left alone to make what she will of her assets. She is the teenage object of Valerian's passion, and nothing substantial is ever expected of her. Valerian's wealth and elevated social position prohibit Margaret's friendship with Ondine, the one person in Valerian's life with whom she is comfortable. With her limited education and experience, she has nothing in common with the wealthy socialites who would be appropriate companions. Margaret is isolated, and having a baby isolates her more. As Ondine surmises, Valerian kept Margaret stupid and idle, and Margaret punished him by sticking pins in his baby. "*Her* baby she loved" (240; emphasis added).

Margaret has no core of self and no culture. She belongs nowhere; she has no roots. Her unnatural mothering has alienated Michael, who apparently loves her but does not want to be near her. At Isle des Chevaliers she is merely a visitor in Valerian's domain. The solitude disquiets her—probably giving her too much time for reflection—and the island sun assaults her too-fair skin. In planning a special Christmas, Margaret attempts to create a cultural context for herself, but she fails. She wants a traditional Christmas with mother, father, son, and friends, a meal cooked by mother's own hands, a turkey, apple pies, and ollieballen, a Dutch bread. These are reassuring symbols of her place in the culture as she knows it. But these symbols are a hodgepodge, an amorphous collection that Margaret cannot assimilate as her own. Her failed Christmas plans suggest the incoherence of her life: Michael will never come home; there are no turkeys on the island; apples have to be imported at great expense; moreover, Margaret cannot cook, especially not a complicated Dutch bread. She is a "cultural orphan," and she has made Michael one as well. That explains his involvement in the struggle for African American and Native American rights or in any struggle that brings him in proximity to people with cultural integrity.

However, Morrison suggests that the burden of guilt that Margaret has borne over the years has positioned her for forgiveness and triumph. That suffering has made her stronger than even she suspects. As Valerian is rendered weak by his seasons of innocence and is therefore in no condition to bear the burden of knowledge (when he hears about Michael's abuse, he collapses into a palsied stupor), Margaret emerges, burnished by the fires of suffering, redeemed and ready to take care of Valerian. She is no longer a visitor on Isle des Chevaliers as she settles into her role of organizer and caregiver. She appears natural and at peace, with her hair falling softly to her shoulders, free of its tortured, teased arrangement, and her face returning to familiarity without its made-up disguise. No longer in flight from herself, Margaret has a coherent identity, finally. And, although it is nearly too late, she may be able to make friends with Ondine and rekindle their brief youthful intimacy. As women—their racial differences notwithstanding—they have a great deal in common, a special bond. Ondine kept Margaret's secret about Michael's abuse because it "was woman stuff" (207). She could not tell Margaret's husband or her own. They would not have understood, but Ondine does. She despises Margaret, judges her, becomes her "mother superior" (72), but only she, as a woman, understands and explains Margaret's transference of anger from Valerian to Michael. Morrison does not exonerate Margaret or minimize her crime. She merely counts it among the museum of horrible acts of which humans are capable. All of Morrison's characters are measured first against the yardstick of humanity and only after that by the rule of historical racial culture.

Sidney and Ondine, too, have interior viewpoints that layer their characterizations beyond thin stereotype. Morrison resists any urge to sanctify them as oppressed servants. They are not immune to the failings that afflict Margaret and Valerian. All are proud, arrogant; all usurp power where they can. Morrison does acknowledge social and racial differences, but these do not diminish the significance of their similarities; they do contribute, however, an abiding and remarkable tension threatening the tenuous boundaries of employee and employer.

Ondine reigns in the kitchen and larder, which are exclusively her domain. For thirty years Sidney has performed his duties as butler and personal attendant with elegant style and attention to detail. Together they administer the domestic chores of the house and yard. Their lives have been spent on the Streets (they have no friends, no children, no social activities outside Valerian's house), but they do not feel exploited. Valerian's financial generosity has made groveling unnecessary, and thirty years of familiarity have softened the roles of master and servant. Indeed, in the end the roles are effectively reversed. In his palsied condition, Valerian has lost most of his authority. Sidney, then, becomes not just Valerian's personal attendant but, like Margaret, a caregiver as well. In that capacity, Sidney has authority, and he does not hesitate to use it.

In some sense Sidney and Ondine are as foreign to Isle des Chevaliers as Margaret and Valerian. They are self-described "Philadelphia Negroes" with a social status that sets them apart and above blacks from the South or from the Caribbean. These other blacks are not Negroes with a capital "N" but strangers, people whose ancestors had not successfully emulated white enterprise and industry as Sidney's and Ondine's people had done in Philadelphia. They have proudly removed themselves from the category of "nigger," synonymous to them with uncultivated and, therefore, unworthy. Valerian is accurate in his fleeting estimation of them as smug and fraudulent in the proprietary pride they take in their employer's property, protecting it from "strangers" on the island. They acknowledge no bond and make no alliance with the other workers hired to maintain Valerian's orderly pace of life. Therese, who does the laundry, and Gideon, who handles yard chores, are merely faceless bodies to Sidney and Ondine. To them, all the island women look alike, and one yardman (the name they assign to Gideon) is as shiftless and unfathomable as the next. When, without first consulting Sidney and Ondine, Valerian summarily fires Therese and Gideon for taking the Christmas apples, the two question Valerian's behavior. It is, they feel, an affront to their position and a violation of their status. They pout and surreptitiously accuse a surprised Valerian of betrayal; only momentarily does his refusal to honor their claim that he owes them remind them that they are, after all, only hired help.

Sidney and Ondine's rank in the Street household is ambiguous at best. They are clearly more than servants, but how much more? Thirty years buys them privileges, but exactly what those privileges are is unclear. Their position is further complicated by the presence of Jadine, their twenty-four-year-old niece. As Sidney and Ondine's surrogate daughter, Jadine is by association with her family a member of the staff. She is also on the staff in deed, hired for a hiatus by Margaret as a companion. The two shop together, exercise together, and generally spend time in some mutual pursuit designed, it seems, to keep Margaret occupied. Jadine's "work" fuzzes the definitions of employer and friend: she takes meals with the Streets and is served as they are by her uncle; her bedroom is upstairs next to Margaret's, far from the servant's quarters Sidney and Ondine occupy near the kitchen. Jadine's anomalous relations are reflected in her quandary over an appropriate Christmas gift for Michael: "Should the—what?—social secretary buy a present for the son of her employer/patron? . . . A gift would embarrass him, probably, because he wouldn't have gotten one for her. Or would he? What had Margaret told him about the household? Even so, would he be offended by a gift from her, however modest?" (77).

Jadine is educated, beautiful, sophisticated, having more in common with Margaret than with Ondine or Sidney. They are her family, but she inhabits a world that is much larger than theirs, one that is closed to them. Yet, Jadine's privilege artificially inflates their status, deceiving them, for a time, into thinking they have more authority than they in fact have. In a crisis Ondine believes that "nothing can happen to us as long as she's [Jadine's] here" (87). They are mistaken, and it is not until Jadine abandons them to their fate with Valerian and returns to Paris that Sidney and Ondine take the initiative in redefining their positions, contouring it to fit their desires.

Encouraged, no doubt, by Valerian's weakened condition and no longer willing to endure the limitations of serving only, the pair (Sidney especially) expand the old limits. In a final scene of the novel, in Valerian's greenhouse, Sidney enters, as is his custom, with a tray of food. Instead of leaving it as he usually does, he stays to handfeed Valerian and to assure him that "we'll give you the best of care. Just like we always done. That's something you ain't never got to worry about" (247). Sidney changes other parts of his normal routine as well. Over Valerian's objections he pours *himself* a glass of wine and, ignoring Valerian's talk of moving back to Philadelphia, decides that he and Ondine like the island's warmth and that moving is out of the question. In taking charge, Sidney unceremoniously revises his and Valerian's roles, and, in response to such revision, Valerian can only half question, half mutter, "What's happening here? Something's happening here" (247).

Meanwhile, back in the kitchen, Ondine and Margaret are revising themselves. Despite the cloud of Margaret's crime hanging over them (or perhaps because of it: since only they knew about it, it bonds them), the women resume the laughter and camaraderie that Valerian had interrupted thirty years earlier because he objected to his wife's intimacy with the cook. Ondine and Sidney (and Margaret) are no longer subject to Valerian's power to preempt their lives. It is they who will take care of Valerian; they will, as Sidney promises, "give him the best of care." Morrison has, in her own words, "enormous respect"[5] for Sidney. Although, as she says, he may be considered "a good old Uncle Tom" by some, Morrison treats his commitment to family and work as a virtue. Indeed, Sidney and Ondine both are familiar as proud people, who, despite making the mistake of calculating their future in Valerian's commercial terms, are progenitors of an African American tradition of pride in accomplishment.

Sidney endures, but Morrison severs the power that Valerian has drawn from his identity as a white male industrialist. Although he has not raised his own hand in abuse of that power, he has stood mute and blind to the systematic abuse of the inherent chauvinism of power in the world. His crime is willful innocence, and for that there is no reparation. Only those who have suffered the sin of crime (child abuse, pride, arrogance) are forgiven and redeemed.

Although the drama of white power and black power keeps Morrison occupied in *Tar Baby,* she is never far from the thematic concerns of black

women: reconstructing themselves, expanding beyond conventional limitations. What price do women pay for the choices they make and for those
they do not make? These and other themes inform Morrison's development
of Jadine's character, which illuminates the opportunities and the dangers of
black womanhood. Jadine is a new kind of character for Morrison. She is not
the rebel, thwarting convention, that Sula is. She is not the mother-woman
that Nel is, standing jealous guard over domesticity. She is not the culture
bearer that Pilate is. Jadine is the modern women, a product of feminist ideology, mistress of the political and social system that ideology once opposed,
embracing the values of that system: business enterprise, social connections,
acquisition. With a graduate degree in art education and a career in high-
fashion modeling, Jadine has realized her goal of transcending the Baltimore
housing project where she was born. The sealskin coat, made from the hides
of "ninety baby seals" and sent as a Christmas present from her Parisian
lover, represents just how far from her childhood she has moved. Jadine is seduced by the blackness of an expensive coat and not by the rhythms of black
Africa. (Both she and the coat are superfluous on a warm Caribbean island
that was once cultivated by the labor of black slaves.) The question Morrison
poses, of course, is how far is too far from Baltimore and her cultural past?
Jadine craves glamour, parties, and cities. In New York, for example, she
feels at home. Its rhythms are familiar and delightful. To her it is a "black
women's town . . . [where] the manifesto was simple: 'Talk shit. Take none'"
(191). This is the language of working women all over New York whose
confidence in themselves defines the city's pulsing beat. And Jadine numbers
herself as one of them.

Although it is earned in some respects, Jadine's confidence in herself is
fragile. It needs the reinforcement of numbers, the assurances of scores of city
women like herself. Without them she is vulnerable to doubts. Without them
she is threatened by her memory of an African woman in a Paris supermarket
who spit at her. Jadine had been transfixed, like everyone else, by the woman's "transcendent beauty" (39) as she glided effortlessly, it seemed, through
the market. She had represented womanhood itself; she was a "woman's
woman," a "mother/sister/she" (39), as all definitions of womanliness found
expression in her air of authority. The woman's insult to Jadine, then, had
had the powerful effect of challenging Jadine's choices: her white boyfriend,
her trendy girlfriends, her parties, her picture on the cover of *Elle*, the way
she lived her life. Jadine hates the woman but cannot escape feeling "lonely
and inauthentic" (40) because of her—except in New York.

Morrison points out the danger in Jadine's choices. The woman in the
Paris market, whether consciously or not, calls attention to something that is

missing in Jadine: she has no connection to her cultural past, and without it, Morrison suggests, she is vulnerable at the very least, and at most she is like the abused Michael, a cultural orphan. Sensing these dangers, Jadine flees Paris and retreats to Isle des Chevaliers, where Sidney and Ondine may offer protection. They are her people, her family, and she seeks them out "to touch bases, to sort out things before going ahead with, with, with anything" (41). But the island offers her no refuge. It is not home, and Sidney and Ondine are only surrogate parents. She has never really lived with them except during summers spent at Valerian's house, and she does not really value their opinions. Jadine's position in the household as Margaret's employee/friend/ guest underscores these ambiguities.

Without ancestors to point the way, Jadine may never discover the path to black womanhood. Like Margaret, she will have no traditions and will have to find a way to live with her feelings of inauthenticity. When it is too late, Ondine tries to guide Jadine, but all that she is really able to do is to express regrets:

> Jadine, a girl has got to be a daughter first. She have to learn that. And if she never learns how to be a daughter, she can't never learn how to be a woman. I mean a real woman: a woman good enough for a child; good enough for a man—good enough for the respect of other women. Now you didn't have a mother long enough to learn much about it and I thought I was doing right by sending you to all them schools and so I never told you it and I should have. You don't need your own natural mother to be a daughter. All you need is to feel a certain way, a certain careful way about people older than you are. . . . A daughter is a woman that cares about where she come from and takes care of them that took care of her. (242)

In their own pride and arrogance, Sidney and Ondine have tacitly encouraged their niece's cultural disconnection as a sign of her and their success. They liked her living in Paris; they liked her acceptance by their employer. But they did not heed the price of such acceptance: becoming someone who is alienated from black culture, someone who prefers Chagall to Entuma masks, a woman who does not know how to be a respectful daughter. Being black, Morrison suggests, is not only a matter of genetics; it is also a matter of culture. Gideon is wrong when he says it is hard for Jadine to choose blackness because she is a "yella" and therefore more white than black. Jadine does not choose blackness because, as Ondine knows, she has never learned what it is; she has not been acculturated. As Morrison notes in

Song of Solomon, without a chorus of mamas and aunts tending her, a black woman may easily lose her way.

Jadine has not learned the things she needs to know to be the "real woman" that Ondine describes. She has never known the "ancient properties" of black womanhood. Morrison observes with regret this aspect of her character's failings when Jadine falls into a tar pit on Isle des Chevaliers. Surrounded by aged trees whose long, mossy growths assume mythic proportions, Jadine rejects the trees' maternal delight in her return to them. As she struggles to free herself, they realize that she is not "a runaway child . . . restored to them" (157). She does not acknowledge her link to their "exceptional femaleness" (157). She does not know "as they did that the first world of the world had been built with their sacred properties; that they alone could hold together the stones of pyramids and rushes of Moses's crib" (157). They marvel at her "desperate struggle . . . to be something other than they were" (157). She does not know, Morrison charges, her place in their history, which is the history of black womanhood, which is "as old as the hills."

Jadine rejects the tree women just as she does the night women who crowd into her room and keep her awake by revealing their breasts. They are joined by the African woman in the Paris market who shows "her three big eggs" (222), symbols of female fertility. These are all the women who have not tried to escape their history. They—her mother, Ondine, Therese, the living, and the dead—come not so much to accuse as to persuade her to follow. These visions are manifestations of Jadine's divided self: she wants to live as a woman of the world, inventing herself as she goes, not tethered to the past, but some part of her needs tradition. Without it her identity is shifting, always in progress; she will never know who she is. Jadine, however, refuses to be initiated into the cult of black womanhood by the night women. She challenges the women's invasion by declaring that she, too, has breasts. When that does not work, she decides to deconstruct the image, "slice it open and see what lay in its belly" (225). She tells herself that the "women looked awful: . . . onion heels, potbellies, hair surrendered to rags and braids. And the breasts they thrust at her like weapons were soft, loose bags closed at the tip" (225). Jadine hopes to outdistance the women by synchronizing her pace to the speed of cities like Paris and New York. In these places she can replace the women with friends whose names—Dawn, Aisha, Felicite, Betty—are, like her own, not cultural throwbacks but emblems of finesse and success.

Jadine's foil in the novel is Son Green. If she is in retreat from black culture, he embodies its deepest currents. On Isle des Chevaliers, with its oozing, rich association with Africa and the Caribbean, Jadine feels misplaced even as Son is easily at home. From the moment he jumps ship, landing feet first in the "soft and warm" (1) island sea, emerging reborn from the "water that heaved and pulsed in the ammonia-scented air" (2), Son is embraced by the water-lady as one of her own. "His skin blended well with the dark [night] water" (1). Later, on the island, unwashed and half starved, he is identified with the rest of nature, poised to [re]claim L'Arbe de la Croix, return it to precolonial wildness, and spoil the superficial harmony (that Jadine labors diligently to maintain) of its residents. Once inside the house, he does just that.

William "Son" Green is a specimen of Morrison's traveling man. He is not a chronic wanderer by nature and by choice as are Ajax and Cholly, "dangerously free" to refuse responsibility for anyone but themselves. Killing his wife by running his car into the bedroom where she is sleeping with her thirteen-year-old lover makes him a fugitive. But for that he would probably have remained at home in Eloe, Florida. Once on the run, he is indistinguish-able, for a time, from the dangerous ones, the "international legion of day laborers" who refuse "to equate work with life" (143). By nature, however, Son is most like Milkman at the end of his journey to self-knowledge. Milk-man discovers the self that Son already knows. Son is rooted in cultural pride; his values are spiritual. He refuses the rituals of success; he refuses "to live in the world their way" (148).

For a time Son is the only one at L'Arbe de la Croix with so honest a representation of himself in the world. But in response to his trespass in Margaret's closet, everyone—Margaret, Valerian, Sidney, Ondine, Jadine—is eventually unmasked, forced to reveal and confront his or her crimes and deceptions. For, as Morrison reveals, the Tar Baby tale seems to her to be about masks, and in her novel all the major characters except Son wear them. His "most effective mask," she says, "is none."[6] At the dinner table, then, on Christmas Day, Son, washed and fed, presides at the other char-acters' unveiling. Sidney and Ondine are the first to lift the edges of their façade as sovereigns in the household. For most of their adult lives, the two have been Valerian's loyal employees. That loyalty has been nourished by an understanding that Valerian appreciates not only their fidelity but their authority as well. When Valerian fires Therese and Gideon without Sidney's and Ondine's knowledge, their identities are called into question. "I may be a cook," Ondine reminds Valerian, "but I'm a person too" (178). The hypocrisy of the pair's position is underscored by the Christmas scene: cook and butler seated at dinner as guests, dressed in their finest clothes, feeling betrayed by their employer, whom they now realize sees them (despite their presence at his table) merely as the help. Having been forced to remove half of her mask, Ondine rips off the remainder. If, indeed, she has no authority, then her loyalty has gone unrewarded, and she is not obliged to remain so. Feeling a reckless liberty and righteous indignation, Ondine in effect reaches across the dinner table to rip away Margaret's mask: Margaret is not the sensitive, inspired mother she believes herself to be; she is a "white freak!," a "baby killer!" who "stuck pins in his [Michael's] behind. Burned him with cigarettes" (179). At first Margaret retreats from Ondine's accusations, but then, like Ondine, she feels an unaccustomed liberation without her mask. She welcomes "the wonderful relief of public humiliation, the solid security of the pillory" (202).

For Margaret, Ondine, and Sidney, Son merely witnesses the unmasking; for Valerian and Jadine, he precipitates it. They hide more and therefore have more to reveal. Son will not permit Valerian, for example, to continue parading the mantle of fair, benevolent employer. He reminds Valerian that he is not entitled to any moral outrage over the apples Therese and Gideon took. Valerian merely paid for the fruit. He had not "row[ed] eighteen miles to bring them here. They did" (177). Now two people would starve so that Margaret "could play American mama and fool around in the kitchen" (177). Stunned by Son's brutal assessment, Valerian no longer perceives himself to be tolerantly amused. He stands exposed as an arrogant colonialist, successor to the French horsemen who once invaded the island and changed its landscape. As Son speaks, "Somewhere in the back of Valerian's mind one hundred French chevaliers were roaming the hills on horses. Their swords were in their scabbards, and their epaulets glittered in the sun. Backs straight, shoulders high—alert but restful in the security of the Napoleonic Code" (177). In anger Valerian struggles to reconstruct the identity he has artfully created. He orders Son to leave L'Arbe de la Croix, and when Son refuses, Valerian declares in disbelief to his wife: "I am being questioned by these people, as if, as if I *could* be called into question" (177).

At the moment Valerian is reconstructing his history with the image of conquering French horsemen, Son is constructing his own history with images of African horsemen and precolonial time on the island: "Somewhere in the back of Son's mind one hundred black men on one hundred unshod horses rode blind and naked through hills and had done so for hundreds of years. They knew the rain forest when it was a rain forest, they knew where the river began, where the roots twisted above the ground; they knew all there was to know about the island and had not even seen it. They had floated in strange waters blind, but they were still there racing each other for sport in the hills behind this white man's house" (177).

Son's moral authority flows from these slaves and descendants of slaves. It is they and he who must inherit the earth and not the Valerian Streets of

the industrial world. That is the disturbing message that Son brings to everyone and especially to Jadine. She, Son thinks, is too available to do Valerian's
bidding. At the dinner table it is she who keeps the assembly going smoothly,
"quietly chastising everybody," "agreeing with Valerian" (176). She has
become too much like a "little white girl" (103), he believes, and he is compelled to "insert his own dreams [of fat black ladies in white dresses and men
in magenta slacks on street corners] into her . . . to breathe into her the smell
of tar and its shiny consistency" (102).

It is Jadine, however, who alters Son's dreams. As a black woman living
in a social world that is mostly white, Jadine is the tar baby of the novel's
title. Like the tar baby of the Uncle Remus tales that the farmer uses to entrap
Br'er Rabbit, Jadine is mistaken by Son, Morrison's Br'er Rabbit, for something she is not. In spite of her upscale lifestyle and extraordinary beauty,
he thinks she is a variety of the women he has known. These were strong
women who faced and usually survived their hard lives in rural Eloe: "Before
Francine was attacked by dogs, she gave him ten points on the court and still
beat him. . . . Cheyenne was driving a beat-up old truck at age nine, four
years before he could even shift gears, and she could drop a pheasant like
an Indian. His mother's memory was kept alive by those who remembered
how she roped horses when she was a girl. His grandmother built a whole
cowshed with only Rosa to help. . . . Anybody who thought women were
inferior didn't come out of north Florida" (231).

In comparison, Son thinks "the black girls in New York City were crying and their men were looking neither to the right nor to the left" (185).
Son sees their gray and colorless faces veiled in heavy plum lipstick. They
are a whole new race of people with no ancestors, no past, no traditions.
He wonders where the old people are. There are no cultural antecedents like
Therese and Gideon in New York. And there are no children, laughing and
spontaneous. Without ancestry and progeny, without a past and a future,
the crying girls have nothing in common with the women of Eloe, the tree
women on Isle des Chevaliers, the night women, or the African woman in the
Paris market. By the time Son realizes that Jadine is of the New York variety
of black woman whose strength lies in the spasms of industry and efficiency
with which she handily negotiates "the First Cities of the world" (230), it is
too late for him to pull back. Like Br'er Rabbit, he is stuck fast.

Valerian, associated as he is with the greenhouse, is no doubt the farmer
who creates the tar baby Jadine. He has paid for her education, influenced
her values, and generally made her style of living possible. He is even expected to underwrite any future business enterprises Jadine might pursue.
Son, as Br'er Rabbit, is a trickster and thief who, when he is hungry, steals

Valerian's food. But, more significant, he is Valerian's antithesis; he threatens Valerian's peace of mind and opposes his material values. As Valerian's protégée, the dangerously attractive Jadine seduces Son into exchanging his African worldview for her (and Valerian's) Western view. At first Son resists; he perceives Jadine as a "tar baby side-of-the-road whore tramp" (189), but he believes he can change that. Instead, he is the one transformed, willing to do "whatever she wants" (235). Seeing through Jadine's eyes the pictures of places and people that he had loved in Eloe, "that used to comfort him so, used to reside with him, in him like royalty in his veins," (253) changes Son. These no longer matter. He willingly replaces his dreams of community and fraternity with Jadine's dreams of getting ahead and getting over. Unlike Br'er Rabbit, Son does not want to escape; he is "stuck in it and revolted by the possibility of being freed" (259), even if that means living "in the garden of some other white people house" (263). In surrender he abandons Eloe and all that he believes about the authority and purity of blackness.

In his present condition, only Therese has the power to release Son and restore his faith in home. When Son entreats her to take him across the bay to Isle des Chevaliers so that he can find Jadine and acquiesce, Therese takes him instead to join the blind African horsemen who are said to have been riding the hills for more than a century. Forget Jadine, Therese advises. "There is nothing in her parts for you. She has forgotten her ancient properties" (263). Therese intervenes to redirect Son away from a foreigner's garden to his own briar patch on the far side of Isle des Chevaliers, where the ancestors await. In the final lines of text—"Lickety-split. Looking neither to the left nor to the right. Lickety-split. Lickety-split. Lickety-lickety-lickety-split"—Morrison calls attention to the rabbit's escape.

The tar baby theme is not as simple as this analysis suggests. Morrison layers meaning to reflect the complex nature of experience. As a flesh-and-blood woman, Jadine has choices. She is not an inanimate tool subject to be molded by Valerian's society: she *chooses* not to be aligned with the "deep dark" (157) tar of the island earth, the ancient properties of the swamp women, the substance of all the black women who have nurtured Son and who generate the smell of tar that he attempts to breathe into Jadine's dreams (102). Jadine eschews the deep dark for the shallow veneer.

Although it may seem so, Morrison is not choosing sides. She renders the difficulties of each point of view and the heartrending consequences for both characters. Jadine, "thought she was rescuing him from the night women who wanted him for themselves, wanted him feeling superior in a cradle, deferring to him; wanted her to settle for wifely competence when she could be almighty, to settle for fertility rather than originality, nurturing instead of building. He thought he was rescuing her from Valerian, meaning *them*, the aliens, the people who in a mere three hundred years had killed a world millions of years old. . . . Each was pulling the other away from the maw of hell. . . . Each knew the world as it was meant or ought to be" (231–32).

Morrison acknowledges the bitter truth of each accusation and the awful necessity of each demand. Perhaps Son (as the infantile appellation implies) has been suckled too long by the night women with their magical breasts. Perhaps, in clinging to Eloe, he is romanticizing the past and home, which to him has always been a "place that was presided over by wide black women" (144). When Therese calls him "small boy" and leads him back in time to the African horsemen and away from a future with Jadine, it is she and not Son who determines his direction. Even to the end he is the suckled. Perhaps Jadine is right when she urges Son to let go, when she advises that "there is nothing any of us can do about the past but make our own lives better. . . . That is the only revenge, for us to get over" (234). Morrison acknowledges this dilemma of the modern woman, thrust into the tiresome either/or scenario: either become a wife and mother or take on the world of work-for-pay "as though," Morrison says, "you can't do two things or do one and then stop it and go do something else."[7] Jadine feels pressed to choose, and she does. In Paris, away from Son, are financial success and personal independence. In leaving Son, she has avoided "wifely competence" and "fertility" (231), and she has "refused to be broken in the big ugly hands of any man" (237). In flight she feels "lean and male" (237). Her fate is not that of the unspayed passive bitch "standing quietly under the paws of a male" (250). In her world, a "grown woman did not need safety or its dreams. She *was* the safety she longed for" (250).

In this profile, Jadine seems akin to Sula, who refuses to care more about a man than she does about herself. And, like Sula, Jadine rejects the role of nurturer; neither woman values community traditions and rituals that seem to abridge the individual's freedoms. With Sula, however, Morrison confines her scope to the tension between the community and the rebel in its midst. There she is concerned with how each finds an uneasy acceptance of the other. With Jadine, Morrison enlarges her concern from matters of self-sufficiency to grander matters of sexual equality. Sula is a pariah who remains within the community; Jadine is a feminist who lives outside. And she is a feminist "without . . . concern for social justice" (78),[8] connected as she is to Valerian and his rape of the earth and its people.

There is little doubt that Jadine has moved too far from the village; she has never found her ancient properties. In getting over, she has sidestepped her place in the line of history. Neither daughter nor mother, she has heed-lessly severed her link to the past and to the future of black womanhood. In dedicating *Tar Baby* to her grandmother, mother, aunts, and sister, "all of whom knew their true and ancient properties," Morrison suggests the im-portance of that link. Morrison does not find fault with Jadine's ambitions. Jadine's fault is in not building on the strength of those who have preceded her, in accepting the either/or interpretation of her choices. Morrison believes that no one should be asked to make a choice between a home and a career. "Why not have both? It's all possible. Like women doing nine things since the beginning and getting to the end of the row at the same time."[9] Perhaps Jadine is right in admiring the kick-ass black women taking charge in New York. But Son is also right in seeing the price they have paid for such power; they have sacrificed the ancestors and the children. Jadine and Son each has a partial answer. "One had a past, the other a future and each one bore the culture to save the race in his hands" (232).

Tar Baby is a fable for these modern times, when the old stories are un-familiar to a recent generation that needs to learn its lessons as much as, if not more than, previous generations. As a paradigm of black/white relations, the tale of a wily rabbit outwitting an unsuspecting farmer has, for blacks, as far back as slavery, confirmed their status as shrewd survivors. Morrison up-dates the tale, revises it to accommodate her form and to reflect her themes. Since, as she reminds us, "We don't live in places where we can hear those stories anymore," a way to get "new information" out must be discovered.[10] In Morrison's estimation, the novel is the best conduit for such information. In this context, "the novel is needed by African Americans now in a way that it was not needed before" to identify the pitfalls of contemporary life for those who are running from the past.[11]

CHAPTER 5

Remembering the "Disremembered"
Beloved

When *Tar Baby* was finished, Morrison expected to stop writing novels. After four successful performances, she was, for a time, without the urgent need to say something that had not been said before. She no longer had a messianic will to tell about people that only she knew, in a way that only she could. In 1974, at the time of her first novel, she was strongly convinced that no one "is going to see what I saw which was this complex poetic life. . . . And no one is going to write from the inside with that kind of gentleness."[1] A decade later Morrison perceived the gap between the black experience and the representation of that experience to be closing. A second renaissance in black literary arts had redressed the paucity of books about women's lives. She could "look at the work . . . and find . . . [herself] properly spoken of in it."[2] Ironically, in this milieu of productivity and creative possibility, Morrison decided not to write anymore, feeling relieved perhaps of the responsibility to shape her special vision of black culture since her subject matter, heretofore sporadically explored, was being confidently, sensitively, and consistently mined by her contemporaries. Morrison could rest, so to speak.

Her hiatus from writing was short lived. Three years after *Tar Baby, Beloved* was published. The old and by now familiar feeling of creating a story unique to her sensibilities had returned. Once more she felt responsible for delineating characters that only she knew, as if she "had the direct line . . . [and] was the receiver of all this information."[3] This time she was "obsessed by two or three little fragments of stories" of extraordinary women. Morrison recalls that

One was a newspaper clipping about a woman named Margaret Garner in 1851. It said that the Abolitionists made a great deal out of her case because she had escaped from Kentucky, I think, with her four children. She lived in a little neighborhood just outside of Cincinnati and she had killed her children. She succeeded in killing one; she tried to kill two others. She hit them in the head with a shovel and they were wounded, but they didn't die. And there was a smaller one that she had at her breast. The interesting thing, in addition to that, was the interview that she gave. She was a young woman. In the inked pictures of her she seemed a very quiet, very serene-looking woman and everyone who interviewed her remarked about her serenity and tranquility. She said, "I will not let those children live how I lived." She had run off into a little woodshed right outside her house to kill them because she had been caught as a fugitive. And she had made up her mind that they would not suffer the way she had and it was better for them to die. And her mother-in-law was in the house at the same time and she said, "I watched her and I neither encouraged her nor discouraged her." They put her in a jail for a while and I'm not even sure what the denouement is of her story. But that moment, that decision was a piece, a tail of something that was always around, and it didn't get clear for me until I was thinking of another story that I had read in a book that Camille Billops published, a collection of pictures by Van der Zee, called *The Harlem Book of the Dead*.[4]

Van der Zee narrates each photograph, giving his subjects stories and contexts. One photograph that intrigued Morrison featured an eighteen-year-old girl lying in a coffin. According to the photographer, the girl had slumped to the floor at a party. When people around her asked what happened, she would say only "I'll tell you tomorrow." The girl died, apparently having been shot by a jealous lover who had entered the party with a gun and a silencer. Of course, the girl knew this, but she kept her story until her lover could escape. She cared for him so much that she could, with one supreme act, forgive him for her murder and protect him from punishment.

This girl's and Margaret Garner's stories seemed to Morrison essentially related to each other. Both women, in Morrison's words, "sabotage[d]" themselves, "displace[d]" themselves for people they loved. Morrison's original plan for *Beloved*, then, was to cement the two stories with a single donnée. Margaret Garner's story would be refracted by the Harlem girl's story when Garner's dead daughter is reincarnated in this life, perhaps as the eighteen-year-old. Morrison explains: "I just imagined her [Garner's

daughter] remembering what happened to her, being someplace else and
returning, knowing what happened to her. And I call her Beloved so that I
can filter all these confrontations and questions that she has in that situation,
which is 1851, and then to extend her life, you know, her search, her quest,
all the way through as long as I care to go, into the [nineteen-]twenties where
it switches to this other girl. Therefore, I have a New York uptown-Harlem
milieu in which to put this love story but Beloved will be there also."[5]

Morrison's plans for weaving the "fragments" into a single continuous
pattern were never completed. At some point during its development, *Beloved* became the contemporary slave narrative that it is, opening and closing on Sethe, the fictionalized Margaret Garner. Intermittently intervening
are the memories that Morrison planned for Beloved, but these never range
beyond 1851 to encompass a dead girl in Harlem. That girl would be the
subject of Morrison's next novel, *Jazz*, which is set in 1920s New York. (The
two novels are part of a trilogy that concludes with *Paradise*, Morrison's
seventh novel.)

Despite revisions in the first blueprint, Morrison does retain in *Beloved*
her concern with a woman's extraordinary capacity for love and sacrifice.
Sethe does kill her two-year-old daughter, and she does attempt to kill the
other three children before she is stopped, because she wants to place them
"where no one could hurt them . . . where they would be safe."[6] This concept of love and safety as motivation for infanticide is a familiar inversion of
conventional thinking in Morrison's work. As no one else can, Morrison renders the terrible moment with perfect reason and clarity. Practiced Morrison
readers may phrase a note of sorrow for the painful inevitability of things,
but they never ask why. The feeble question "what she go and do that for?"
(150) is left to the sadistic slave master, Schoolteacher, and his nephews.
(Paul D and the black community ostracize Sethe but not because they cannot understand why she acts; they question her right to do so.) These same
people take false comfort in easy explanations: Sethe lost her reason because
she couldn't take a little "mishandle[ing]" (150).

But Morrison's queries in *Beloved* are not about what Sethe does or why.
These answers are available to anyone with knowledge of slavery. Morrison
asks who. Who is the woman capable of making such a choice? Who is the
woman with such audacity? In her search for Sethe, Morrison returns to the
first flashes of insight stirred by the "fragments": Sethe is the kind of woman
who "loved something other than herself" so much, she has placed all of the
value of her life in something outside herself in her children.[7]

Morrison renders Sethe, then, almost completely as mother—not in any
predictably pejorative meaning of the role but as a woman whose love for

her children has absolutely no limits in spite of slavery, which subverts all relationships and kinships. Sethe, like many children born into slavery, had not
known her own mother. Raised communally by the plantation's wet nurse
(after two weeks with her mother), she had no rights to the scared woman
who had briefly and surreptitiously identified herself as Sethe's mother and
who was later hanged. At Sweet Home, Sethe's children fared better; they
had a mother and a father. The Garners created the illusion of security for
their slaves, and through diligence and persistence Sethe managed to mother
her children and protect them from environmental dangers: fire, the well,
animals. When Garner dies and Schoolteacher takes over, the illusion is
shattered, and Sethe is forced to face a brutal reality of slavery: her children
do not belong to her. They are property, subject to be sold, traded, raped,
beaten, disposed of. In order to make them safe, she and they would have to
escape. And they do. First the children and later Sethe, pregnant with a baby
that she delivers in route to freedom, run off.

Escape is Sethe's emphatic rejection of slavery's power to circumscribe her
motherhood. Barefoot, bleeding, hungry, exhausted, disoriented, Sethe struggles to reach Ohio, not so much to save her own life as to save "the life of
her children's mother" (30). Only she has milk enough in her breasts for her
two-year-old, who had gone ahead, and for her newborn. Sethe suffers with
the knowledge that "little white babies got it [her mother's milk] first" (200)
and she got what was left. She "knows what it is to be without the milk that
belongs to you; to have to fight and holler for it, and to have so little left"
(200). By the time she reaches her babies, she will have "milk enough for all"
(100). In Ohio, under the expert care of her mother-in-law, Baby Suggs, Sethe
begins to claim herself and her children. She nurses the baby girls and kisses
the boys from "the tops of their heads [to] their tight round bellies" (94). For
twenty-eight days—the cycle of preparation a woman's body needs to begin
a new life—Sethe's motherlove is unrestrained. She remembers that her love
felt "good and right . . . and when I stretched out my arms all my children
could get in between. I was *that* wide. Look like I loved em more after I got
here. Or maybe I couldn't love em proper in Kentucky because they wasn't
mine to love" (162).

When Schoolteacher (named, according to Morrison, to reflect the
scholarly way in which racism was pursued in theology and in biology in
the Darwinian theory of evolution), his nephew, and the sheriff enter Baby
Suggs's yard to reclaim Sethe and, worse, to take her children back into
slavery, Sethe revolts.[8] In an instant she is transported back to the brutal
beating she endured in the hours before her escape and to her deepest violation: suckling Schoolteacher's nephews, being "handled" (200) as if she were

a goat, being robbed of the milk that belonged to her babies. Stirred by her memories, Sethe resolves that "nobody will ever get my milk no more except my children" (200). Threatened by Schoolteacher's arrival, she collects "every bit of life she had made, all the parts of her that were precious and fine and beautiful" (163) and carries them to the woodshed. Finally, they would all be "over there. Outside this place, where they would be safe" (163).[9]

Sethe's action places her outside the Ohio community of former slaves. She becomes one of Morrison's outlaw characters—much like Sula and Pilate (but unlike them also)—in conflict with communal values. After the woodshed, she must give up Baby Suggs's healing care, and all ties of friendship developed over twenty-eight days are severed by those who fear her determination. They "understand Sethe's rage . . . but not her reaction to it" (256). They had not responded to their own unspeakable and unforgivable insults so outrageously. Ella had survived the sexual sadism of her master and his son, who had taken turns with her. Stamp Paid had steeled himself to the rage he felt when he had "handed over his wife to his master's son" (184). By not killing the master, his wife, or himself, he had stamped any debt he or any slave owed to the institution as paid. Like Stamp and Ella, Baby Suggs had outlived an intolerable life. She neither condones nor condemns Sethe, but, unlike her daughter-in-law, she has learned not to mourn the seven children she bore but was not allowed to keep. Like the others, she understands the "nastiness of life" (23). Slavery made love risky, even dangerous, according to Paul D, the last of the Sweet Home men, "especially if it was her [a woman's] children she had settled on to love. The best thing, he knew, was to love just a little bit; everything, just a little bit, so when they broke its back, or shoved it in a croaker sack, well, maybe you'd have a little love left over for the next one" (45). Sethe, however, does not love so timidly. She rejects any compromise of her maternity. She had "birthed" them, "got em out," and "it felt good" (162). She would not see them returned to slavery. "The best thing she was, was her children. Whites might dirty *her* all right, but not her best thing, her beautiful, magical best thing—the part of her that was clean" (251). Her job was keeping them away from what she knew was terrible. "I did that," she declares.

Sethe's exercise of power is, in effect, a declaration of independence from an unsympathetic community, and the ensuing clash informs a latent tension in the novel that is unresolved until the final pages. Community finds expression as traits of character in Morrison's novels. Its values and beliefs shape the background against which the individual's behavior is assessed and defined. As a repository of cultural traditions, the community is usually necessary to the individual's wholeness and identity, and those who do not embrace it are incomplete, as is Jadine in *Tar Baby*. But sometimes the role of community is not so easily justified. In such instances, its function as cultural arbiter is tainted by a smugness and pettiness, which the individual who would be free is, like Sula, compelled to resist. The case is similar in *Beloved,* when the community abridges its natural function through spite, jealousy, and meanness. Before Sethe arrives in Ohio, the black community maintains the integrity of its purpose with Baby Suggs at its moral core. Her house, 124 Bluestone, was the gathering place, the community center. There, people came to discuss "the true meaning of the Fugitive Bill, the Settlement Fee, God's Ways, and Negro pews; antislavery, manumission, skin voting, Republicans, Dred Scott, book learning, Sojourner's high-wheeled buggy, the Colored Ladies of Delaware, Ohio, and the other weighty issues" (173) that concerned them. In the clearing behind the house, Baby Suggs taught the people to dance, to laugh, and to love themselves. In this setting, for twenty-eight days Sethe had "women friends, a mother-in-law, and all her children together" (173). When these same people betray Baby Suggs and her family by failing to warn of what they instinctively know is trouble when white men come to town asking questions, the community fails its obligation to the individual. Baby Suggs is mortally disillusioned. She abandons her ministry of love and slowly gives up life. "To belong to a community of other free Negroes—to love and be loved by them, to counsel and be counseled, protect and be protected, feed and be fed—and then to have that community step back and hold itself at a distance—well, it could wear out even a Baby Suggs, holy" (177).

Like the individuals who constitute it, the community is collectively subject to character flaws: envy of Baby Suggs's generosity and of Sethe's youth and deftness flowers into meanness. After holding themselves at a distance and not warning Sethe, people in the community gather but do not raise their voices in the customary unifying ceremony of song when Sethe is taken to jail. Later they rumor doubts about Sethe's past: did she really escape from slavery in her condition? Was Baby Suggs's son really the father of her children? Ten years later, after Baby Suggs's funeral, they congregate in the yard, eating the food they brought and leaving Sethe's untouched. After that time no one visits 124, and, rankled by Sethe's independence and self-sufficiency, "Just about everybody in town was longing for Sethe to come on difficult times" (171). For nearly two decades Sethe and Denver (and, later, Paul D) are left to themselves, solitary figures living at the edge of the community.

Morrison does not censure or judge the community for its treatment of Sethe. Most crimes in her fictional world are redeemable. Despite its coldness, for example, the community does not entirely expel Sethe, and, in the end, when she is haunted by the ghost of her daughter and is no longer self-supporting, it reclaims her as its own.

In the interim Morrison explicates the tension between Sethe and her neighbors to illuminate Sethe's character: she is impenitent and tough. She refuses to seek the community's approval, and each act of community disapproval evokes a corresponding defiance from Sethe. The community members hold themselves distant when Schoolteacher comes; Sethe holds herself aloof from the crowd when she is taken to jail and remains aloof when she is released. Many years later, when Baby Suggs dies, they set up tables of food in the yard because no one will enter the house; Sethe will not attend the funeral service and will not join in their singing at the graveside. Back in the yard of 124, they do not eat Sethe's food, and she does not touch theirs. Nearly a month of fellowship is followed by nearly twenty years of alienation. The uncommunal action of holding back begets an unbroken pattern of mutual spurns. The community erred, Sethe rebuked it, and neither will relent.

These social dynamics are different from those in *Tar Baby*. The earlier novel dissects Morrison's abiding interest in the individual's initiation to mythic and folk culture in the community. Without initiation, Morrison warns, self-knowledge is imperfect. The communities (Eloe and Isle des Chevaliers) in *Tar Baby* do not hold themselves back; they strive to assimilate Jadine into cultures of black womanhood. In choosing to live in Paris, however, Jadine cuts herself off from black people and in doing so deprives herself of an identity as a black woman. She may be, as she stubbornly asserts, self-dependent, but without assimilating historical culture she is fundamentally incomplete. This is the dilemma of contemporary life. Community dynamics in *Beloved* are not so apocryphal. In *Beloved*, with its 1850s setting, Morrison is not, as she was in *Tar Baby*, warning of the dire consequences of a failure by the individual to be acculturated by the community. Sethe is not in danger, as Jadine is, of losing her identity as a black woman (she is endeavoring to *make* an identity as a black woman).

Indeed, in denying historical identity, Jadine, in effect, denies her link to Sethe and her struggle. Sethe's conflict with her neighbors is virulent but not as lethal as Jadine's. Sethe continues in the community (even if on the periphery) and is reconnected with it when the women save her from the child ghost who threatens to replace Sethe's life with its own. Sethe knows, as Jadine does not, that her fight is not with these people with whom she has so much suffering in common. Her struggle is against Schoolteacher, his nephews, and the system that enslaves, degrades, and defines.[10]

In Morrison's work, Sethe is the prototypical womanist, one of the first of Morrison's women to demand the privilege of defining herself. (In the novels' historical time the earliest such character is *A Mercy*'s Florens in seventeenth-century Virginia.) Contemporary women like Jadine are expected to make these demands, but Morrison demonstrates that these recent combatants owe much to their predecessors. The particular demands have changed—Jadine sees motherhood as inhibiting, and Sethe sees it as necessary—but the essential struggle for self-definition is the same. Sethe, like her mother, Baby Suggs, and all slave women, can never be wife and mother. She is biologically female, and she is a breeder, but she is exempt from all ideological considerations as woman. She is no more than a cow or goat, subject to "milking" like any other beast. Schoolteacher and his pupils confirm these categories by compiling a list of Sethe's animal characteristics for study and evaluation. Sethe resists this nonhuman suborder by proving herself capable of thinking for herself and by insisting upon the right to determine her own and her children's fates in life and in death. She will not have them liable to Schoolteacher's demeaning measurements of their "animal" qualities. Sethe had "felt what it felt like and nobody walking or stretched out" was going to make her children feel it too (203). Sethe acts, then, alone—sending her children along the underground a week before she escapes. Morrison calls attention to the magnitude of Sethe's defiance by accenting her aloneness. All the men at Sweet Home who were supposed to run away together and take Sethe and the children are either dead or in chains. Six-o was burned alive, one Paul had been sold, two killed, and Paul D was locked in the barn with a bit in his mouth. Halle, Sethe's "husband," unable to rescue his wife from the vile nephews who take her milk, cracks under the strain and sits near the butter churn, spreading creamy fat over his face. Sethe takes no refuge in insanity: "Other people went crazy. . . . Other people's brains stopped, turned around and went on to something new, which is what must have happened to Halle. And how sweet that would have been: the two of them back by the milk shed, squatting by the churn, smashing cold, lumpy butter into their faces with not a care in the world. . . . But her three children were chewing sugar teat under a blanket on their way to Ohio and no butter play would change that" (70).

For Sethe, the duties of motherhood are not dissolved by mental disarrangements. Sethe savors the size of her accomplishment: "I did it. I got us all out. Without Halle too. Up till then it was the only thing I ever did on my own. Decided. And it came off right, like it was supposed to. . . . Each and every one of my babies and me too. I birthed them and I got em out and it wasn't no accident. I did that. I had help, of course lots of that, but still it was me doing it; me saying. *Go on,* and *now.* Me having to look out. Me using my own head" (162). Schoolteacher's arrival threatens to reduce Sethe again to a list of parts and jeopardizes her self-confidence. But, more than exposing Sethe to these dangers, Schoolteacher's insistent presence forces her to stake her claim as a mother who is capable of defending her children's lives.

That responsibility is abridged only once. Briefly, Sethe had placed "the responsibility for her breasts . . . in somebody else's hands" (18); Paul D had relieved her of their burden. For the first time since the woodshed, she could "trust things and remember things because the last of the Sweet Home men was there to catch her if she sank" (18). Sethe, however, overestimates Paul D's empathy for her struggle. He is sorrowful for those indignities of Sethe's experience that his own suffering corroborates. But, perhaps as a man, he cannot fully accept the maternal weight of her breasts. He had first "held them as though they were the most expensive part of himself," (21) so eager was he to absorb Sethe's pain, but after their first lovemaking (as if to foreshadow his abandonment), Paul D is repulsed by Sethe's breasts. In these moments he symbolically rejects Sethe's protean identity as woman and mother. He cannot understand a "used-to-be-slave woman['s]" love for her children, and he fears Sethe's determination to protect her daughter "while I'm live and . . . when I ain't" (45). Paul D has no context for Sethe's independence or for her "thick" love (164); he is incapable of measuring its heft and, in his own helplessness, feebly reminds her that she has "two feet . . . not four" (165), intimating that only a beast could kill its young. His words are harsher than his intent, but once they are spoken, "a forest sprang up between them" (165). Sethe will not tolerate any reduction of her selfhood (from Schoolteacher's listing her parts or Paul D's counting her feet). She rebuffs all attempts to minimize her victories as a woman, as a mother. And so she takes back from Paul D the responsibility for her breasts that she had given a short time earlier.

Sethe never questions her womanhood as Paul D does his manhood. He has endured the sadism of slaveholding and survived its hellish aftermath; yet he cannot commit himself to Sethe and share her sorrow. He has taken his own advice to Sethe and learned not to love too much, because if one loves too much, one or the object of that love may be destroyed. Paul D wonders, then, if he is the man he always thought himself to be. At Sweet Home, Garner had encouraged his defiance, independence, and decision making. He and the others had been allowed to "buy a mother, choose a horse or a wife, handle guns, even learn reading if they wanted to" (125). But these privileges of humanity were available only at Sweet Home and only under Garner. "One step off that ground and they were trespassers among the human race" (125). The day Schoolteacher puts a bit in his mouth for trying to escape is the day Paul D comes to terms with these certainties. He tells Sethe that on that day, as the last of the Sweet Home men, "wasn't no way I'd ever be Paul D again, living or dead. Schoolteacher changed me" (72). In order to continue with his life, Paul D replaced his "red heart" with a "tobacco tin buried in his chest. . . . Its lid rusted shut" (72–73). In that condition he comes to Sethe but cannot remain. Sethe's heart, on the other hand, is conditioned by motherlove. She does not doubt its function. Children are incarnate proof of her woman's identity.

Morrison's implicit contrast of Sethe and Paul D is not a faultfinding mission against Paul D or against men in general but rather is a delineation of Sethe's character. She uses Paul D in much the same way she does the community: to set Sethe's extraordinary strength in relief. Conflict becomes a strategy. Like the community, Paul D eventually returns to rescue Sethe. When she sinks under the burden of responsibility she has borne alone for so long, Paul D is there to offer relief once more, but this time he does not waiver. Once before he had embraced her life with the force of masculine intent and desire: arousing Sethe's sexual passion; criticizing her daughter, Denver; evicting the baby ghost; proscribing Sethe's responses. This time, however, his presence is conditioned by feminine principles of compassion, nurturance, and patience. He offers to bathe Sethe, including her "exhausted breasts" (172), Sethe hopes. This time Sethe can tell him things that women "only tell each other." She can transcend the bounds of her rebellion against Schoolteacher (which informs the bravado of her first explanation to Paul D of what happened in the woodshed) and cry for the absent sons and her dead daughter, who was her "best thing" (272). This time Paul D does not judge Sethe or feel betrayed by her stamina: "He wants to put his story *next* to hers" (273; emphasis added). This time he does not count her feet but reminds her that she is her "best thing." He can accept her yesterdays and share her tomorrows.

Despite his early retreat from deep feeling, Paul D is a nurturer at his core. He is "the kind of man who can walk in a house and make the women cry. Because with him, in his presence, they could" (272). But, like other men in Morrison's work, he has the spirit of a wanderer. He is another of Morrison's traveling men who resist domesticity. He is compulsively mobile "because he didn't believe he could live with a woman—any woman—for over two out of three months. That was about as long as he could abide one place" (40). Slavery has birthed a fear of place that is quieted only when he is moving. Like Cholly and Ajax, he is conditioned by oppressive circumstances to crave freedom. Paul D is different from them, however. He is not dangerously free like Cholly (who, when he is overcome by pity for his daughter's pathetic helplessness, rapes her), nor is he as self-absorbed as

Ajax (who loves but one woman—his mother). Paul D's wanderlust spawns less debilitating character defects and ends at 124 when his compassion for Sethe quells his fear of being entrapped.

Paul D's presence in *Beloved* serves Morrison's second literary goal (the first is to delineate Sethe's identity as a strong woman who so much loved something other than herself): to portray the lives of slaves in a way that has not been done before. As a black woman and a student of American history (both the canonized and the revised versions), Morrison is familiar with slaves' lives as those lives are presented in memoir.[11] These narratives recount the cruelty and inhumanity of slavery. Morrison notes, however, that, in their efforts to be objective, not to "offend the reader by being too angry, or by showing too much outrage, or by calling the reader names," slave narrators pulled the veil over "proceedings too terrible to relate."[12] Morrison aims to remove that veil and to recreate "the interior life" that was deliberately excised "from the records that the slaves themselves told." The reader should not merely *know* about the horror of slavery but *feel* what it was like.[13] The extent to which she does this is the extent to which she writes beyond the record of slavery. The published account of Margaret Garner's crime is totally subordinate to the unpublished interior life, just as the published recollections of male narrators do not go as far as Paul D's truth; Morrison fills in and updates.

Unlike the narrators, Morrison is under no constraint to please her audience. Neither is she constrained by the narrators' need for verity, to keep facts straight. She has artistic freedom. In one view, then, the difference between slave autobiography and *Beloved* is the difference between autobiography and fiction. In effect, *Beloved* is directed by the creative process that holds all good writers in tow by engaging the author's imagination and demanding attention to her characters' interior lives. But Morrison's relationship to her subject and characters is not entirely explained by the art of fiction. She does acknowledge that her work is imaginative, but, more important, it is also truthful. "Truthful" does not require a recounting of verifiable details of specific events, places, and people as in the approach that Morrison calls the "oh, yes, this is where he or she got it from school."[14] It does require absolute fidelity to the subject. In *Beloved* this means fidelity to the slaves' experiences. The truth of slavery is its contamination of humanity, its agency of evil, and that truth lies beyond the specific details of suffering of any individual. Truth transcends time, place, and audience, and it gives universal insight. It is more spiritual than intellectual. It is the difference between Margaret Garner's personal truth and humanity's impersonal truth. Morrison arrives at this truth through her own memory—not particular memories of slavery, of course, but a personal (and seemingly unrelated) memory that gives her almost clairvoyant access to the interior lives of characters. For Morrison, then, writing Paul D, Sethe, and the community of *Beloved* was more than a mental exercise acted upon by the imagination to turn thoughts into art. It was, through inclusion of her memories, an act of writing a part of herself into the narrative. The result is a view of slavery not undertaken before. As she says, "they [her characters] are my entrance into my own interior life."[15]

While *Beloved* was in progress, for example, Morrison had a recurring image of corn on the cob that evoked converging memories of her early life: the house where she grew up in Lorain, Ohio; her parents' working in the garden; eating hot and cold corn in the summer in the midst of extended family and neighbors who stopped in. The corn is sweet finger food, Morrison remembers.[16] "The picture of the corn," she says, "and the nimbus of emotion surrounding it became a powerful one" in *Beloved*.[17] Morrison does not say what scenes that emotion prompted, but perhaps the sweet corn of her childhood became the succulent blackberries picked by Stamp Paid, and perhaps the "easy" mood of her summers in Ohio became the satisfying fulfillment of those invited to Baby Suggs's community party to eat berry pies. The mood of that moment of celebration (which begins with a bucket of blackberries and explodes into a feast of pies, pan-fried perch, rabbit, corn pudding, chicken, and watermelon punch) stands out in its stark contrast to other moods in the novel. During an afternoon and evening, ninety former slaves please and indulge themselves with an uncommon abandon. Then celebration turns to vexation, to envy, and finally to malicious withdrawal. Those who had enjoyed Baby Suggs's generosity were suddenly too resentful to warn her of the coming danger. In her signature style, Morrison portrays the contradictory emotions that drive human behavior: ninety people eat so well and laugh so much they become not joyful but angry; simultaneously, they savor Baby Suggs's liberality and punish what they believe is the arrogance that begets it with their own arrogance.

That scene takes less than two pages to tell, but its brevity belies its strategic importance. It becomes the radiating "nimbus" of Sethe's conflict with the community and of Baby Suggs's defeat. And it subtly but distinctly colors the murder, heightening the sorrow. The knowledge of betrayal by the community haunts the scene and challenges readers' credulity: how, the reader asks, could people have behaved so? Schoolteacher's pursuit of Sethe and her children is no surprise, but her own people's withdrawal reverberates throughout the text. The story strains toward an explanation and resolution. Not surprisingly, Morrison offers no explanation. She understands the authority of ambiguity in the human experience. Resolution comes many years later, in the final pages, when the community of women prevents Sethe from committing another murder. Weakened and disoriented from her ordeal with the incubus, Beloved, Sethe sees Edward Bodwin drive into her yard and imagines that Schoolteacher has returned for her best thing. She turns upon the unsuspecting Bodwin with an ice pick, but, before he is even aware of any danger, the women knock Sethe to the ground. This time they save Sethe from death and murder and, in so doing, return to their natural function as a refuge and a reservoir of knowledge for the individual. They understand, even if Sethe does not, the power of the incubus, and they do not fear it. Their own collective will is greater. At last they gather before Sethe's house, not in recalcitrant silence but with raised voices, searching "for the right combination, the key, the code, the sound that broke the back of words. Building voice upon voice until they found it and when they did, it was a wave of sound wide enough to sound deep water and knock pods off chestnut trees. It broke over Sethe and she trembled like the baptized in its wash" (261). Sethe is reborn in a primordial ceremony of engulfing sound. For her the women's "loving faces" (262) recall the twenty-eight days of fellowship she had once known in their midst. It is as if Baby Suggs's ministry of love has finally come to fruition and is nourishment for Sethe.

Unveiling these interior lives of her characters carries with it titanic responsibility for Morrison. She is continuing an unfinished script of slavery begun more than two centuries ago by the first slave narrative, and she must do it truthfully and with integrity. Morrison's characters stand in for all those slaves and former slaves who were "unceremoniously buried" without tribute or recognition. She feels chosen by them to attend to their burial "properly, artistically."[18] *Beloved* is her effort to do that. It is an act of recovering the past in narrative, to "insert this memory that was unbearable and unspeakable into the literature."[19] Only then is it possible, Morrison believes, for black people, for society, to move on. This need to remember before moving on is reflected in the epilogue, where, after having passed on Beloved's story, Morrison writes in contradiction that "this is not a story to pass on" (275). It threatens peace of mind and must be resisted. To protect itself, the community forgot Beloved: "Disremembered and unaccounted for, she cannot be lost because no one is looking for her, and even if they were, how can they call her if they don't know her name? Although she has claim, she is not claimed" (274). This is not a story to pass on, and yet Morrison acknowledges that, ironically, "it is not a story to pass by."[20] Only by remembering the past can we be liberated from its burden.

Although the setting and scope of *Beloved* are primarily slavery in the American South, Morrison wants to recover all facets of the slave's story—

from Africa to America. Brief images of Sethe in a place where she "take[s] flowers away from leaves [and] . . . puts them in a round basket" (210) suggest an Africa of beauty and freedom before white violence and enslavement.[21] Morrison also captures the heartbreak of the middle passage, the slave route from Africa to the West Indies, during which many perished in cargo holds or jumped from ships to death in the sea. This, Morrison thinks, is the least examined aspect of slavery. "No one praised them, nobody knows their names, nobody can remember them, not in the United States nor in Africa. Millions of people disappeared without a trace, and there is not one monument anywhere to pay homage to them, because they never arrived safely on shore. So it's like a whole nation that is under the sea."[22] Beloved inhabits this place under blue water before she is reincarnated at 124, and, as Karla Holloway notes, she is "not only Sethe's dead daughter returned, but the return[ed] of all the faces, all the drowned, but remembered, faces of mothers and their children who have lost their being because of the force of that EuroAmerican slave-history."[23]

Writing *Beloved* required a modicum of emotional risk for Morrison. Recovering truth was sometimes "very intense," she says. She would "write a sentence and . . . jump up and run outside or something." This kind of story "sort of beats you up."[24] But during the difficult times she reminded herself: "All I have to do is to think about the people who lived there, who lived through it. If they could live it, I could write about it."[25] That is the way Morrison works—with an intensity and a focus that can be isolating: "There is a temptation to draw away from living people, people who are extremely important to you and who are real. They're in competition a great deal with this collection of imagined characters."[26] Morrison converses with her characters, literally speaks aloud to them; they become a collection of "graphic presences." She acknowledges that this is not "the vocabulary of literary criticism," but it is, she claims, the way any writer whose work she respects speaks about her work. And it is often the vocabulary of black women writers.[27]

"The work that I do," Morrison says, "frequently falls in the minds of most people, into that realm of fiction called fantastic, or mythic, or magical, or unbelievable."[28] She is "not comfortable with these labels" because they suggest a breach with truth, and her "single gravest responsibility (in spite of that magic) is not to lie."[29] Morrison names this aspect of her work "enchantment" and says she uses it "simply because that's the way the world was for me and for the black people that I knew. In addition to the very shrewd, down-to-earth, efficient way in which they did things and survived things, there was this other knowledge or perception, always discredited but nevertheless there, which informed their sensibilities and clarified their activities."[30] *Beloved*

gives a context to these comments. It has been pointed to as an example of
Morrison's magical real style. Indeed, a toddling infant who is reincarnated
as a young woman with new skin, rudimentary language, breath like new
milk, and the cravings and temper of a child is fantastic—but it is also artistically credible. It validates Sethe's claims that she is a tough mother who will
protect her children in life and in death. She sent her daughter not to death
and nothingness but to another life from which she returns "of her own free
will" (200). This scenario saves the novel from becoming a melodramatic tale
of murder and pathos (although one could not imagine Morrison authoring
such stuff).[31] Sethe transcends the limitations placed upon her in slavery and
becomes the agent of her own fate. In this plot Sethe is not subject to any
authority outside herself—not Schoolteacher's, Paul D's, Stamp Paid's, or
anyone else's in the community. By the same token, she is also not subject
to any conventional punishment. She may be jailed and ostracized, but she
remains steadfast in the rightness of her action until Beloved's return. Only
then does she weaken, in the presence of the only one capable of tormenting
her, "the one and only person she felt she had to convince, that what she had
done was right because it came from true love" (251).

Of course, Beloved, though she is twenty-one, is temperamentally the
child whose emotional growth was arrested in the woodshed. She is selfish,
demanding, greedy for Sethe's love, her attention, her self. Her demands
drain Sethe to the point that "Beloved . . . looked the mother, Sethe the . . .
child . . . confined to a corner," (250) muttering feebly to an implacable
ghost. Ironically, the very love that earlier gives Sethe the strength to save
herself for her children betrays her into a sacrifice of self. And it is a different
sacrifice from going to the gallows for killing her children to "save them."
This sacrifice is born not of conviction but of guilt and fear. This sacrifice
erodes her identity. By the time the thirty neighborhood women appear in her
yard, Sethe has "yielded up her life [to Beloved] without a murmur" (250).
Beloved's return, then, gives Morrison an opportunity to explore the circum-
ference of Sethe's character. Endurance joins halting fear. As resilient as she
is, she is also vulnerable, and her strength and weakness emanate from the
same stream of love. "It's peculiar to women," Morrison believes, that "the
best thing . . . in us is also the thing that makes us sabotage ourselves."[32]

The love that gives Sethe courage in the woodshed and bitter triumph
over Schoolteacher and slavery makes her vulnerable to the manipulations of
a ghost child. She had been willing to die with and for that child to keep her
from slavery; years later, she willingly enslaves herself to the incubus who she
continues to believe is her best thing. The love that sustained her threatens to

consume her. Perhaps this is retribution; even righteous crimes such as Sethe's have a reckoning. But Sethe's journey does not end there. When the novel closes, she is on the verge of new understanding. Her children are free, and finally it is possible for Sethe to learn that, as Paul D tells her, she is her best thing.

CHAPTER 6

City Blues

Jazz

Five years after the publication of *Beloved,* Morrison returned to the image of the dead girl in Van der Zee's photograph collection, *The Harlem Book of the Dead.* In *Jazz* (1992) eighteen-year-old Dorcas Manfred embodies Morrison's curiosity about a young dying woman who sacrifices herself to save her lover by refusing to name him as her murderer.

Morrison's original interest in the story related to a broader fascination with women's unselfishness—the willingness of some to value people they love more than themselves. By the time she wrote *Jazz,* however, Morrison's focus had changed. (She had, after all, just finished writing about Sethe, a woman who loves too much, in *Beloved.*) Dorcas is neither noble nor selfless. She is shallow and manipulative. When shot by her married lover, she bleeds to death because she will not seek medical help. Any magnanimity demonstrated by shielding her boyfriend's identity is spoiled by a foolish insistence upon waiting until morning for treatment. She apparently fears discovery of her transgressions more than she does death.

Dorcas, then, is not a sympathetic character whose life and death, if they were given the exemplary Morrison treatment, have the potential to both inspire and disgust. That role goes to fifty-four-year-old Joe Trace, a married man who loves his wife, seduces and falls in love with an eighteen-year-old girl, and then shoots her when she leaves him. Joe shares the role with his wife, Violet, who crashes Dorcas's funeral to attack a girl who is already dead. Dorcas's death and funeral center the story and characters, serving as a recurring point of return and reference, but once the crime is named, typically, Morrison moves to a review of the criminals. Crime and punishment do not concern Morrison, but people and motivation do.[1] What kind of man desires a girl young enough to be his daughter, even his granddaughter? Why does he harm her? What kind of woman walks into a funeral in progress and assaults a dead body with a knife? If they are not psychopaths (and they never are in Morrison's work), then they are merely interesting people and extraordinary specimens of the human condition: they are good people who do bad things. "The combination of virtue and flaw, of good intentions gone awry, of wickedness cleansed and people made whole again," interests Morrison. She does not judge characters by "the worst that they have done" or by the best, but the "combinations . . . are the best part of writing novels."[2]

Joe and Violet are two lonely people whose love for each other cannot penetrate dense walls of disappointment and pain. When he can no longer turn to his wife for companionship and intimacy, Joe looks for someone else and finds Dorcas. In a way, Violet also finds her. After the shooting, Violet obtains a photograph of the girl and places it on the living room mantle, where she and Joe take turns alternately admiring it and being moved to tears by it. For each the picture is a reminder of lost opportunities for living and loving: Dorcas is the mother Joe was never able to love and protect, and she is the daughter Violet never bore. In a peculiar way Dorcas's death is the bridge that links their paths back to each other. Sorrow bonds them, and ultimately they are reconciled with their losses and renewed in life and love.

Morrison does not brand Joe Trace an immoral man. He and Violet are good people whose circumstances shape their bizarre behavior. Shooting Dorcas is the exception in his otherwise unblemished life. Before and after, Joe is

> [a] nice neighborly, everybody-knows-him man. The kind you let in your house because he was not dangerous, because you had seen him with children, bought his products and never heard a scrap of gossip about him doing wrong. Felt not only safe but kindly in his company because he was the sort women ran to when they thought they were being followed or watched or needed someone to have the extra key just in case you locked yourself out. He was the man who took you to your door if you missed the trolley and had to walk night streets at night. Who warned young girls away from hooch joints and the men who lingered there. Women teased him because they trusted him.[3]

For the most part Joe lives up to this summary assessment of his character. With Dorcas he is paternal, kind—not exactly in the way of a doting, indulgent father but more like a wise, generous lover. He brings her gifts, confesses his deepest doubts and fears, and, perhaps as the best evidence of his love, accepts her as she is. With Violet he is also touchingly affectionate. By the time Joe finds Dorcas, his marriage is routine, lonely, and silent—Violet speaks only to her birds; there is no intimacy. Joe cannot even remember the way their lives used to be when they were young and in love. He recalls events, "but he has a tough time trying to catch what it felt like" (29). Despite Violet's distance, however, Joe continues to care about her. He may have lost the energy of his love, but the affection remains. His passion for Dorcas does not threaten that affection. He would never intentionally hurt Violet.

And he does not *intentionally* or with deliberation hurt Dorcas. Morrison does not provide explicit reasons for Joe's violence, and yet the emotions that propel him toward Dorcas on the night of the shooting are entirely comprehensible. They are not the ordinary passions of violence: rage, fury, malice, anger. In fact, on that evening he feels and thinks very little. The hunter that he was in youth emerges, and he follows Dorcas's trail instinctively, doggedly, across New York's boroughs. In the beauty parlor, women speculate about a man Joe's age asking questions with embarrassing urgency about a girl barely out of high school. A neighbor looks with a knowing and disapproving smile at his foolish demeanor. The search is pathetic, hopeless, sorrowful. For five days he traces her movements, reviews her scheduled appointments, analyzes the discrepancies. Finally, he tracks her to a crowded apartment where she is locked in a dancing embrace with a new, younger lover, swaying back and forth to the steamy music. At that moment, Joe's "rambling . . . rambling all through the City" (130) is over. He has the gun, but he believes it is the hand with which he wants to touch her. When he heard "the gun go thuh!" he wanted to "catch her before she fell and hurt herself" (130).

The tempest is hardly discernible. Joe loves Dorcas before, and he loves her after—and most likely he loves her at the instant he aims the gun and pulls the trigger. Unable or unwilling to leave her, as Dorcas had urged him to do, Joe tracks her to "help" her clarify their need for each other, to help her realize that he is "a mild man" (183) who "know[s] how to treat a woman," who "never would mistreat one. Never would make a woman live like a dog in a cave" (182). He needs her acknowledgment that he belongs to her. But, like Joe's mother—the naked woman who lived wild in the caves and woods of Virginia while he was growing up—Dorcas abandons him, does not claim him. In searching for one, Joe also searches for the other. The trail across the streets of New York becomes, in Joe's mind, the viney, treacherous Virginia woods where he hunted the woman who was said to be his mother, in order to be granted a glimmer of recognition. Joe never finds his mother. After the third abortive search, his hurt feelings compete with feelings of anger and humiliation that his mother would choose a cave and not him. He does, however, find Dorcas. But she, too, has chosen not to give her love to him or to receive his love. Perhaps shooting Dorcas discharges the pent-up misery and humiliation of his past.

Any convenient psychoanalytical view of Joe's repressed intentions (no matter how much such a view is supported by the text) should not obscure Morrison's characterization of him as a kind man and, more important, as a sane one. Before the day he sets out to locate Dorcas with a gun in his pocket, he is level-headed, prudent, discreet, reasonable. Those essential ingredients of his character do not change in the course of the narrative; they are only temporarily arrested. Morrison suggests, as she always does of deranged episodes in otherwise rational lives, that no definitive, easy-to-grasp explanation exists for the exception. Some experiences are paradoxical and irreconcilable. As Morrison's mysterious narrator observes in *Jazz*, "trying to figure out anybody's state of mind" (137) is risky.

For that reason perhaps (and also because Joe is not directly responsible for Dorcas's death; she could have saved herself by getting medical help), Morrison does not send Joe off to prison for his crime. Obviously, banishment would not serve Morrison's structure, which situates her characters within a community, nor would it serve her perennial interest in the individual's relationship to that community. Instead, she gives Joe an opportunity for redemption. In self-imposed detention in his apartment, Joe spends his days crying and his nights staring at the photograph of Dorcas that sits on the mantelpiece. Through heartfelt anguish and grief Joe discovers forgiveness and peace of mind. His punishment is the knowledge that even if he "didn't kill her outright; even if she made herself die" (212), he is to blame. As he says, "It was me. For the rest of my life, it'll be me" (212). But, as he stares into Dorcas's picture, he sees in her face no regret, no accusation: "No finger points. Her lips don't turn down in judgment" (12). In time Joe accepts this dichotomy of guilt and innocence and moves forward with life.

Joe is a variation on Morrison's prototypical male. At the core this kind of man likes women. Even the most embryonic, emotionally unevolved male protagonist in Morrison's fiction has at least a kernel of this unlibidinous affection for women. In Joe this quality achieves maturity. After observing him, Dorcas's young friend, Felice, innocently compares him to other men she has known and to her father. Joe is the domestic sort who trims his wife's hair, whose generosity and warmth are reflected in his eyes, which allow an observer to "look inside him" and which look "inside you" (206). When Joe looks at Felice, she feels "deep" as if her feelings and thoughts "are important and different and . . . interesting" (206). She concludes that Joe "likes women" without "flirt[ing] with them" and that, contrary to prevailing community sentiments, Joe especially "likes his wife" (206).

Violet, Joe's wife, is a study in madness, the type of contained craziness that suggests a strenuous but unsuccessful effort to keep one's life in balance. In consequence, the fabric of Violet's once cohesive, conventional existence persistently unravels into loose threads of lunacy. Attacking Dorcas in her coffin represents one of several frayed edges. Helpless to stop herself, Violet watches as a woman she recognizes but does not know elbows her way through the mourners in a crowded church, stops at the coffin with her knife raised, and, before she is wrestled to the floor by ushers, manages to nick the dead girl's neck. Another time, she had stopped on her way to an appointment and sat in the street. "She didn't stumble nor was she pushed: she just sat down" (17). Violet is also tormented by "a renegade tongue yearning to be on its own" (21). Sometimes she has no control over it, and she hears speech that is without context or rational meaning. Fearful of these times, Violet retreats into silence, relying upon "'Oh' or 'have mercy' [to] carry almost all of her part of a conversation" (24). Over time the only time she feels safe speaking is when she speaks to the caged parrot in her apartment.

Violet was not always pathetic. Her days were not always punctuated by public and private craziness. As a girl and young woman in Virginia, she had hauled hay, broken cane, chopped wood. As a married woman in New York, "She had been a snappy, determined girl and a hardworking young woman, with the snatch-gossip tongue of a beautician. She liked, and had, to get her way. . . . She had butted their way out of the Tenderloin district into a spacious uptown apartment promised to another family by sitting out the land lord, haunting his doorway. She collected customers by going up to them and describing her services ('I can do your hair better and cheaper, and do it when and where you want'). She argued butchers and wagon vendors into prime and extra ('Put that little end piece in. You weighing the stalks; I'm buying the leaf')" (23). But by the time she is fifty, Violet is transformed from nervy ambition to cracked silence.

Morrison renders Violet's lapses from normalcy without judgment, as though emotional exigency is just another aspect of the human predicament, as though huge allowance must be made for the variances of conduct. Once such allowance is made, no eyebrow need be raised in condemnation. On the contrary, Morrison exhibits a regard for Violet and confers on her the madwoman's insight. For example, Violet rightly observes, without malice, that Dorcas "was ugly. Outside and in" (205). She visits Alice Manfred,

Dorcas's aunt, not to apologize—for anything—but rather innocently to find answers, "to see what kind of girl" Joe would choose over her (82). Indeed, between Alice and Violet, "No apology or courtesy seemed required or necessary. . . . But something else was—clarity. . . . The kind of clarity crazy people demand from the not crazy" (83). Because Violet has lost so much— peace of mind, focus, direction—she has little to fear from hearing and speaking truth. With Violet the always proper Alice can forgo the façade of social convention. She can be "impolite. Sudden. Frugal" (83), but mostly she can be honest. With Violet, Alice is forced to see not only her niece's lie with Joe but also her own deceptions. She can no longer set herself apart, pretend to be different from other women—common women, who are enraged and deranged by a husband's betrayal. In the face of Violet's assertion that Dorcas is her enemy even in death and that that is why she attacked her, Alice suddenly, reluctantly remembers repressed images of violence against the other woman in her own married life. Thirty years earlier, she had craved not her husband's blood but death and torment for the woman he had chosen instead of her. Alice had not acted but had con- tented herself with murderous dreams. And because she had been restrained then, now Alice is fearful of women like Violet who are not—until she gets to know Violet and comes nose to nose with their similarity to each other.

In some ways Violet's life is Morrison's window for viewing the lives of all black women who have been wronged. Morrison calls them "armed" and "dangerous" (77) because many carry "folded blades, packets of lye, shards of glass taped to their hands" (78). Those who do not arm themselves are "attached to armed men" (78). Still others "become pistols" organizing "leagues, clubs, societies, sisterhoods . . . [designed to] bail out, dress the dead, pay the rent, find new rooms, start a school, storm an office, take up collections, rent the block and keep their eyes on all the children" (78). These are the resolute women who are united in struggle. Whether they struggle to keep a man, whether the fight is for room and board or for personal dignity, is unimportant. For Morrison they detail a single composite pattern.

That is the point Morrison makes with Alice and Violet's relationship. Despite their differences—Alice is one of the "pistols" organizing charitable women's dubs; Violet is one of the armed; Alice's niece is shot by Violet's husband—they find unlikely comfort and friendship with each other. Alice is prepared, when Violet first comes to see her, to look down from a moun- taintop of superiority and propriety. But Violet will allow no such unexam- ined response: "We women, me and you. Tell me something real. . . . I'm fifty and I don't know nothing" (110). She means, "Do not judge me or dis- miss me; look at your life and tell me what lessons, if any, you have learned in fifty-seven years that can help make my life intelligible." To such frankness and vulnerability, Alice can only moan, "Oh Mama" (110). And Violet does the same. In that moment they are linked by mutual compassion to each other and also to ancestral women. In that moment they occupy a space in the line formed by generations of struggling black women.

Perhaps Alice is remembering some particular aspect of her mother when she responds to Violet. Certainly, Violet is remembering her mother, who had fought for life and lost. Rose Dear had scratched out a living in Virginia after her husband left. But, with five children and no help, she did not last long. When the sheriff came and took everything, including the chair Rose was sitting in, she was defeated. Four years later she jumped to her death down a well shaft. Violet recalls her mother's desperation in the wake of her own, and the recollection prompts her to ask, "Mama? Is this where you got to and couldn't do it no more?" (110). Was there one final assault that pushed you beyond the edge of endurance and made suicide the best choice?

Violet does not contemplate suicide, but she is nevertheless facing a crossroads of decision: should she leave Joe or should she take another lover? (After Dorcas's death she had halfheartedly taken one whose name she cannot remember.) Should she fall back in love with Joe and try to repair her broken life with him? Violet puts these questions to Alice, who advises her to "mind what's left to you" (113) because "little bitty life" is too "small and quick" (113) to do anything less. Alice has learned this the hard way. Not until it is too late does she realize that with her niece she had substituted policing for nurturing. She had tried in vain to forestall Dorcas's maturing into a woman because she feared the youthful passions that might claim Dorcas and transform her into one of the other women. Ironically, her fears are realized in Dorcas's fatal rebellion. Alice warns Violet not to allow her fears about the future with Joe to boomerang. As if to underscore her point, Alice unintentionally burns a blouse that she is pressing when she leaves the iron on the fabric too long. The scorched spot is like a painful episode in a life. At first the women stare at the ruined material in shocked disbelief, and then they disintegrate into healing laughter. "Crumpled over, shoulders shaking, Violet thought about how she must have looked at the funeral, at what her mission was. The sight of herself trying to do something bluesy, something hep, fumbling the knife, too late anyway. . . . She laughed till she coughed and Alice had to make them both a cup of settling tea" (114).

Violet and Joe fix what is wrong in their lives and continue on together. Like those of many other Morrison characters, their crimes are redeemed by suffering and by spiritual enlightenment. Joe comes to understand that although he had been *in* love twice, he "didn't know *how* to love anybody" (213;

emphasis added). He would not squander a third opportunity. Violet realizes that sleeping with a doll to satisfy the hunger for a baby and permitting herself other acts of lunacy have a high price. When she awakens from self-induced oblivion, "her husband had shot a girl young enough to be that daughter" (109) she hungers for. In the future she will "mind" what is left to her. Joe and Violet find love again—not the first love of passion and desire or the follow-up love of anguish and regrets—but a kind that is tranquil and deeply satisfying, a love of long walks, good meals, afternoon naps in each other's arms. "A lot of the time . . . they stay home figuring things out, telling each other those little personal stories they like to hear again and again" (223).

Morrison's novels are said to be about place and displacement, referring to her communities, which are strongly evocative of mood, culture, and psychology, and to her characters, who are often alienated from the people and places that give them identity. In these ways, *Jazz* is typical of Morrison's work: the place is New York City, and Morrison's characters are both seduced and repulsed by it. Joe and Violet moved to New York from the South like many others between the turn of the century and World War I. And, like these others, they were motivated to move by political and economic hard times in the South and by the hope of better times in the North. For the most part their hopes were realized. At first Violet found domestic work until she settled on doing hair, and Joe "worked everything from whitefolks shoe leather" to cleaning fish and toilets before finding better work conditions and better pay as a full-time hotel waiter who sold lady's cosmetics on the side. They moved four times in about seven years, the fourth time to Lenox Avenue in a Harlem that is now just a memory. "The buildings were like castles in pictures" (127) with five-, six-, and ten-room apartments. Joe and Violet "had birds and plants everywhere," and they "made sure the front was as neat as the inside" (127). The city offered them possibility, the chance to remake themselves in the images of their dreams, which had been fueled in part by long-distance reports of Baltimore from those who had gone there and believed they had found a new promised land:

The money to be earned for doing light work—standing in front of a door, carrying food on a tray, even cleaning strangers' shoes—got you in a day more money than any of them had earned in one whole harvest. White people literally threw money at you—just for being neighborly: opening a taxi door, picking up a package. And anything you had or made or found you could sell in the streets. In fact, there were streets where colored people owned all the stores; whole blocks of handsome colored men and women laughing all night and making money all day.

Steel cars sped down the streets and if you saved up, they said, you could get you one and drive as long as there was road. (106)

For Joe and Violet the dream place was New York and not Baltimore, but it too was wonderful. In 1906 they boarded a northbound train. As they approached the city, it "was speaking to them. . . . And like a million others, chests pointing, tracks controlling their feet, they stared out the windows for first sight of the City that danced with them, proving already how much it loved them" (32). When they "danced on into the City . . . they knew right away that perfect was not the word. It [New York] was better than that," (107) especially for a couple who had no children and did not want any— "citylife would be so much better without them" (107). Being on Lenox Avenue was "worth anything" because it marked the boundary of a pulsing black world of economic progress.

At some point, however, during twenty years of keeping the beat of city rhythms, Joe and Violet lose their way. Violet is first, and then Joe. The city deludes Violet into thinking she can be who she is not: "White. Light. Young again" (208). These are childhood longings nurtured by her grandmother's stories of the little blond Golden Gray, the child of Miss Vera Louise and a slave boy on her father's plantation. True Belle, a slave herself, had taken care of Vera Louise and later her golden-haired son in Baltimore, where the three of them had gone when the daughter was no longer welcome at the plantation. In going to Baltimore, True Belle left behind a sister, a husband, and two daughters, ages eight and ten. Twenty-two years later, when one daughter, Rose Dear, gave up on life, True Belle returned with ten dollars, "Baltimore tales for granddaughters," and descriptions of life with the wonderful Golden Gray: "How they bathed him three times a day, and how the G on his underwear was embroidered with blue thread. The shape of the tub and what they put in the water to make him smell like honeysuckle sometimes and sometimes of lavender" (142). In Violet's little-girl imagination, Golden Gray was sometimes transformed into a young girl, always living inside her "mind. Quiet as a mole" (207), dormant until in New York old stories of city glamour, golden beauty, and privilege surfaced and began to shape her needs. By the time she realizes the deception, her life is already "messed up" (208). She is a lonely, silent woman craving the child (a daughter, she thinks) she once aborted. Before she "came North . . . [Violet] made sense and so did the world. . . . [She] didn't have nothing but . . . [she] didn't miss it" (207). At fifty, in the city, she and her world are incoherent. "Twenty years in a city better than perfect" (111) is not what Violet thought it would be.

Joe is correspondingly desolate. Living an empty routine with a woman who carries a doll to bed and talks only to a parrot leaves Joe feeling more alone that he ever did in "his fields and woods and secret lonely valleys" of Virginia (107). This simple need for belonging that makes Joe the neighborly, trustworthy man that he is and that the city cannot obliterate finds distorted expression in Joe's relationship to Dorcas. With her he is no longer lonely, but, paradoxically, with her he also violates himself. He becomes the kind of man who *"knew* wrong wasn't right, and did it anyway" (74). Joe had gone to New York in search of his new self, his better self, but the quest is derailed. In Tyrell, Virginia, he had been a sharecropper. In New York he expected to find dignity and spirit. He would be swept up on the tide of black evolution. If Booker T. Washington could eat a sandwich in the president's house, he and Violet could make the city their own. The price of such ownership is high, however. In giving themselves over to their dream selves, they become people neither recognizes: a childless couple, alienated from community in the big city.

Their problems could merely be the consequence of a weary familiarity that threatens any long marriage after years and years of sameness. But Morrison implicates the city in Joe and Violet's failings. Neither anticipated so much anguish in a city better than perfect. In essence, they are betrayed by the city's wonderful promise of perfection.

Morrison signals their recovery as a new affection for each other and for the city. Long hours of replenishing leisure replace obsessive work: "They walk down 125th Street and across Seventh Avenue and if they get tired they sit down and rest on any stoop they want to and talk weather and youthful misbehavior to the woman leaning on the sill of the first-floor window. Or they saunter over to the Corner and join the crowd. . . . Once in a while they take the train all the way to 42nd Street to enjoy what Joe calls the stairway of the lions. Or they idle along 72nd Street to watch men dig holes in the ground for a new building" (223). In the city they have found a sense of community and a way to be themselves. In Felice they have found a daughter. Older and saner, Joe and Violet are not what they imagined themselves, nor is the city what they imagined it to be. They can enjoy its excitement and opportunity without losing the best of their original selves. Perfection is not possible, but transcending imperfection is.

The New York that Morrison conceives is based upon the city's historical character as a final destination for southern blacks fleeing increasing discrimination and oppression, lynchings, and other violence against them during the early 1900s. They came in search of a refuge from want:

Some were slow about it and traveled from Georgia to Illinois, to the City, back to Georgia, out to San Diego and finally, shaking their heads, surrendered themselves to the City. Others knew right away that it was for them, this City and no other. They came on a whim because there it was and why not? They came after much planning, many letters written to and from, to make sure and know how and how much and where. They came for a visit and forgot to go back to tall cotton or short. Discharged with or without honor, fired with or without notice, they hung around for a while and then could not imagine themselves anywhere else. Others came because a relative or hometown buddy said, "Man, you best see this place before you die"; or, "We got room now so pack your suitcase and don't bring no hightop shoes." (32)

Many who came did not find the mecca they sought. Work was not always available, and living conditions were sometimes miserable.

Morrison does not delineate these aspects of city life. They contribute to the novel's historical accuracy but not to its themes. Morrison is most concerned with developing the city's subjective, nonmaterial identity in the way that she develops identity of place throughout her work (the Bottom in *Sula,* a sultry Ohio community—on the periphery of a thriving segregated town—almost perversely surviving the effects of long-entrenched patterns of racism; Shalimar, Virginia, in *Song of Solomon,* where women wear loose-fitting dresses and do not carry purses, reflecting a rural community and an inelegant, natural way of life; Isle des Chevalier with its primal forests and mythic undercurrents). In *Jazz* there is the seductive New York where "a colored man floats down out of the sky blowing a saxophone" (8) whose jazzy notes make one forget about "little pebbly creeks and apple trees" (34). Children, men, and women like the Durnfrey sisters forget about southern origins. Graceful and "citified," the sisters have become "stuck up," having retreated from their beginnings in Cottown, Tennessee. In the city "they feel more like the people they always thought they were" (35); they feel "stronger," "riskier" (33).

One of Morrison's metaphors for the city's bewitching magnetism is its night sky—not the starry expanse that can be observed on a clear evening in the country but a starless interior space "booming over a glittering city" (35). Sometimes it "can go purple and keep an orange heart," imparting to everyone on the street below an enchanting glow. Most often, however, its oceanic depths are dark and mesmerizing. Contemplating this darkness is like penetrating the city's soul, which is both unfathomable and revealing, both "welcoming and defensive at the same time" (9). Morrison does not say it, but perhaps it is these contradictory, competing messages that confuse people and make them "think they can do what they want and get away with it" (8) in the city. Perhaps it is the lack of certainty that gives them a sense of possibility and informs their stronger, riskier selves. Subliminally, the city sky infects the psyche in much the same way that the phases of a moon are thought to affect personality and behavior. Throughout the novel Morrison back- and foregrounds her characters with images of city sky. During the late afternoons when Joe, for example, meets Dorcas, "the Iroquois sky . . . crayon-colors their love" (38). And by evening, at the end of their lovemaking, "the city sky is changing its orange heart to black" (38), becoming an accomplice to Joe's uncharacteristic daring.

The other metaphor for the city's mystique is music, which permeates the narrative in subtle but haunting ways. It is, to borrow a phrase, the music of the night, "the lowdown stuff" (56) played by "men in shirtsleeves [who] propped themselves in window frames, or clustered on rooftops, in alleyways, on stoops and in the apartments of relatives" (58). It is the powerful blues of the 1920s, which insinuates itself into the brain until called into service to chronicle a transgression or to explain life itself. Everywhere the "belt-buckle tunes [were] vibrating from pianos and spinning on every Victrola. . . . There was no place to be where somewhere, close by, somebody was not . . . tickling the ivories, beating his skins, blowing off his horn while a knowing woman sang ain't nobody going to keep me down you got the right key but the wrong keyhole you got to get it bring it and put it right here, or else" (59–60) or where "a woman with a baby on her shoulder and a skillet in her hand" might sing "turn to my pillow where my sweet man used to be . . . how long, how long, how long" (56).

Like the city, the music sends competing messages. It is simultaneously happy and hostile. While its "sooty" rhythms invite a correspondingly rhythmic response (head shake, foot pat, dance step), its lyrics register complaint. Even the raunchy, edgy humor in lines like "hit me but don't quit me" (59) and "when I was young and in my prime I could get my barbecue any old time" (60) belies a subtext of lamentation. The music's excitement masks a "complicated anger" of wronged lovers, of betrayed veterans of World War I who returned from war in Europe to white violence, and of a generally disillusioned existence. But the music also registers audacious endurance. Under the influence of the music, people do "unwise disorderly things" (58): the music may have been responsible for the confusion in Joe's thoughts on the Saturday he tracked Dorcas to a room with someone else and shot her. The music also shaped Violet's attempt "to do something bluesy, something hep" like assaulting a dead girl. It was the "seeping music" of the city "that begged and challenged [Dorcas] each and every day. 'Come,' it said 'Come and do wrong'" (67).

All of the facets of New York—its excitement, its promise of a better life, its seduction, its repressed hostility and blue mood—coalesce in the personality of Morrison's unidentified narrator. She (slight textual clues and strong intuition points toward the narrator's identity as feminine) is the voice of the city: sassy, gossipy, prescient, and more. "I'm crazy about this City," she declares early in the novel (7). "A city like this one makes me dream tall and feel in on things. Hep" (7), she continues. From this point forward, she interprets the city with intimacy and understanding, describing the physical and nonphysical landscape, its past and present, advising of its dangers and attractions, commenting upon the lives of its inhabitants. She knows the city uptown, where "wealthy whites, and plain ones too, pile into mansions," (8) as well as she knows it downtown on Lenox Avenue, where "everything you want is right where you are; the church . . . the party . . . the bootleg houses . . . the beauty parlors, the barbershops, the juke joints . . . the number runner . . . brotherhood [and] sisterhood" (10). The city, she admits, is not "pretty" (8), but it can be hospitable if one is "clever" (9) enough to figure it out. "Do what you please in the City, it is there to back and frame you no matter what you do. . . . All you have to do is heed the design—the way it's laid out for you, considerate, mindful of where you want to go and what you might need tomorrow" (9). She warns, however, that those who cannot decipher its design and avoid pitfalls lose their way and (literally and metaphorically) "end up out of control" (9), as Joe and Violet are for a time.

The narrator's observations are sometimes made as a disembodied consciousness whose perspective of city life is without borders: "When I look over strips of green grass lining the river, at church steeples and into the cream-and-copper halls of apartment buildings, I'm strong. Alone, yes, but top-notch and indestructible—like the City in 1926 when all the wars are over and there will never be another one. The people down there in the shadow are happy about that" (7), she confides. From somewhere above and beyond, the narrator's ubiquitous field of view distinguishes her from the people and things she observes "down there"; she knows more and sees more. Her view of the city is integrated, authoritative.

And yet, Morrison's narrator is not omniscient or infallible (all wars were not over in 1926). On the contrary, as a first-person narrator, at times she seems to be a character participating in the sequence of events and interacting with other characters. In the opening lines of the novel she introduces Violet and Joe in a familiar, colloquial voice, admitting that "I know that woman. She used to live with a flock of birds on Lenox Avenue. Know her husband too" (3). Like a neighbor or acquaintance with recriminating secret details of a scandal, the narrator recounts a complete story of alienation, seduction, and violence, intermittently interjecting her uncharitable judgments: Violet is "skinny" and "mean"; Dorcas is "hard-headed as well as sly"; Joe is a "rat," although sometimes she takes a kinder view of him as a "nice, neighborly, everybody-knows-him man" (73); and Alice Manfred is repressed. Such conclusions are drawn from the narrator's apparent involvement in the day-to-day experience of these characters. She comments as if she is one of the crowd gathering to look on as Violet sits in the street or as one in the church as Violet crashes the funeral or as one of the flirting ladies attending lunch at Alice's house the day Joe comes to sell his beauty products and takes notice of Dorcas for the first time. "If I remember right," she says, "that October lunch in Alice Manfred's house, something was off" (71). She continues with a review of the eating, conversation, and personalities in a detailed but speculative way. She thinks Alice was "probably" distracted about Dorcas during lunch that day because, as she says, "I always believed that girl [Dorcas] was a pack of lies. . . . Maybe back in October Alice was beginning to think so too" (72). She wonders also if Alice "had a premonition of Joe Trace knocking on her door" (72) and desiring her niece. The narrator has many questions but few answers. As any other person at that lunch might do, she theorizes about what happened. The narrator's point of view is often restricted to time and place. In such instances she is left to imagine, to doubt, to think, to express an opinion, or even to admit that she does not know.

The dichotomy of her narrator's identity—as omnipresent on the one hand and as restricted to what she directly observes on the other—was new for Morrison, who in previous novels serves as storyteller relating events and point of view, free to move and to comment at will. The narrative perspective in *Jazz*, however, is more complex. Events are narrated in the first person even though the narrator is not a character. And although the narrator is free to move and comment at will, her comments are not always reliable. She compares her narrative force to the eye of a storm: as narrator she is at the center of storytelling; she gives it momentum—controls sequence, shapes perspective, manipulates meaning. Her characters are like "hens starving on rooftops," awaiting a rescue. "Figuring out what can be done to save them since they cannot save themselves" (219) is her responsibility. "It's my storm," she declares. "I break lives to prove I can mend them back again. And although the pain is theirs, I share it, don't I?" (219). The answer to that question is no, she does not. At the conclusion of her story the narrator confesses that she has little control over her characters' lives. At every turn "they contradicted" (280) her. She "invented stories about them—and doing it seemed . . . so fine" (220). She was certain, for example, that either Joe or Violet "would kill the other." She prepared herself and the reader for their violence. But they were too "busy being original, complicated, changeable—human" (220) to be so predictable, so easily manipulated. It never occurred to the narrator that her characters "were thinking other thoughts, feeling other feelings, putting their lives together in ways [she] never dreamed of" (221). The narrator's "know-it-all self" is really a fallacy. In the end she faces this deception; she is capable of psychological growth.

Clearly, Morrison's narrative voice in *Jazz* is a personification of the impersonal authorial voice. It is not the voice of the author occasionally stepping outside her role as omniscient observer to contribute an opinion—an awkward intrusion at best. It is the author incarnating—as God might take on human form—fictional muscle and bone, giving herself a consciousness and a presence in the text. She does not interact; she exists in a parallel space, chronicling Joe and Violet's story and to some extent telling her own. She characterizes herself as introverted, living "a long time in . . . [her] own mind . . . close[ing] [herself] off in places," (9), but longing for the kind of public affection Joe and Violet have found in the calm after their storm. When she gives up authorial powers for personal identity in the text, the narrator, like other characters, is subject to the aspirations and urges of humankind.

Morrison's personification of the impersonal authorial voice dramatizes the undivined aspect of the creative-writing process. During the course of composing, minor plots and characters may take on an unexpected primary focus as planned themes recede and vice versa. Mark Twain's familiar account of what happened to the musical twins who started out headlining his novel *Pudd'nhead Wilson* facetiously illustrates the point. The novel's original title was *Those Extraordinary Twins*, but somewhere in the composition process their story was subsumed by another. Twain explains: "I meant to make it very short. . . . But the tale kept spreading along, and spreading along, and other people got to intruding themselves and taking up more and more room with their talk and their affairs. . . . When the book was finished and I came to look around to see what had become of the team I had originally started out with . . . they had disappeared from the story some time or other. I hunted about and found them . . . stranded, idle, forgotten, and permanently useless."[4]

Kate Chopin's tongue-in-cheek response to criticism of *The Awakening* is similar. Censured for Edna Pontellier's decision to leave her husband and children to seek fulfillment as a woman and artist, Chopin says, "I thought it might be entertaining (to myself) to throw them together and see what would happen. I never dreamed of Mrs. Pontellier making such a mess of things

and working out her own damnation as she did. If I had had the slightest
intimation of such a thing I would have excluded her from the company.
But when I found out what she was up to, the play was half over and it was
then too late."[5] Morrison's view of a writer's relationship to her characters is
expressed in less cavalier terms than Twain's and Chopin's views. Her characters are "very carefully imagined." She knows "all there is to know about
them." She knows that they "have nothing on their minds but themselves"
and are capable of getting out of a writer's hands. But Morrison feels that
"you can't let them write your book for you."[6] She does not give up authorial control because that would mean a sacrifice of her art. And yet, she does
have a regard for the unanticipated quality of writing. Without losing sight
of her controlling image,[7] Morrison does not fear the tough choices that her
characters sometimes compel her to make for them if she is to write truthfully about them. To some spiritual extent it is her characters and not she
who write books, and she must follow the story path where they lead. She
has been chosen by them to represent them, to tell their stories, exhibit their
experience.

These authorial responsibilities and limits of storytelling shape Morrison's
conception of narrator in *Jazz*. Like Morrison, the narrator is charged with
interpreting and presenting the truth of her character's lives, and, like Morrison, she must be intuitive enough to receive these truths (the narrator as
storyteller mirrors Morrison as storyteller). If she is not, the characters create their own reality in spite of her, and the narrative is false. (Of course, as
author Morrison has more leeway here. Without her, her characters have no
recourse. They must live with her failure.) "What was I thinking of?" (160),
the narrator asks after failing to perceive a character's true motivation. "How
could I have imagined him so poorly? . . . I have been careless and stupid and
it infuriates me to discover (again) how unreliable I am" (160). She resolves to
be more attentive in the future: "Now I have to think this through, carefully,
even though I may be doomed to another misunderstanding. I have to do it
and not break down" (161). She "want[s] to be the language that wishes him
well, speaks his name, wakes him when his eyes need to be open" (161). Her
language will construct his experience. Unfortunately, the narrator repeats
her failures—with other characters. Hers is a process of trial and error, like
an artful jazz improvisation inventing itself from a stated harmonic theme,
which, indeed, was Morrison's controlling image of *Jazz* as she composed it:
a book "writing itself. Imagining itself. Talking. Aware of what it is doing,"
willing "to fail, to be wrong" like a jazz performance.[8] *Jazz*, Morrison says,
"predicts its own story. Sometimes it is wrong because of faulty vision. It
simply did not imagine those characters well enough, admits it was wrong,

and the characters talk back the way jazz musicians do. It has to listen to the characters it has invented, and then learn something from them."[9]

It also listens to or is certainly aware of its audience. In that sense *Jazz* advances Morrison's ideas about the reader's participation in making meaning in her novels. The text should promote complicity, Morrison believes, between author and reader. It should elicit the reader's interpretation and activate her imagination. That is the narrator's missive to readers in the final lines of the novel. Having provided a parting view of Joe and Violet in denouement—a calm loving after their storm—the narrator turns to the reader with a declaration of intimate vulnerability: "I have . . . surrendered my whole self reckless to you. . . . I love the way you hold me, how close you let me be to you. I like your fingers on and on, lifting, turning. I have watched your face for a long time now, and missed your eyes when you went away from me. Talking to you and hearing you answer—that's the kick" (229). An act of reading rendered as an act of lovemaking becomes a moment of mutual creation. You may choose to "make me, remake me," the narrator concludes, and "I am free to let you" (229). That is the reader's privilege and the author's promise.

CHAPTER 7

Utopia and Moral Hazard
Paradise

Morrison says that she "was lucky to be working on *Paradise* when she won the Nobel—to avoid the writer's block a friend called 'the Stockholm curse.'"[1] She received the Nobel in 1993, and five years later her novel appeared. *Paradise*, like other Morrison novels, explores the intellectual questions she, as well as, perhaps, the rest of us, contemplates. In *Paradise* (her publisher's choice of title; Morrison wanted to call it *War*),[2] she made what she calls a "two-pronged" inquiry. The first proceeded from her observation that one's political ideals often become jaundiced with increasing age; political activism seems to be a province of the young self, while caution and stability have more appeal in later life. What explains this difference, Morrison wondered, "between the young and the old" in their political and moral passions? The second question, about "the idea of paradise," flowed from a second observation about the limitations of utopian societies: they are seductively safe but dangerously cloistered. As Morrison says, "the isolation, the separateness, is always a part of any utopia."[3] These double inquiries at first appear unrelated, Morrison admits, but in *Paradise* they converge as multiple and competing visions of the ideal community unfold, largely along the axes of age and experience. The novel portrays a youthful vision of a race-conscious community in solidarity with emergent black power against a backdrop of social tradition and hostility to change. Morrison pays respect to tradition, but she sees social agility as the more essential human asset. Absent change, "you freeze history, and you simply just pass it off as preformed, already made, already understood, already furnished."[4] Morrison accepts that "the fight, when one is young, for social justice or for the good life is a struggle for a kind of paradise,"[5] but she suggests that each subsequent generation must commit to struggle for its own vision. One generation's paradise may be the next generation's prison. An inherited paradise is lifeless, a community frozen in time. It might provide a measure of security for its creators, but it also forestalls the possibility of social evolution and regeneration for everyone.

Ruby, Oklahoma, founded by blacks in 1950, is what Morrison calls her "meditation" on the two sides of paradise as both sanctuary and fortress. In a generous reading, Ruby is paradisiacal—"full of bounty, where no one can harm you."[6] Visually stunning, everywhere, "Front yards were given over to flowers. . . . The red bands drinking from sumac competed with the newly arrived creams and whites that loved jewel flowers and nasturtiums. Giant orange wings covered in black lace hovered in pansies and violets" (90). And when Deek Morgan drives through Ruby's streets, he notes, with no small pleasure, "quiet white and yellow houses" occupied by "elegant black women at useful tasks" (111). Prosperous and long lived, Ruby's residents have not recorded a death in twenty years. Yet, in a less generous prospect, Ruby itself is dead—a casualty of its own social engineering. With few exceptions, new people and ideas are censored or otherwise purged. The present looks much like the past, and that is the hazard of paradise that Morrison examines.

The conceit for this singular town in which to interrogate the "idea of paradise" formed from historical study and from a story fragment that, Morrison explains, is a warning to freedmen heading west after war: "Come prepared or don't come at all." What struck Morrison was a historian's observation "that 200 ex-slaves came and they didn't have enough money, they didn't have enough resources and were turned away." And that, she says, "is what compelled me to wonder about what might happen to ex-slaves being turned away by other ex-slaves."[7] The answer, as Morrison imagines it, is fierce self-sufficiency, exclusivity, and insularity—hence the novel's segregated setting. One hundred fifty-eight proud but bedraggled freedmen left Louisiana and Mississippi in the 1890s and were rejected by one Oklahoma town before settling another. The story of that journey and, in particular, the "Disallowing" in Fairly, Oklahoma, shapes a defining narrative for successive generations. By 1975, the "Disallowing" is Ruby's sole narrative. The rage of that rejection and the obsessive interiority that results find ritual reenactment at the town's annual Christmas pageant and in each incident of a newcomer being chased or killed. The gospel of "holy families" turned away is the town's only knowledge of itself. In Richard Misner's words, "over and over and with the least provocation, they pulled from their stock of stories tales about the old folks, their grands and great-grands; their fathers and mothers. Dangerous confrontations, clever maneuvers. Testimonies to endurance, wit, skill and strength. Tales of luck and outrage. But why were there no stories to tell of themselves? About their own lives they shut up. Had nothing to pass on. As though past heroism was enough of a future to live by. As though, rather than children, they wanted duplicates" (161).

The past should inform present and future, but it cannot replace them. In *Song of Solomon*, Milkman is inspired by his ancestor's flight of daring will, but he is also liberated to choose differently from Solomon. He is free to improvise, and he does. As Morrison warns, "You can romanticize [the past] to such an extent that you cannot join the modern world. You can find it as overwhelming and so frightening and so wicked that you can't separate yourself from its wickedness. . . . So there's kind of a negotiation that has to take place between one's self and one's national past, one's cultural past, one's personal past and one's racial past."[8] That negotiation is dramatized in *Paradise* through generational conflict. Ruby's youth respect the past, but, to their elders' dismay, they want to reinterpret it in the context of their present lives and to propose new understandings. Instead of believing in the Old Testament translation of the Oven's text as "Beware the Furrow of His Brow," they read the words first as "Be the Furrow of His Brow" and then "We Are the Furrow of His Brow," growing in their advocacy and exchanging the fearful command of obedience for an activist's call to new purpose.

This fourth generation envisions history as encompassing more than the town's past. History is inclusive, fluid, and immeasurable. As Richard Misner, Ruby's progressive young preacher, teaches, it extended "past your great-great-grandparents, past theirs, and theirs, past the whole of Western history, past the beginning of organized knowledge, past pyramids and poison bows, on back when rain was new, before plants forgot they could sing and birds thought they were fish, back when God said Good! Good!—there, right there where you know your own people were born and lived and died" (213). History is national, cultural, personal, and racial. It is primordial, Africa, slavery, freedom. And it is recent: "four teenagers arrested in Norman and charged with possession, resisting, arson, disorderly, inciting and whatever else the prosecution could ferret out of its statutes to level against black boys who said No or thought about it" (206). But in Ruby, only the town's past has agency. Pat Best speaks for community when calling Africa just another foreign country, and, in Ruby's way of thinking, four jailed teenagers are "little illegal niggers with guns and no home training [who] need to be in jail" (206). Reductive and hateful, the town's "voices [will not] bespeak civilizations gone [nor those] yet to be."[9]

Old oppose young; progressives confront preservationists. Morrison, however, is interested not just in difference but in change, especially when that change feels like loss, what she describes as "how one moves from liberation to conservation . . . how you can make a liberationary gesture and how it can make you end up as the world's most static conservative."[10] Many in Ruby ask, in retrospect, how an exalted vision could turn so thin. To the extent that Morrison answers that question, the novel is a dissection of moral regression, an unraveling of communal consciousness.

The original one hundred fifty-eight had practiced scrupulous community. "They had denied each other nothing" following the Fairly rebuff. "Afterwards the people were no longer nine families and some more. They became a tight bond of wayfarers bound by the enormity of what had happened to them" (189). The symbol of that unity was the Oven; there was comfort in a "community kitchen" (99). People gathered there "for talks" and "for society" (15). It "stayed alive"; its fire never died. Nearly nine decades later, in Ruby, the Oven is a shrine to the past and the object of strife. Cohesion has given way to self-centered resentments and repeated transgressions of human kindness. First, Delia Best was allowed to die in childbirth. Offended by her pale skin, hazel eyes, and light hair, Ruby's men refused the ride she needed to a hospital that might have saved two lives. Then the town ostracized Delia's granddaughter and namesake, sacrificing her to its intolerance. In the interim, Menus, the town's barber and weekend drunk, loved outside, too, and was forced to return the "pretty sandy-haired girl from Virginia." "Forced" also "to give up the house he'd bought for her," Menus "hadn't been sober since" (195).

The burden of these failures is borne by Deek and Steward Morgan, twin brothers who value money and property, mostly. It is their bank's foreclosure that nets Deek Morgan Menus's house. Significantly, when Anna Flood asks Steward why his brother had not rescued a disoriented Sweetie Fleetwood, troubled to the point of "marching" out of town, he "stared at Anna as though he couldn't believe her words. 'He was opening up the bank, girl'" (124). Under Morgan authority, "fertility shriveled" in Ruby, "even while the bounty multiplied. The more money, the fewer children, the fewer children, the more money to give to the fewer children" (193). Their grandfather, Zechariah, was a man of vision and insight. Guided and sustained by his walking god, Zechariah sought self-sufficiency and independence but not demagoguery. Probably born Kofi, aka Coffee, he renamed himself in freedom, not after Joshua, the successor "king," but "after the witness to whom God and angels spoke on a regular basis" (192). He understood the importance of showing "mercy" and "compassion" and knew that the punishment for having neither was forfeiture of family and identity. In Lone DuPres's view, the Ruby community has squandered that knowledge: "There was no pity among its leaders. . . . They did not think to fix [a problem] by extending a hand of fellowship or love. They mapped defense [and murder] instead" (275).

Killing women is an extravagant perversion of the ancestor's narrative. In the beginning, repeated rejection had made Zechariah and his freedmen voluntary outcasts. They altered routes, avoiding towns and trouble, and each effort at isolation made them "stiffer, prouder" (14). Generations later, pride is arrogance, isolation is exclusivity, and those who had inscribed the narrative of disallowance are disallowers themselves. The story of their ancestors' survival, committed to memory and ritual, confers outsized power. Delia Best and Menus's wife were certainly a rehearsal for the more elaborate drama. Perhaps it should not be a surprise that "they shoot the white girl first." Was hers the mistake of other light-complexioned women who coupled with eight-rock men—those unadulterated, tall, "blue-black people," so designated by Pat Best for a purity akin to the "deep deep level in . . . coal mines" (193)? Was choosing K.D. Morgan the white girl's fatal error?

The Convent is Ruby's opposite. It is women's space, holistic, healing and compassionate. As community devolves in Ruby, it evolves in the Convent. Broken, inchoate girls, always at odds with each other, take up residence over the years, but by the July morning when the men arrive, weak girls have transformed themselves into authentic, composed women. And, "unlike some people in Ruby," they "were no longer haunted" by a tortuous past (266). The evening before, as if in preparation for the next day's inferno, they had been baptized in a "hot sweet rain" that sloughed off the profane and left "enchantment" in its place. The next morning they awaken at four "to prepare for the day." In mindful concert, they work: "one mixes dough while another lights the stove. Others gather vegetables for the noon meal, then set out the breakfast things. The bread, kneaded into mounds, is placed in baking tins to rise" (285). Four previously discordant lives have entered into harmony and community. The men's intrusion at that point is criminal, but it is also a sacrilege informed by another of Morrison's story fragments—this one recounting a murder in Brazil in which a posse of local men killed a community of black convent nuns who took in abandoned children. The men were outraged over the practice of "candomblé, an Afro-Brazilian religion." For Morrison, the story (which turned out not to be true but was still useful) places "women, defenseless and threatening [as] interlopers [in] male conclaves," and "when we [women] get ourselves together and get powerful is when we are assaulted."[11]

The Convent, Morrison illustrates, is sacred terrain—not because it had once been occupied by nuns but because it is a place of miracles. The man-god appears there as he had to Zechariah, and Consolata discovers Truth there as she comes of spiritual age. Consolata is timeless, the daughter of Mary, Eve, Piedade. In her, the erotic, the maternal, the sacred, and the heroic converge. Born in Brazil but given no biological ancestry, Consolata assumes supernatural proportions. Morrison develops her as sovereign and transcendent, someone who reconciles the conventional dualities of good and evil, spirit and flesh, God and man. Her story of childhood rape, of spiritual devotion, of human love and abandonment, of "stepping in" to retrieve life from death is a series of connected events, no matter how seemingly contradictory, that she assimilates. Consolata's lesson is "Never break them [the temporal and eternal] in two. Never put one over the other. Eve is Mary's mother. Mary is the daughter of Eve" (263). Beware of the divided self, she warns. Her love of God on the one hand and her practice of pagan spirituality on the other do not condemn her to a "half cursed, half blessed" condition (248). As Lone DuPres sees it, to "separate God from His elements" (244) is to divide Him from His works and unbalance His world.

Consolata's other achievement is the integration of female and male, which she completes not long before her death during an early evening in the garden. In a pivotal moment, which traces Consolata's awakening, she appears to be meeting herself as a man with eyes "as round and green as new apples" and "Fresh, tea-colored hair," both features like Consolata's own, approaches her. His familiar "come on, girl. You know me" and "Don't you know me better than that" suggest intimacy. During their exchange, Consolata adopts his language and "flirtatious" mood, "which was full of secret fun" (252). He moves closer to her "without having moved" (252). They are synchronized—god-human, female-male. With Deek Morgan all those years earlier, she had experienced male and female as oppositional. He had feared that their union would be more than sexual, that she would take him in and consume him; hers was a "gobble-gobble love" (240). Theirs was never a convincing partnering as indicated by barren fig trees and a burned-out meeting place. In the garden, however, male and female are not antithetical but integrated, and, as the embodiment of both, she is sufficient and complete. Coming to this understanding of divinity, Consolata is literally transformed by new knowledge and remade. She has "higher cheekbones, stronger chin. . . . Her hair shows no gray. Her skin is smooth as a peach" (262). The years fall away. She is ageless, no longer subject to corporeal effects. She loses all fear of death, loneliness, and responsibility, and she does not require Deek to validate or partner. She complements herself.

This is the knowledge to pass on. Consolata summons the four brooding women in her charge to witness her new narrative agency: "I call myself
Consolata Sosa," she announces. Placing the (last) sumptuous supper on the
table (going forward she feeds them "bloodless food and water alone" [265]),
she invites the women to her as disciples. They will behave, eat, sleep as she
directs them. In return, she promises, "I will teach you what you are hungry
for" (262)—how to gather all the parts of themselves. They will be the fruit of
her encounter in the garden. She assures them that, when they are complete,
"someone [the human-god, an emissary of wholeness] could want to meet
you" (262). Following Consolata's model, the women speak their painful
stories; each one inhabits all the others in the way of extraordinary sisterhood
(a sister would not abandon, they assure Seneca: "no sister would do such
a thing" [262]). In vibrant floor paintings, they represent their experiences
in repeated images and fall in love. Writing a more compassionate script for
Reverend Mother than that of the hegemonic CHRIST THE KING SCHOOL, pur-
porting to bring God and salvation to native girls in exchange for despising
themselves, Consolata ushers her novitiates through affirmation of self and
to redemption. Unlike Ruby's residents, the women are no longer tethered to
a punishing past that sabotages present and future. After months, the women
Consolata once labeled frightened, lying girls are strong and assured.

Consolata's death finishes the evolution of community at the Convent
(and the devolution of community in Ruby) and makes visible the true paradise, one not defined by disallowing. Her final smiling words, "you're back,"
directed high above the men's heads, suggest not Deek Morgan's return as
it might at first seem but the return of him she had met in the garden. The
Convent is now holy ground, the men's obscene acts notwithstanding. The
women's rituals of forgiveness have redeemed them and the place. Consolata's last word is "Divine," evocative in its multiple meanings: Pallas's baby,
who is named Divine after Pallas's mother; an inspired act of forgiveness,
since Consolata knows the men might kill the baby; divine love, of which
she is capable even in the moment of her destruction. Perhaps "divine" is her
description of the glimpsed paradise to come, where, at the close of the novel,
she finds solace in the arms of the black mother-goddess.

Paradise found, however, is not the perfection Consolata once envisioned
in which white sidewalks met the sea and fish the color of plums swam alongside children. This paradise is a place where "discarded bottle caps sparkle
near a broken sandal. A small dead radio plays the quiet surf" (318). There is
rest and safety here, but there is also "endless work" and ordinariness. Ships
bearing the "lost" and "disconsolate" find reception in a paradise intended
with a small "p." "The whole point," Morrison says "is to get paradise off its

pedestal, as a place for anyone, to open it up for passengers and crew." She wants "all the readers to put a lowercase mark on the 'p.'"[12] Consolata, then, is Morrison's consummate woman. She is a revision of Eve in the garden with the difference that she is visited by a god who imparts self-knowledge that is validating and empowering. She is Mary, mother of all who come to her for help. Perhaps she is also destined to replace Piedade, the maternal figure in the true paradise, whose ancient fingers are now "ruined."

Consolata's mythic, transfiguring role is in strong contrast to the women of Ruby, who are static in the way of not linking to the maternal past or future, to either ancestors or progeny. Grandmothers are not featured in the founding narrative, and young women are in rebellion, like Billie Delia, or indifferent, like Arnette. Ruby women evince little sense of themselves as part of a female lineage. They may have insisted on naming the town after one of their own, "that sweet, modest laughing girl whom . . . Deek and Steward had protected all their lives" (113), but, paradoxically, Ruby is patriarchal, its authority passed from one generation of male to the next, as with the five generations of Morgan men, the last of which is K.D.'s infant son. In Pat Best's charts, Ruby women have only one name or "generalized" last names; their "identity rested on the men they married" (187). Idealized by the men, they are imagined as passive, pious, and innocent like the mothers and grand-mothers who sang "He will take care of you . . . [in their] pure sopranos" (15–16) or like Deek's nineteen summertime ladies in pastel dresses and pale hats from his childhood whose "creamy, sunlit skin excited him" (110). In-elegant women threaten the paradisiacal order. Thus, Steward Morgan can entertain the thought of his fist in the face of a certain kind of woman, like the streetwalker knocked down and kicked by white men. And he can put a bullet in the head of another.

Paradise is not merely a standoff between town and Convent or between male and female, it must be said. The contrasts among these are clear but complex. Morrison makes the point, for example, that, although Ruby women are not like Consolata, they are also not exactly like their husbands; they are better and more interesting. Most would not have transplanted the Oven to their new town, unaffected as they are by its power to command blind allegiance: "They resented the truck space given over to it—rather than a few more sacks of seed, rather than shoats or even a child's crib. Resented also the hours spent putting it back together—hours that could have been spent getting the privy door on sooner" (102). In the early days of Ruby's settlement, the women confronted their husbands in an effort to save Delia Best and the child when those husbands refused to get help for a woman with "sunlight skin" and "racial tampering" (197). The women who did not drive

had to beg men, who gave excuses. During the Convent killings, their inter-
vention again meets with little success. Tears and incredulity are not enough.

Soane and Dovey Morgan, especially, have great unrealized potential to
be absolutely free of Ruby's restrictive ideological boundaries. Morrison is
clearly fond of them. Self-assured, often independent, the sisters sit in distant
disapproval of their husbands' acquisitive nature:

> Almost always . . . when Dovey Morgan thought about her husband it
> was in terms of what he had lost. His sense of taste one example of the
> many she counted. Contrary to his (and all of Ruby's) assessment, the
> more Steward acquired, the more visible his losses. The sale of his herd
> at 1958's top dollar accompanied his defeat in the statewide election
> for church Secretary because of his outspoken contempt for the school-
> children sitting in in that drugstore in Oklahoma City. . . . In 1962 the
> natural gas drilled to ten thousand feet on the ranch filled his pockets but
> shrunk their land to a toy ranch, and he lost the trees that had made it
> so beautiful to behold. His hairline and his taste buds faltered over time.
> Small losses that culminated with the big one: in 1964, when he was forty
> . . . they learned neither could ever have children. (82)

Dovey wonders if a wealthy man can be good, and the sisters are two of the
three people in town willing to parent the ostracized Billie Delia, if only for
a short time. They "treated her with easy kindness. . . . If it had not been for
them her teens would have been unlivable" (151). Soane, in particular, seems
liberated in her friendship with Consolata, the woman who had once loved
Soane's husband. She even invites the Convent to the wedding reception at
her house. Although generous and wise, however, the sisters are too deeply
bonded to the town and their husbands to choose something different. It is
not long after the women arrive at the reception that Soane realizes, "'There's
no place for them.' The strange feathers she had invited did not belong in her
house" (155). Similarly, decades earlier, as a young woman, Soane had believed in her husband and his vision enough to threaten abortion if Consolata
did not stop seeing him. Consolata remembers that Soane "was a mother . . .
saying a brute unmotherly thing that rushed at . . . [her] like a forked tongue.
She dodged the tongue, but the toxin behind it shocked her" (239). Soane
had miscarried and not aborted—a girl; that choice falls to Arnette, the
"quietly sullen" next generation of Morgan wife. Soane longs for the past,
when community was a feeling as well as a place, when a girl could receive
confirmation and blessing from that community. A riverside baptism symbol-
izes such harmony for her: They were "baptisms to break the heart . . . when
the pastor held the girls in his arms, lowering them one by one into newly

hallowed water, never letting go. Breathless, the others watched. Breathless, the girls rose, each in her turn. . . . Hair and face streaming they looked to heaven before bowing their heads for the command: 'Go, now.' Then the reassurance: 'Daughter, thou are saved'" (103). Now Soane lives with an emptiness where "her little girl . . . who would be nineteen years old" should be. That daughter would not have called a meeting of a town as had one of Pius DePres's daughters. She would not have lectured them on whites, Africa, and a way of understanding both. She would not have wanted to rename the Oven or change the meaning of its inscription (102). Morrison makes us wonder what Soane would have taught her daughter. Could she have helped her be a woman in the 1970s? The answer might come in knowing that, despite her long friendship with Consolata, Soane backs her husband following the killings just as Dovey defends hers, and the sisters separate. Their link to the men in their lives is stronger than their link to community and to each other as sisters and women. Morrison does not set them up to be fabulous or mythic as is Consolata, but she does advance their progress toward Truth ahead of their husbands, even if in the end they fall short.

Like the sisters, Lone DuPres is imperfect yet appealing, connected as she is to both Ruby and the Convent, historical Christianity and magic. Lone understands that it is women "never men [who] dragged their sorrow up and down the road between Ruby and the Convent." She knows what it means for the Convent residents to "choose themselves for company" (276). Still, she embraces the "Disallowing" and the Oven's Old Testament interpretation. At the annual founders' play, hers is the strong voice of assent as the holy families point forefingers at enemies and chant "God will crumble you. God will crumble you" (211). Like the men, she has faith in the Oven and warns that "they had better hurry up and fix its slide before it was too late" (298). Lone interprets the Convent massacre in the self-interested terms of God's relations with Ruby: the missing bodies, she thinks, represent a God-given second chance. In such a scenario, the murdered women are reduced to human pawns—God's way of admonishing his chosen people.

Billie Delia and Anna Flood are the women of Ruby's future. Both have experience of the Convent's transcendent values—Billie Delia while in exile there and Anna as a visitor following the carnage. Both see the problem with Ruby's rigid rules; both have lived away from Ruby, and both embrace change. They are women of the time. Billie Delia's is the way of youthful militancy, someone who engages the struggle to define her independence. She imagines the Convent women acquitting themselves as warriors and returning to crush the town. "She hoped with all her heart that the women were out there, darkly burnished, biding their time" (308). Anna, a little older and less angry, sees the women in a nuanced way. She understands that the floor images are not satanic or pornographic, as the men assert, but denote "the turbulence of females trying to bridle, without being trampled, the monsters that slavered them" (303). Anna, however, unlike the Convent women, will not step outside her history into an eternity. When a door opens in the Convent garden, she stands "transfixed for a long moment" with Richard Misner before backing away and running to the car. The question is "What would happen if you entered? What would be on the other side? What on earth would it be? What on earth?" (305). The answer, perhaps, is that she would find Consolata, Seneca, Grace, Mavis, and Pallas there. Misner calls it "neither life nor death" but a place of splendor (307). Before the murders, the women had been healed in the baptism of rain and made holy—and fully human. Afterward, they remain complex. Morrison does not render them placid and ethereal; she does not romanticize them in life or death. Through them Morrison reinforces Consolata's message of the integrated self, her warning to resist false dichotomies. They can be holy as well as armed, no longer weak and vulnerable. Gigi is dressed in camouflage and carrying a gun. Pallas, with baby Divine strapped to her chest, carries a sword and a good pair of leather huaraches. Pallas Athena, the Greek goddess of warfare and wisdom, seems to be Morrison's model for that image, suggesting a stunning triumph of woman's body and spirit. Perhaps Consolata's final word, "Divine," is the blessing conferred on a baby girl who will know what she needs to survive as a woman in Morrison's imagined paradise with a small "p."

Anna's place is on this side of the door. In 1976 Anna synthesizes the aims of feminists and black activists to rewrite the dominant narratives of race and gender in America. A businesswoman—the only one in Ruby—young and successful, Anna is independent of the Morgan bank and its often ruthless capitalist agenda. Set up as a cooperative, the bank operates as an extension of the twins' power to control the town. Having steered through whatever discontent sent her north to find "something real" and the subsequent confusion of all "talk [and] running around" in Detroit, Anna is back in Ruby as an advocate for the latest generation, whose frustration with inflexible codes she shares. Her unstraightened hair identifies the epistemological split in the town: most of the older generation hated it; "most of the young people admired it" (119). She asserts a different narrative of Ruby's founding premise, which she insists was the pursuit of honest community. In that narrative, the bank was never intended as Deek and Steward's private domain but was to be a communal enterprise, with everyone contributing and benefiting. Anna worries that the "kids need more than what's here" in Ruby. She even supports their revision of the Oven's meaning.

Yet Anna likes the Morgans even as she rejects their overbearing style. A defining memory for her is of coming of age in the company of Ruby's men. They build shelving in her father's store; she builds mountains in the path of industrious ants nearby. Steward's gentle scorpion lesson shapes her understanding of timid power and its abuses when she sees young policemen with guns in Detroit. Anna's affection for these men softens the politics of gender in the novel. Morrison is not drawing hard ideological lines with obtuse men positioned on the wrong side of wise women. She sets Deek Morgan onto the path to enlightenment after he looks through Consolata's eyes and sees the ruin in his life; he has become a person to shame the ancestors. He will be guided on the journey by Misner, an apostle of forgiveness and love. Where Anna sees a closed door in the convent garden, Misner sees an open window, whose invitation he willingly accepts. Steeped in historical Christianity, Misner preaches that "life after life is everlasting" (307). Through the window he sees there is also life "in between." He is capable of intuiting multiple truths.

It falls to Misner to offer the final hopeful assessment of Ruby: its leaders are misguided, but its people are "outrageously beautiful, flawed and proud" (306). Misner is Morrison's most spiritually, psychologically, and intellectually evolved man. She admits that he is "closest to her sensibility about moral problems."[13] He is of a different sort and generation from other nurturing men such as Paul D and Joe Trace, who are older and at peace with the world as it is. Any change they might expect will come from within themselves. As the face of public difference in Ruby, however, and as someone whose unflinching reading of the town's past and present provokes debate, Misner possesses a subtle power to effect social change and spiritual healing. His optimistic reading of Ruby's future replaces the old narrative of hatred. He sees the end of isolation and the beginning of growth and openness. There is no value in Ruby's version of paradise, for, as Morrison says, that sort of place is "designed by who is not there, by the people who are not allowed in" (156). In Misner's reckoning of a new Ruby, "Outsiders will come and go, come and go" (306). And if some are women, they will not be hunted down, for, as we're told earlier, "Misner despised males who [were] brutal with females" (62). Misner, then, pledges to do battle for Ruby's youth and the town's future because "there was no better battle to fight, no better place to be" (306).

Paradise completes Morrison's historical trilogy, the three novels scanning successive eras of African American experience. Speaking about historical emphases in her work, Morrison has said, "I'm interested in the way in which the past affects the present, and I think that if we understand a good deal more about history, we automatically understand a great deal more about contemporary life."[14] Each novel in the trilogy, then, focuses, at fifty-year intervals, on major forces that have shaped and continue to shape African American and national identity. *Beloved* recounts the aftermath of slavery during 1870s Reconstruction. *Jazz* examines a 1920s Harlem of optimism and possibility, and *Paradise* explores aspects of social and civil tension in the 1970s. The novels present a rich milieu in which history is reimagined and reinterpreted for a contemporary audience.

Woven into these historical landscapes is Morrison's repeating subject: the ethics of love. "The [trilogy] question," Morrison says, "is, how are we able to love under duress, and when we can, what distorts it for us and how can we negotiate the various kinds of claims on love that we choose in order to make it include ourselves, the love of the self that is not narcissistic, not simply selfish. And also how do we love something bigger than ourselves in a way that is not martyrdom—not setting oneself aside completely. How do we negotiate between those two extremes to get to some place where the love is generous?"[15] Generous love in the trilogy is nonjudgmental. It is love without jealousy or the desire for revenge, and it is healing. It reconciles past suffering with present insight and makes one's life good, even happy. That's the moral measure for each of the texts: the capacity of generous love to rehabilitate the tortuous past and to validate the individual and community. Baby Suggs knows this when she invites damaged bodies and souls to an Ohio clearing for social and spiritual rebirth in the presence of her and their expansive love. Suggs's "great heart" is the catalyst. It inspires her gospel of love, which she hopes will recreate community and remake individuals. Suggs implores each person individually and everyone en masse to love purposefully and emphatically. Love the body first, she advises. "Love it. Love it hard."[16] But love the beating heart, too. "For that is the prize." More important than a life-giving womb or life-sustaining lungs or other parts of the "deeply loved flesh," the great heart facilitates free, authentic life.

The clearing is a place of geographical and spiritual refuge. "Yonder," beyond the clearing, Suggs tells them, "they do not love." Slaveholding "breaks heartstrings" (88). But so does the community, it turns out. Beyond the clearing, out of Suggs's presence, the community loses what Martha Nussbaum calls "love's knowledge."[17] When Schoolteacher arrives for Sethe and the children, meanness and resentment take the place of love and moral duty. In response, Suggs abandons her ministry of love; she dies sad and grief stricken. Morrison does not condemn these failings; still, as ethical readers, we imagine acting better than the community toward Suggs, given our antipathy to slaveholding and to Schoolteacher. Morrison, however, helps us understand the community's complex human response by giving it historical and moral context. Accustomed to loving small or not at all in the face of certain loss, Ella and the others are dazed by Suggs's extraordinary capacity to do what does not seem humanly possible in that place: to love her family and friends fearlessly. Only God could do as much.

Sethe's choice is given broad context, too. She claims credit for engineering her own and her children's escape from Sweet Home plantation. "I did it. I got us out," Sethe tells Paul D. Her love is deep. Morrison calls it "this all-consuming love" that is "fierce, unhealthy, distorted."[18] Love is a powerful determinant of behavior, especially in terms of how we exercise duty or responsibility. The claims made by love are as strong as those made by moral law, according to the philosopher Harry Frankfurt.[19] And it is possible, even probable in some circumstances, for two claims to conflict and for both to be "absolute": Sethe's need to be a mother to her children and keep them safe on the one hand and her need to resist slavery on the other, for example. Sending them to the next life, even if it means death in this one, satisfies both claims for Sethe. But the moral dilemma she instigates is clear. She commits murder, but, in doing so, she "saves" her children from death in slavery. She was right to do what she did, but she had no right to do it, to paraphrase Morrison. With Sethe, Morrison says, she "was trying very hard as a writer to put into language the theatricality and the meaning of these kinds of distortions [of love] in order to reveal not only their consequences but what one should be warned against, what we should look out for, what we should be wary of."[20] In the end, community does restore the love it withheld from Sethe. Captive to Beloved's enervating demands, Sethe is rescued by the women's voices "baptizing" her in healing sounds. "It was as though the clearing had [finally] come to her" in the "loving faces" (261) of thirty neighborhood women. Still, they cannot make Sethe whole, and there is only a possibility of her capacity to reconcile love of self with love of the other.

The second installment in the trilogy, *Jazz,* Morrison says, is about "the notions of *romantic love* in the so called 'jazz age.'"[21] Such love is inventive and unpredictable, as the narrator realizes when, contrary to her thinking, Joe and Violet Trace don't kill each other. Their "past," the narrator believed, "was an abused record with no choice but to repeat itself at the crack and no power on earth could lift the arm that held the needle."[22] But Violet and Joe surprise the narrator and enlighten readers as they settle into a way of loving each other that renders the past less like the crack in a record and more like a sorrowful blue note—the familiar blues sound—in an improvisational jazz composition. Their loving incorporates the childhood pain of parental abandonment—Wild leaving the newborn Joe to return to life in her cave, Rose Dear jumping to her death in a yard well. Their loving also acknowledges Violet's seduction by the city and Joe's by Dorcas. These recurring blue notes are a reminder, a kind of warning from the past that presses the urgency of taking pleasure in the present—the spontaneity of days that go "however they want . . . [them] to"—short naps, long walks, train rides, babysitting a neighbor's children, playing bid whist and "telling each other those little personal stories they like to hear again and again" (223).

Joe and Violet's is a "grown people," "old-time love." In 1920s New York, they are expansive with life and love for each other, Felice, their new young "daughter," and the city. No longer wishing she were someone else, Violet is herself—the woman her "mother didn't stay around long enough to see." Joe is the man who encourages a woman's true self. They arrive at self-knowledge and a conception of how they want to live—what Nussbaum calls "a conception of the good."[23] Through Joe and Violet, Morrison "wanted to work and work out the problems of *that* kind of love . . . as compared to our notions of romantic love these days."[24]

Morrison's moral vision of what it means to be human in a Godly community unfolds in *Paradise*. "Love of God is what the book is about," Morrison says. "It's about spiritual love—how it gets played out and how it gets corrupted."[25] What is the human responsibility to love God and man, Morrison asks. Richard Misner, an apostle of forgiveness and love, provides the answer. Misner's ethics elevate him above Ruby's religious dogma, hypocrisy, and fear. Misner "loves God so much it hurts, although that same love sometimes made him laugh out loud."[26] A clarifying instance for him and for the reader is the long moment he stands with the cross held high at K.D. and Arnette's wedding, in defiance of Reverend Pullium's hellfire and brimstone, eager to heal fissures in the community, committed to a future in which young people have a role and compelled by love: "The cross he held was abstract; the absent body was real, but both combined to pull humans from backstage to the spotlight, from muttering in the wings to the principal role in the story of their lives. This execution made it possible to respect—freely, not in fear—one's self and one another. Which was what love was: unmotivated respect. All of which testified not to a peevish Lord who was His own love but to one who enabled human love. Not for His own glory—never. God loved the way humans loved one another; loved the way humans loved themselves; loved the genius on the cross who managed to do both and die knowing it" (146). Ruby's leaders are misguided, he believes. Human love and acceptance are a form of the divine.

Morrison's concern is spiritual love and self-love. Commenting in the publication year of *Paradise*, she said, "I think for those of us who live in 1998, male or female, the problems of trying to love oneself and another human being at the same time is a serious late-twentieth-century problem, a very serious problem."[27] Morrison is especially interested in the problem as it relates to women. She explains that "since I began the *Beloved* trilogy . . . I have been wondering why women who are twenty, thirty years younger than I am, are no happier than women who are my age and older. What on earth is that about, when there are so many more things that they can do, so many more choices? *All right,* so this is an embarrassment of riches, but so what. Why is everybody so miserable?"[28] The answer, Morrison thinks, is the conflict in women's lives between the requirement to nurture others and to simultaneously make themselves whole.[29] The trilogy tracks that discord back to a beginning. For Sethe, there is not resolution. To care for her children, she sacrifices herself. In her historical circumstance, in or out of slavery, her life is impossible. And the nature of that dilemma does not end with the institution of slavery, as Rose Dear's situation illustrates. Still, the solution for Violet is not, as she wrongly believes, to refuse children because life is so much easier without them. Morrison offers no such release from a woman's work as culture bearer in passing self-empowering knowledge to the next generation. Violet's relationship with Felice underscores the point. Anna Flood, too, in her historical moment, will negotiate multiple roles and duties. But not until Connie, Gigi, Pallas, Mavis, and Seneca transcend the historical moment to be resurrected in the place of enchantment are the imaginative possibilities of female and human apotheosis glimpsed. No longer in thrall to the demands of an-other, each is free and each is generous. "Count on me, Sal," Mavis says to the daughter she once feared would murder her. For now, Mavis declares, "I'm perfect." Fearless and whole, she has knowledge of love.

It isn't clear that Morrison's thematic concern with the ethics of love is what organizes the trilogy form of the novels exclusively or that ethical love is exclusive to the trilogy. Michael Silverblatt is correct, no doubt, in seeing all of Morrison's novels, beginning with *The Bluest Eye* and up through *Paradise,* "take the impaired self into the world where attempts at love are made."[30] So, also, are *Love,* which follows *Paradise,* and *A Mercy,* Morrison's ninth novel, concerned with the agony and truth of love. Certainly, the complications of loving another without denying oneself are a thematic concern in all the books, not just three. Still, these three are unified by their author's expressed aim to treat the theme in deliberate, successive periods of African American and human history.[31]

The trilogy, then, examines the primacy of love in human happiness and suffering and recommends a strategy for living and for loving. In his final conversation with Deacon Morgan, who recounts the story of a brother's betrayal, Misner advises, "Lack of forgiveness. Lack of love . . . that's worse than the original shame" (303). The novels are a source of moral knowledge and education, a thought experiment, a narrative that stirs reflection and analysis and embodies what philosopher Noel Carroll calls "moral, psychological and social knowledge."[32] Each one of the novels "has a pedagogical impulse," according to Morrison. "That is what the creative enterprise is about—helping people see the world."[33]

In speaking about her life and work in the values context, Morrison has said her teaching is indeed values laden: "Through anything I say, write and do, however I may try to stand between, to the side, or over issues of ethics and value when discussion is underway [*sic*], my position is either known or available to be known. If I encourage strictly and only aesthetic readings of literature, then I have left an indelible message of where I place the persuasive, historical aspect of literature. If I insist upon solely political understandings of these readings, that too is a teaching value."[34] Here Morrison is seeing her work in the broader arena of values education in the academy. The title of her commentary is "How Can Values Be Taught in the University." And she accepts the assumption that they should, since "explicitly or implicitly, the University has always taught values" and always will, she believes.[35] Morrison continues that academic tradition as a teacher and as a writer of novels that explore value in self-sustaining relationships.

As her mission relates to the trilogy, Morrison says that "whatever the historical background, my hope was that the relevance of these people, whatever race, whatever region, whatever their historical circumstances were, they would resonate powerfully with contemporary difficulties."[36]

CHAPTER 8

The Language of Love

Love

Morrison's eighth novel is a love story that does not read like a love story. Instead of idealism, there is a pointed emphasis on the underside of loving: betrayal, violence, deception, and unfulfilled longing. Tenderness and generosity surprise occasionally, but love is in short supply even though there is a pent-up demand. Only in the final, powerful scenes does the novel appear to earn its title, confirming what Morrison calls "that human instinct to care for somebody else."[1] Until that point, *Love* is, more than it is not, a tale of exploited childhood, squandered youth, and the ridiculous aging of two clever women approaching their last years. Christine and Heed Cosey were the kind of childhood friends who "fall for one another. On the spot, without introduction."[2] Since childhood, however, they have been guerrilla warriors. But as L, Morrison's wise, farseeing narrator, explains in the conclusion,

> if such children find each other before they know their own sex, or which one of them is starving, which well fed; before they know color from no color, kin from stranger, then they have found a mix of surrender and mutiny they can never live without. Heed and Christine found such a one.
>
> Most people have never felt a passion that strong, that early. If so, they remember it with a smile, dismiss it as a crush that shriveled in time and on time. It's hard to think of it any other way when real life shows up with its list of other people, its swarm of other thoughts. . . . Heed and Christine were the kind of children who can't take back love, or park it. When that's the case, separation cuts to the bone. And if the breakup is plundered, too, squeezed for a glimpse of blood . . . then it can ruin a

mind. And if, on top of that, they are made to hate each other, it can kill a life way before it tries to live. (200)

Marvelously insightful and important, L's ontology of unsullied love— "pre-gendered, pre-sexual," in Morrison's words—as vital and animating contextualizes the novel's internecine battles: they are really expressions of thwarted love. And the passage effectively stages *Love*'s final movement of reconciliation and redemption when Heed and Christine discard the old festering grievances and speak the language of love for the first time in adult life and then, later, in death.

Still, much of *Love* examines emotions other than love: Christine's and Heed's bitterness, May's blinding vengeance, Junior's insatiable hunger—all centered on each one's connection or imagined connection to Bill Cosey, the story's deceased epic villain and hero both. As Morrison puts it, "what sucked up all their ambition about loving one another was turning their attention to him. He was the one who authenticated them. He was the one whose legacy they would all fight over. He was the one who ruined their lives beyond repair. And they lied about it to themselves all the time."[3] Narrating those self-deceptions is the women's work in the novel, and that female-centered narrative strategy is Morrison's method of organizing portions of the story.[4] Each of the nine sections—Portrait, Friend, Stranger, Benefactor, Lover, Husband, Guardian, Father, and Phantom—is an aspect of maleness or what Morrison sees as the universal "idea of maleness" that is too often the center of women's stories about themselves and each other.

All but three of the sections comment, primarily and through memories, on the women's earlier hopes and expectations of Bill Cosey's role in their lives. "Stranger" and "Lover," two of the three segments not specific to Cosey, feature fourteen-year-old Romen and the evolution of twenty-one year-old Junior's determined seduction. These sections chart the escalating thrill of a couple's sexual recognition and attraction. First, Junior surveys a stranger from Heed's window, and later, as lovers, she and Romen probe the limits of erotic fantasy and desire. "Guardian," a third non-Cosey section, focuses on the relationship between Sandler Gibbons and Romen. Sandler recognizes and guides the adolescence's journey into manhood and personhood. Concerned for his grandson and an astute observer of human nature, Sandler catches the signs of dysfunction in Romen's involvement with Junior. Learn the difference between a "good good woman" and "a scary one," Sandler advises (154–55): "Looks like you hooked yourself up with somebody who bothers you, makes you feel uneasy. That kind of feeling is more than instinct; it's information, information you can count on. You can't always pay attention to what other people say, but you should pay attention to that. Don't worry about whether backing off means you a wimp. It can save your life" (154). Sandler is one of Morrison's good men; "caring, and fussy and important," she says.[5]

In the other six divisions, Bill Cosey comes gradually into full focus, if not full comprehension. His portrait in the first segment arrests Junior and sets her dreaming about the "Good Man" who will love and protect. Through her eyes we see "a handsome man with a G.I. Joe chin and a reassuring smile that pledged endless days of hot, tasty food; kind eyes that promised to hold a girl steady on his shoulder while she robbed apples from the highest branches" (30). From a different angle, remembering him as a perfect friend, Vida, Sandler's wife and Cosey's former employee, dismisses the women in his life and elevates him to a position as Lord of the Realm: in her thinking, "Mr. Cosey was royal. . . . All the rest—Heed, Vida, May, waiters, cleaners— were personnel fighting for the prince's smile" (37). Over her husband's ob- jections, Vida insists that Cosey's "laugh, his embracing arm, his instinctive knowledge of his guests' needs smoothed over every crack and stumble" (34). In yet another view, Heed's face-saving, revisionist presentation of Cosey as benefactor poses as many questions as it satisfies. "Knowing she had no schooling, no abilities, no proper raising, he chose her anyway," to everyone's shock and, in some cases, resentment (72). Heed never asks why. She accepts her husband's assurance that "all she needed was him." She feels "safe with him" despite understanding that he is at another woman's beck and call. May, Cosey's daughter-in-law, and Christine, her daughter, also assume that Cosey will be the benefactor. But his marriage to Heed produces doubt about his character and his commitment to them. Indeed, the benefactor does not leave a proper will, and the women's contested claims of inheritance devolve into subterfuge and worse. In "Husband" Heed's and Christine's call and response provide some additional clarity. An eleven-year-old was chosen by her friend's grandfather, and enmity soon replaced the initial confusion. When Heed returned from the three-day honeymoon, a trip that Christine had wanted to share, Heed had stories to tell her friend. Naively, she even offered Christine her wedding ring to wear. Later that wife was put across her husband's knee and spanked in public for disobedience. In retrospect, Christine does acknowledge Heed's victimization, that "there's virgins and then there's children," and that Bill Cosey "was the Big Man who, with no one to stop him, could get away with it and anything else he wanted" (133). Heed, nonetheless, remains, in Christine's thoughts, "his cheap little bitch- wife" (135). Complementing "Benefactor," the "Father" segment explores the consequences of absent fathers—for their daughters and for the mothers of their unborn children. In her youth Christine rationalized seven abortions by telling herself "revolutions needed men—not fathers." Fruit, the would-be father, had not "stopped her or suggested she do otherwise" (164). The "unborn eye" that accompanied her after the seventh signaled the beginning of the end of her revolutionary ideal. The actual end came in the event of a young girl's unavenged rape. Christine calculated that "Fruit could upbraid, expel, beat up a traitor, a coward, or any jive turkey over the slightest offense. But not this one—this assault against a girl of seventeen was not even a hastily added footnote to his list of Unacceptable Behavior since the raped one did not belong to him"—not his mother, wife, sister, or daughter (166). And that realization had been preceded by the girl's insistence that her father be spared the truth. In Christine's words, "Good Daddy Big Man mustn't know" (166). By that time, Christine understood well the complications of failed father-daughter expectations. She had lost her father at age five and remembered "the half-closed eyes," his not answering when she called, the sensation of "how sudden, how profound, loneliness could be" (168). And the benefactor who should have replaced father, her grandfather, had "abandoned his . . . kin" without apology (168). In the same section, Heed's hopes, perhaps, of "Father," begin with a memory of her twenty-eight-year-old self standing in an upstairs window observing a nursing mother on the lawn below. She is on the eve of an affair that leaves her elated and pregnant. The man, Knox Sinclair, disappears, but Heed cheerfully recovers from the disappointment: "she would trade a father for a child any day" (173). Her cynicism is most certainly the result of having been sold by her father for the sum of two hundred dollars to a man who spanked her as he might his child but exploited her as no father should—an unholy hybridism.

Bill Cosey's proportions are fully shaped by the final "Phantom" section. All that is left is Heed's and Christine's acknowledgment of the shadow that shape has cast in her life and, most critical, in the life of the other. They speak out loud their knowledge, as is required for those of Morrison's characters who would find redemption and healing. Together, no longer cross-talking or contradicting, they reconstruct the coordinating narrative of their experiences: in 1940, on a day of summer play and picnicking at the beach, a little girl on an errand for forgotten jacks encounters her friend's grandfather in a hallway. The grandfather talks, questions, smiles, "touches her chin, and then—casually, still smiling, her nipple, or rather the place under her swim-suit where a nipple will be if the circled dot on her chest ever changes" (191). Minutes later or perhaps earlier, the little girl's friend sees her grandfather standing in her bedroom window "his trousers open, his wrist moving with the same speed L used to beat egg whites into unbelievable creaminess"

(192). Ashamed of themselves, neither tells the other her experience. Each believes, "without knowing why, that this particular shame was different and could not tolerate speech" (192). Over the years, these unexpressed feelings are echoed in fits of arson, greed, florid confrontation, and, finally, delusion and silent machinations. Eventually, both are isolated in humiliation, and the burden contracts their humanity and leaves them without speech for more than a half century.

Speech, here, refers to the transparent communication that engenders trust. Left to themselves, children perfect that connection. Christine and Heed had existed together in a private world they made complete: the keeled-over rowboat they cleaned and furnished—a blanket, driftwood table, two broken saucers, emergency food, and a made-up language. That imagined, guileless place ended where Cosey's might began. Nothing of their private universe survived his force—certainly not the exotic language of childhood intimacy. Christine last used it to hurl an angry accusation at Heed, who returned from that honeymoon trip with the saved stories Christine refused to hear. Only decades later, when one friend is dying, can they speak honest words to each other, and "language, when finally it comes, has the vigor of a felon pardoned after twenty-one years on hold. Sudden, raw, stripped of its under-wear" (184): each tells the hurt of having never been parented; they indict Bill Cosey for taking their childhood and their love but also accept that they squandered the rest. In Christine's view, "we could have been living our lives hand in hand instead of looking for Big Daddy everywhere" (189). Morrison confirms that "they were complicit in that movement of constantly making him the big daddy, the one who did it all. And everything was his fault and therefore, *you* did this, and *you* did this, and *you* did this, until they finally exorcise him" by returning to the unfinished narrative begun in childhood innocence and by telling the whole truth. Christine can say "Love. I really do." Heed can respond "Ush-hidagay. Ush-hidagay" (194).

Morrison says she thought "a lot . . . about the connection between love and language" in the novel. "We human beings distinguish ourselves from other beings through the fact that we have the power of speech, and that we can love."[6] We take both for granted, Morrison suggests, in vacuous talk and, especially, in the promiscuous utterance of the word "love." In the text, L is the only one who understands that "it takes intelligence to love . . . softly, without props" or sex. And she is the only one who speaks the word, until Christine and Heed rediscover friendship even in the midst of their suffering. "And that's when [they] can say L-O-V-E."[7] Morrison succeeds in "giv[ing] back to the worn-out word 'love' the emotions that it has lost through eternal presence."[8] Her point is twofold. First, women's identities in the 1940s were linked to the power of their men. Second, women enabled that subordination. In the case of Bill Cosey, Morrison says, "this man . . . would not have had all this power if the women had not given it to him."[9] Her women, therefore, must (re)possess their own authority and voice; they are on a journey of insight.

Lucidity for characters and readers is facilitated, structurally, by what Morrison describes as "the idea . . . of the way crystal forms. . . . You have a small piece and then it expands to another. And another layer comes on in a different shape, but it's all the same material. And when you get finished it's different facets, different light looking at one simple thing."[10] Fragments of stories from multiple characters and perspectives aggregate to form the whole of meaning. That process allows readers to come close to understanding, for instance, why Bill Cosey would want an eleven-year-old wife. Seeing herself during those childhood years and after all the conflict she has endured since, Heed believes Cosey "picked her out of all he could have chosen" because she had stamina and a strong instinct for survival. "Everybody else thought she could be run over" (72–73). Female guests at the resort, too, made unkind speculations about Cosey's reasons. Unflattering views of Heed's lack of sophistication—her being "sort of physical [and] . . . jungle-y"—led to the conclusion that marrying Heed was "Protection. From what? Other women" (75). Implications are that anyone could serve the purpose of providing the political cover that marriage would offer a philanderer. In Sandler Gibbons's practiced interpretation of Cosey, "after years of eligible widowerhood, he hoped to end [bachelor behavior] by marrying a girl he could educate to his taste" (110). L, who knew Cosey best, discounts his public declaration that he married because he wanted children. That is what "he told his friends and maybe himself," she says. "But not me. He never told that to me because I had worked for him since I was fourteen and knew the truth. He liked her" (139). But more complex than that is L's belief that marrying Heed was a strike against Dark, his father, and an apology to a sad little girl whose shame he had once witnessed and ridiculed. Oddly similar to L's explanation, Junior's conjecture about the marriage reflects a sadness for her own desperate upbringing in the "Settlement" with an indifferent mother and vicious uncles. In one of several imagined talks with Cosey, she declares, "You married an eleven-year-old girl. I ran away when I was eleven. . . . If you'd known me then, nobody would have messed with me. You'd have taken care of me because you understand me and everything and won't let anybody get me." And then she asks, "Did you marry Heed to protect her. Was that the only way?" (156). Christine's final inference is that her grandfather took her friend because he could. There was no one to object. Perhaps none but more likely all of these perspectives combine to convey a truth about Cosey that defies easy understanding.

Indeed, the story's meaning comes less from unfolding plot than from these integrated points of view. An evolving chronology keeps the novel's present time of Junior's arrival, her residence at One Monarch Street, the multiplying deceptions, and culminating fatality. But more significant are the multiple perspectives that function to fix the outsized dimensions of Bill Cosey's behavior, his place and time. This crystalline vision is also a paradox: particles of narrative adhere to form a composite whole, but, as the whole takes shape, individual voices are rendered less consequential on their own. Thus, no one view of Cosey's motivation taken alone is wholly convincing. Without omniscient or seamless first-person access, the story builds through an accretion of nonsequential narratives that overlap, shed light on one another, and illuminate some piece of the whole.

The meaning of a novel is in the structure, according to Morrison.[11] In *Love* she sought to represent the realism of transforming human experience into knowledge and insight. Experiences multiply chronologically, one after another, but insight and self-knowledge come over time, when perspective and maturity allow one to fit myriad experiences into meaningful patterns. It takes a lifetime for Heed and Christine to reach the liberating understanding of the seminal events that shaped their choices and losses. Readers, too, must see the patterns and themes in discordant voices. Of course, narrative organization is an engaging and defining feature of all the novels, each inviting analysis and commentary. *Song of Solomon*'s mythic quest, for instance, advances the novel's coming of spiritual age theme. *Beloved*'s opening in medias res promotes its mystery and dramatic disclosures. *Jazz*'s self-conscious, unreliable narration mimics orality and improvisation. In general, nonlinearity supports Morrison's project for fiction. "Just writing the beginning, the middle, the end is . . . not very interesting . . . because it's not really life-like," she says.[12] The thematic shards of one's life don't, by their nature, connect sequentially or proportionally. In *Love* the pieces build around Cosey. We come to know characters and they know themselves and each other by their relations with him. Morrison is certainly critical of such a man's influence, but she is more focused on the telling and, occasionally, the interpretation of that influence, especially by the women: Christine, Heed, Junior, and Vida.

L is the exception. Continuing the crystal metaphor, L illuminates others' facets. As a part of the story, if not the plot, since she is dead, L has first-person narrative prerogative, exercised infrequently and judiciously. Not a gossip or chatterbox, she transcribes and assesses events and persons fairly though shrewdly, and her extensive knowledge makes her a useful trope for Morrison and a reliable interpreter for readers. As a character, she is a maternal figure whose moral substance garners everyone's respect, even her employer's. "He never lied to me," she asserts (67). As a narrator, L is authoritative and spiritually seductive, someone who suggests the human potential for self-dependence. She answers to no other and acts with conviction. Wise and compassionate, L supplies *Love*'s metanarrative—its background and motivation for characters in thrall to the destructive passions of rage, envy, punishing love, and fear. In speaking about these isolating instincts, Morrison says her characters "may feel separate, but everything they do and think is connected to the behavior, or what they think was the reason for the behavior of somebody else."[13] L's stories interweave all of those connections and thus humanize otherwise monstrously flawed people. From her we get a unifying narrative of characters and events—that Bill Cosey chose rebellion against Dark, the miserly father who sold police information about black people. Cosey never forgot that he had once been his father's unwitting spy and the source of a little girl's distress. David Robert Cosey "withheld decent shoes from his son and passable dresses from his wife and daughters, until he died leaving 114,000 resentful dollars behind" (68). His son spent it on the things his father hated. Cosey avoided his granddaughter, Christine, "because she had his father's gray eyes" (139), and yet he had a tender love for his first wife, Julia, and, after she died, he transferred that feeling to their twelve-year-old son. L claims that "only a wide heart like his could care that much for a wife and have so much room left over" (100). When that son died, the father gave up on life for some time, until he chose Heed. After three years with her and no children, he returned to Celestial, the sporting woman who cast a spell that "neither could break" (106). Cosey's decisions devastated his daughter-in-law, May, L reports. May's devotion to her husband and to her father-in-law was exhaustive. Billy Boy's death only intensified the commitment. L declares that "if I was a servant in that place, May was its [willing] slave" (102). Her reward, as L sees it, was Cosey's announcing, "I'm taking a wife. You know her. Christine's little friend" (138). May turned strategic. A "sweet-tempered daughter of a preacher . . . bred to hard work and duty," a "devoted, not calculating, girl" became so. When L speculates about why May died smiling, she can conjure only one explanation: the smile was about "the hatchet she threw between Heed and Christine when they were little girls. That stuck, cleared the ground they stood on" (141). L sees a complex intergenerational webbing of motivation that is unavailable to the others, captured as each is by his or her particular provocation.

In conceiving L's role as narrator, Morrison planned that "the interior narrative of the characters, so full of secrets and partial insights, would be interrupted and observed by an 'I' not restricted by chronology or space—or the frontier between life and not-life. Thus the character called 'L' is meant to exhibit and represent the imaginative and transformative nature of her name along with its constructive and destructive talents" (xi). L is love, of course, "the subject," in her words, "of First Corinthians, Chapter 12" (199). Accordingly, "Love is patient and kind; love is not jealous or boastful; it is not arrogant or rude. Love does not insist on its own way; it is not irritable or resentful; it does not rejoice at wrong, but rejoices in the right. Love bears all things, believes all things, hopes all things, endures all things."[14] L loves the women, unconditionally, generously. "But her love for Bill Cosey," Morrison says, "is another level. . . . It is slightly maternal, but not really. It is totally acceptable. It is Jesus at his best."[15] L is clear-eyed, however, about transgression and accountability. In her summarizing assessment, May is held responsible for "the hate she put in" Christine and Heed, and Bill Cosey is at "fault . . . for the theft" of their love (200). Cosey's final attempted theft is the women's inheritance. Poisoning him is not punishment or vengeance but L's way of protecting the Cosey women and stopping the man. Her scribbled fake will refers to the "sweet Cosey child," intended, perhaps, as acknowledgment of the parts of themselves Christine and Heed had lost. L calls Bill Cosey "a good bad man or a bad good man" (200). He is not Satan but "an ordinary man ripped, like the rest of us, by wrath and love" (200). It is poignant that she murders the man who had awakened her to love at age five when she had her first sight of him standing in the sea with Julia. Observing him holding Julia close as he carried her ashore, seeing "all that tenderness coming out of the sea" (64), made a tearful lasting impression. But at eighty-one, Bill Cosey is prepared to leave his estate to Celestial and to turn his family out of doors, and L concludes that "he wasn't fit to think, and . . . he wasn't going to get better" (201).

It is not clear that we care very much about L's crime and Cosey's death—not because we agree or disagree with her decision. But L's circumstance is not rendered as morally complex as is Eva's or Sethe's; Cosey does not elicit our sympathy, and the killing does not strike one as morally compelling. L reconciles any apparent contradiction in her or Cosey's behavior satisfactorily enough: they and we are pulled by the difficult dichotomy of wrath and love. "Real" love, she says, the "better" kind is shaped by moral pragmatism "where losses are cut and everybody benefits" (63).

That kind of love endures, Morrison seems to say. L's affection for the Coseys survives in death, where she keeps a watchful eye on Christine and

Heed, hoping they will "figure out how precious the tongue is" (20) and return to the language of love, and where she visits Bill Cosey's grave. Endurance is not joy, however. Betrayal and suffering, accompanied by wrath, are long lived, also. The tombstone fiction "Ideal Husband. Perfect Father" enrages and marginalizes Celestial in death as she had been in life. Her plaintive plea, "come back, baby. Now I understand. Come back, baby. Take me by the hand," infects even L, who joins in. She, too, wants something back, "Something just for me" (202). In a life and beyond of sacrifice, she is tempted to self-interest at least once. Heed and Christine are able to salvage what is left for them, but the best loving promises no rewards. Not interested in romanticized clichés, Morrison advises that caring for another is tough work. She seeks to "give the word [love] . . . its girth and its meaning and its terrible price and its clarity."[16]

Appropriately, L and Celestial are linked in death. In life both offered Bill Cosey the kind of durable devotion that gives the novel its deepest meaning— Heed and Christine's relationship notwithstanding. Through them, Morrison suggests that love is indeed a worthy, if costly, enterprise. L clearly foregrounds the theme; Celestial is opaque but just as significant. Morrison called the novel "The Sporting Woman" for years, after Celestial,[17] intimating, perhaps, the power of her presence in the story for Morrison and the reader. In the alternate title, Celestial would have been the wanton, dangerous sort. Christine and Heed would have been another sort, "not in the sense of a prostitute, but a woman of courage."[18] That program, however, did not work, Morrison says. The result, it appears, is the revisioning of Celestial as a woman of courage and the emergence of Junior as dangerous. Neither is especially wanton. Celestial's name, for example, is certainly not ironic or contradictory as it might at first appear. Prostitution does not summon the heavenly, divine, or angelic, but, according to L, Celestial "did it in such a quiet, reserved way you would have thought she was a Red Cross nurse" (106). Symbolic of her spirit, perhaps, her teeth "were white as snow" (106). Even innocent little girls admire a woman whose "profile was etched against the seascape, her head held high" (188), and for a lifetime "Hey, Celestial" acknowledged "a particularly bold, smart, risky thing" for Christine and Heed (188).

Celestial and L are associated with water—primal, strong, and substantive. L claims to have moved "from womb water straight into rain" (64). Later, she adopts a sensuous conceit of the ocean as the "man" in her life: "He knows when to rear and hump his back, when to be quiet and simply watch a woman. He can be devious, but he's not a fake-hearted man. His soul is deep down there and suffering. I pay attention and know all about him. That kind of understanding can only come from practice" (100). For L

the sea is companionable. "I sit on the steps or lean my elbows on the rail-
ing," she says. "If I'm real still and listening carefully I can hear his voice"
(106). Similarly, the sea is connected to Celestial's enigmatic life force, represented by L's recollected image of her walking into the night ocean, naked and
unafraid of ominous clouds "or of anything." In that liberating movement,
"she [confidently] stretched, raised her arms, and dove" (106). Celestial is
less sanguine than L about a reassuring masculine voice reaching out to her
from the waters. The sound she uttered when she returned to shore that
evening was likely her protest against masculine power. Cosey had just left
her to return to the hotel whose steps "she was not permitted to mount"
(201). L could not identify the sound "as word, a tone, or a scream" (106).
It was, however, desperately alluring. It is not clear whether L responded
that evening on the beach, but she does in their next lifetime. As different as
they are, a deep knowledge of love's prerogative and suffering informs their
shared sensibility, if only in a brief space of sound. From these lonely scenes
and sounds of the ocean, *Love* inherits a melancholia, and, like Whitman's
speaker who learns "the low and delicious word DEATH," L and Celestial
have become interpreters of the sea and the man, for their relationship to the
sea mirrors that with Cosey. For them the low, delicious word is love. It is
possible that only those who choose love over all else enjoy an afterlife. That
would explain May's and Bill Cosey's silence.

The ocean is historical setting as well as motif. The Bill Cosey Hotel and
Resort, a seaside retreat and playground, is a prop in Morrison's portrayal
of a decades-long drama of racial politics. The resort, L declares early on,

> was the best and best-known vacation spot for colored folk on the East
> Coast. Everybody came: Lil Green, Fatha Hines, T-Bone Walker, Jimmy
> Lunceford, the Drops of Joy, and guests from as far away as Michigan
> and New York couldn't wait to get down here. Sooker Bay swirled with
> first lieutenants and brandnew mothers; with young schoolteachers, land-
> lords, doctors, businessmen. All over the place children rode their fathers'
> leg sharks and buried uncles up to their necks in sand. Men and women
> played croquet and got up baseball teams whose goal was to knock a
> homer into the waves. Grandmothers watched over red thermos jugs with
> white handles and hampers full of crabmeat salad, ham, chicken, yeast
> rolls, and loaves of lemon-flavored cake. . . . Handsome single men from
> outside Atlanta or even Chicago . . . came partly for the music but mostly
> to dance by the sea with pretty women. (6)

The sea and its surrounds offered respite, freedom, and good times. Vida
recalls men in "beautiful shoes" and perfectly creased linen trousers holding

chairs for elegant women in "moiré and chiffon and trailing jasmine scent in their wake" (34). "Ocean breezes" kept guests happy and hopeful (34). "Up Beach" from the resort, blacks lived in shacks and worked grueling, low-wage cannery jobs. They could not afford accommodation at Cosey's, but they "prized it" just the same and "felt a tic of entitlement" (42) in black ownership.

Cosey's evokes an era in which rising middle- and upper-class blacks all over the country, but especially in what St. Clair Drake and Horace Cayton called Black Metropolis in 1945—black community in Chicago and other cities—traveled and vacationed at black-owned beaches in the North and in the Jim Crow South.[19] In the words of the 1949 edition of *Green Book*, an international travel guide for blacks, "the Negro traveler's inconveniences [were] many and . . . increasing because . . . many more [were] traveling, individually and in groups."[20] Black-owned businesses mitigated those inconveniences and provided valued social and cultural security. In that year, at least thirty resorts existed across the United States, nineteen of them on the East Coast, from Florida to Maine.[21] One of those boasting the "soft" weather of Cosey's was Atlantic Beach in South Carolina. Known as the "Black Pearl of the Grand Strand," it was a popular haven for blacks in the thirties, forties, and fifties. Perhaps the best-remembered is Idlewild, "The Black Eden of Michigan." Today, fewer than six of the original thirty hotels operate as resorts; the rest were casualties of expanded social access for blacks. As L explains, "folks who bragged about Cosey vacations in the forties boasted in the sixties about Hyatts, Hiltons, cruises to the Bahamas and Ocho Rios" (8). And the children of those former guests were "preoccupied with boycotts, legislation, voting rights" (171).

Integration came at a price to black community, Morrison suggests. The politics of revolution after midcentury required commitment and courage. But the progressive social and economic policies wrought by radical and moderate movements were a trade- off for cultural cohesion and identity. May's hysteria over civil rights aside, something of value was lost: a pursuit of intraracial excellence that defied legal segregation; the steely self-worth that is nurtured in black enclaves; a unifying communal sensibility. For Vida, Cosey's Resort was more than a playground; it was a school and salon where people "debated death in the cities, murder in Mississippi, and what they planned to do about it other than grieve and stare at their children" (35). She is grateful for housing provided by the U.S. Department of Housing and Urban Development and for hospital aide work, but the "good fortune of her current job . . . did not prevent her from preferring the long-ago one that paid less in every way but satisfaction" (35). Sandler, too, each year becomes fonder of the neighborhood he and Vida had moved from (39). Clearly, husband and wife are in the throes of nostalgia, but Morrison is also exploring a point of tension between racial autonomy and inclusion. Assimilation was "a good move," but, in consequence, "pretty much all the black stores disappeared [and] the black schools are desperate for money. That's what you pay if you want this other," she believes.[22]

Many blacks did not want change, and Morrison examines that position. The friction between May and the adult Christine centered on the debate over cultural politics. May, on the side of what Morrison calls "racial uplift," took earnest possession of Bill Cosey's invented ancestry of "a long line of prosperous slaves and thrifty freedmen—each generation adding to the inheritance left by the previous one. . . . They kept low, no bragging, no sass—just curry and keep close relationships with the whites who mattered" (136). May's baseline objection to Heed was her family's failure to resemble that fiction. The Johnsons were "shiftless," "savage," and "brain-dead"—an undisputed threat to May's pride in racial progress: her defense of "colored-owned businesses, the benefits of separate schools, hospitals with Negro wards and doctors, colored-owned banks, and the proud professions designed to service the race" (80). Christine, on the opposite side of her mother, was for a time a committed revolutionary. Her deepest conviction was service to the cause of insurgence against the arrogant injustice of whites and the misplaced complicity of blacks like May. Christine, of course, was on the right side of history. May had been duped by a false and condescending narrative of racial uplift. But the contrasts are not quite so neatly outlined. Revolutionary ideals are subject to perversion, too, as a disillusioned Christine learns. In 1973 "the good work of disobedience was merging with disguised acquiescence" (167). This jaded view of the revolutionary settling into life as a risk-averse traditionalist is examined earlier in the 1970s-era intergenerational drama of *Paradise*. There the political divide is integration versus self-imposed separation. Here, Morrison presents the divide through May and Christine's conflict over civil rights and the doctrine of separate-but-equal. For Morrison the divide continues in contemporary schisms—debates over the legitimacy of affirmative action and new thinking by "a small but certainly very vocal group of Americans who are questioning the value of this liberal aggressive move that sweeps away everything and has its own agenda."[23] Sheryll Cashin, a law professor at Georgetown University, puts this twenty-first-century ambivalence toward integrated society into sharp focus:

> Black people . . . have become integration weary. Most African Americans do not crave integration, although they support it. . . . There is

much evidence of an emerging "post-civil rights" attitude among black folks. . . . In opinion polls, the majority of African Americans say that they would prefer to live in integrated neighborhoods; but for some of us integrated now means a majority-black neighborhood—one where you are not overwhelmed by white people and where there are plenty of your own kind around to make you feel comfortable, supported, and welcome. Across America, wherever there is a sizable black middle-class population, suburban black enclaves have cropped up that attest to the draw of this happy "we" feeling.

This is not separation in the classic sense. Black people want the benefits of an integrated workplace; we want the public and private institutions that shape opportunity to be integrated. More fundamentally, we want the freedom to chart our course and pursue our dreams. We bang on the doors and sometimes shatter the ceilings of corporate America not because it is largely white but because this is how to "get paid." We want an integrated commercial sector because we want banks and venture capitalists to lend to us and invest in our business ideas. We want the option of sending our children to any college we desire but for many of us Howard, Morehouse, or any number of historically black colleges are at the top of our list. We want space on the airwaves for our music, preferably aired by black-owned radio stations. (xii–xiii)[24]

For Morrison, some form of the tension between racial autonomy and racial assimilation is perennial. The story of integration is continuing, and she is not certain of the outcome. "I am just sort of inching up on contemporary life as I do these books," she says. "You know, 1996 was about all I could do for *Love,* because that was as far as I could see."[25]

Without romanticizing the cultural past, ambivalence is permitted, Morrison seems to be saying. In her words, "beneath (rather, hand-in-hand with) the surface story of the successful revolt against a common enemy in the struggle for integration (in this case, white power) lies another one: the story of disintegration—of a radical change in conventional relationships and class allegiances that signals both liberation and estrangement" (xi). Social justice is not negotiable; legal segregation is abhorrent. But in the womb of suffering, innovation, self-reliance, and moral authority are born of cultural knowledge and integrity; in the absence of economic, political, and social access, all was not bereft in black community. Morrison makes that point with Sandler, whose clarity regarding Cosey and his era is second only to L's. He is fifty-two years Cosey's junior when the two begin taking fishing trips together. Perhaps in choosing Sandler, despite the age and economic differences,

Cosey is aligning with the younger man's incorruptibility: a cynical, regretful, middle-aged man commands the company of his opposite. Sandler feels some compassion for someone who did not know his own son very well, hated his father, and too often carried his position in the community as a burden. But Sandler speaks truth and has little patience for what is not. Only once did he attend a Cosey boat party. Afterward, he promised himself that he would never go again. "It was the talk, its tone, its lie that he couldn't take. Talk as fuel to feed the main delusion: the counterfeit world invented on the boat; the real one set aside for a few hours so women could dominate, men would crawl, blacks could insult whites. Until they docked. Then the sheriff could put his badge back on and call the colored physician a boy. Then the women took their shoes off because they had to walk home alone" (111). In looking back, Sandler respects Cosey's achievement but is embarrassed by his politics. In the 1940s racial uplift did not improve white attitude, and social revolution in the second half of the century changed laws and increased material opportunities but devastated black community.

Sandler is the ancestor in *Love;* L is its metaphysician. Empowering the next generation falls to him. It is Sandler's words of advice that Romen echoes in his flight from Junior to rescue Heed and Christine at the abandoned resort: "You not helpless Romen. Don't ever think that" (195). In that spirit, Romen finally discovers the difference between teenage swagger and personal authority that feels less like license than like respect, responsibility, kindness, and caring. Indeed, Romen's instinct for loving relationship helps shape the defining theme. Morrison says she wrote the rape scene first in which Romen "keeps faith with his heart" and rather than be the seventh in line to violate a girl being held in restraints, he surprises himself and the others by releasing her hands and delivering her to the porch and to freedom (xi). Without parenting, Christine and Heed learn that lesson nearly too late. But Romen, "chased by the whisper of an old man," is the hopeful future. Junior is his counterweight, whose fate Morrison does not predict. She "was hoping to suggest that the future for her is not clear," but she also "didn't want to close off Junior's possibilities."[26] L calls Junior a "needy, wild woman" (200), one of the sporting women—all victims who "never could hide their innocence . . . can't hide the sugar-child, the winsome baby girl curled up somewhere inside . . . under the heart" (4). Indications are that Heed, Christine, or "both" will take her in, one of them referring to her with a measure of affection as a "little rudderless, homeless thing" (198). Perhaps parenting and love will rescue her from the ominous Police-heads (*"dirty things with big hats who shoot up out of the ocean to harm loose women and eat disobedient children"* [5]), which Romen sees gathering when he turns to look back at the house. Celestial, fearless and alone, had escaped them. Junior is determined, but whether she is brave enough to open her heart like the others is an unanswerable question in the end.

CHAPTER 9

The Race[ing] of Slavery
A Mercy

Morrison does not object to *A Mercy* being called a prequel.[1] For her ninth novel, rather than advance a storyline beyond *Love*'s 1996 setting, she turned the focus back to a historical beginning when seventeenth-century America was still a place of possibility and the social order—on the cusp of a systematic and systemic race code—was what Morrison calls "fluid" and "ad hoc": "From one year to another any stretch [of territory] might be claimed by a church, controlled by a company or become the private property of a royal's gift to a son or a favorite."[2] Western European nations contested each other and native peoples for New World geography, and a European upper class, religious and secular, grabbed wealth and privilege, both of which were contingent upon the stolen labor of indentured servants and slaves. Morrison explores that familiar historical dynamic but briefly postulates, even if the story does not fully accomplish such a vision, a more progressive economic and social regime in which character trumps ancestry, and all individual industry, regardless of one's race, color or creed, has its rewards.

Jacob Vaark shoulders the weight of Morrison's enlightened regime. He is the story's projected American hero, possessed of self-knowledge and a strong moral imagination. In 1682, during the novel's opening scene, Vaark rides on horseback through the Virginia colony "breathing the air of a world so new" that it was "almost alarming in rawness and temptation. . . . He saw forests untouched since Noah, shorelines beautiful enough to bring tears, wild food for the taking" (13). This is a place, Vaark believes, where courage still has the advantage of rank. Despite the similarity, Morrison is not foreshadowing here the American of myth partly spawned in Crevecoeur's eighteenth-century formulation of the romanticized autonomous American who, in Crevecoeur's words, "acts upon new principles . . . entertain[s] new ideas . . . and form[s] new opinions"[3] just by virtue of an association with the country's expansive atmosphere—a kind of European everyman who trades misery in the Old World for personal liberty and justice for all in the new. Vaark is more believable. He is a realist or perhaps an idealist with a postmodern sensibility. He is easily, for example, aware of the deep social, economic, and psychological contradictions of life in the colonies: thinking slaves "judging the men who judged them" (25); the doorman at Jublio plantation who is simultaneously "deferential and mocking" (17); America as a vast land claimed by many but rightfully owned by "certain natives" (28). And most disjunctive for Vaark is the ménage à trois arrangement of religion, wealth, and slavery. It made whites cruel and blacks silent, but with an ominous "roar he could not hear" (26). "My trade is goods and gold, Sir," he tells D'Ortega, the Portuguese slaveholder and master of Jublio. "Flesh was not his commodity" (25).

Vaark is repulsed by Senhor D'Ortega, his wife, their sons, and their obtuse manner of living. Obsequious, foppish, unmanly in Vaark's estimation, D'Ortega has no useful knowledge or skill and therefore no rightful place in the New World. Worse is that Catholicism gives D'Ortega a false estimate of his own worth: living in an "untamed world" and being responsible for "recalcitrant labor" was his "unbearable connection to God's work and the difficulties [his family] endured on His behalf" (20). Vaark winces at D'Ortega's self-righteous indulgence—the "sly, indirect" patter, the brutish lasciviousness, the entire "sordid and overripe" self. Vaark surmises that "Access to a fleet of free labor made D'Ortega's leisurely life possible. Without a shipload of enslaved Angolans he would not be merely in debt; he would be eating from his palm instead of porcelain and sleeping in the bush of Africa rather than a four-post bed" (30). Vaark "sneered at wealth dependent on a captured workforce that required more force to maintain . . . [and] recoiled at whips, chains and armed overseers. He was determined to prove that his own industry could amass the fortune, the station D'Ortega claimed without trading his conscience for coin" (30).

Vaark inspires joyous admiration; he just seems to position himself on the correct side of seventeenth-century geopolitics. Principled, even kind, he accepts seven-year-old Florens in partial payment of D'Ortega's debt, but, more than that, he rescues the child in a clear acknowledgment of her mother's fear and hope. He "was struck by the terror in her [the mother's] eyes" (30). A decade earlier, he had rescued Sorrow, a ship captain's orphaned daughter, in much the way he frees the hind leg of a trapped raccoon on the journey to

D'Ortega's Maryland: "The raccoon limped off, perhaps," Vaark thinks, "to
the mother forced to abandon it or more likely into other claws" (12).

Propertied and, to an extent, privileged, both of which conditions he believes must be earned, Vaark is the archetypal American individual, unaligned
and self-dependent. He has come into patronship through inheritance, but
that advantage is less a factor in the development of his character than the
strong imprint of a survivalist work ethic carried over from an impoverished
English childhood—"years spent with children of all shades, stealing food
and cadging gratuities for errands" (38). These experiences have shaped his
humanity. Thus, in Vaark's estimation, a black man with skill is not less a
man than he. In moments of their casual intimacy, "Sir," in Lina's words,
"behaved as though the blacksmith was his brother," and, just as effortlessly,
the blacksmith reciprocated. With the same extraordinary liberality for a
man of his time and place, Vaark views Florens as "a human child, not pieces
of eight" (195). Taking her from D'Ortega "was a mercy" (195). At home his
wife might "welcome a child around the place," having lost her own, who
would have been about the same age as Florens. Vaark's dependents—four
women and two men—form a multiracial family of interdependent relationships: the women perform as wives, mothers, daughters, and sisters, the men
as brothers, husbands, and fathers. He had worked first with Lina, a Native
American, purchased by him to create a farm and prepare for wife Rebekka.
Then had come deliverance of Sorrow and Florens. Scully and Willard are
not residents, but the farm and its inhabitants constitute the whole of their
meaningful relations.

Vaark is without racial hatred. Morrison makes him sympathetic on that
point and celebrates his potential to change the course of seventeenth-century
history. But, as a Morrison character, he is not without tragic fault. And that
is the subject of his development: human failing. Modestly successful as a
farmer, Vaark has neither the skill nor the temperament to be better. He is an
adventurer. Abandoned as a child and with no family prestige to claim, he
finds that inheriting land "softened the chagrin of being both misborn and
disowned," but it does not dim his determination or his earnest ambition for
wealth, a factor that decisively informs his ruinous resolution to make his
fortune in the production of West Indian rum. The Barbadian plan, Vaark
muses, "is as sweet as the sugar on which it was based. And there was a profound difference between the intimacy of slave bodies at Jublio and a remote
labor force in Barbados" (40). The enterprise succeeds financially, and the
proceeds pay first for small extravagances and then for a grand house.

Thus, even as Vaark condemns the source of D'Ortega's sordid wealth,
he covets the emblems of that wealth—the house, the gate, the fence. And,

although Vaark cannot see it as such, his own conspicuous edifice, when finally acquired, conveys a similar kind of sordidness: killing trees, in Lina's words, and replacing "them with a profane monument to himself," financing construction with the profits of slave labor. The house embodies a lost virtue that began with gifts, less practical than whimsical, which brought "a glint" to his eye in the unpacking, and ended with a serpent gate of intricately worked iron that marks the entrance to "the world of the damned," again according to Lina. The prelapsarian garden that had been a stark contrast to Jublio falls. "Serpents, scales and all . . . ending not in fangs but flowers" points to Vaark's self-deceit, his contradictory impulses (176). What he intended as a "pure, noble" structure is, rather, a testimony to vanity, envy, and perverted pride. The American Eden is destroyed by its American Adam. Death, when it comes to Vaark, seems earned, like a punishment, an inevitability, a just dessert. "The fever of building was so intense . . . [Rebekka] missed the real fever, the one that put him in the grave" (104). Fevers of soul and body are equally lethal. A decent man, Vaark has not the good fortune of D'Otega's easy wickedness. The obsession, then, with wealth and status and an unsuccessful determination to parse a difference between Maryland slavery and a West Indian "labor force" transform Vaark. In Lina's final estimation, "it was not a sudden change, yet it was a deep one. The last few years he seemed moody, less gentle" (51).

Still, Morrison devotes only a small space to what Vaark refers to as these "new arrangements" in his business affairs (103). Morrison agrees with her character in principle (if not with his misapplication of the principle) that slavery and race hatred can be distinctly different. One may be solely economic; the other is always pathological. Indeed, slavery is not Morrison's primary concern in the novel. As she says, "there was no civilization that did not rest on some form of enslavement. . . . Owning the labor of people was a constant in the world."[4] Vaark, then, turns out to be more a disappointment than evil.

In *A Mercy* Morrison presents a cosmology in which class and not race defines social status and access. She wishes to separate race from slavery and to ask whether it is possible to be a slave and not raced. She concludes that for a brief span of decades it was. In that period, for example, a free black man, a skilled blacksmith and artist, could command liberty and wages, while indentured servants had neither. Of twenty-three men working tobacco fields in Virginia, Willard, indentured and, in effect, enslaved, recalls that six Englishmen, one native, and twelve Africans developed a "camaraderie . . . sealed by their shared hatred of the overseer and the master's odious son" (175). Years could be added to an indentured term at the master's will and his advantage. Black slaves and white servants alike escaped via underground networks. And masters seeking to buy or rent labor had choice and variety. One printer's advertisement read,

> A likely woman who has had small pox and measles. . . . A likely Negro about 9 years. . . . Girl or woman that is handy in the kitchen sensible, speaks good English, complexion between yellow and black. . . . Five years time of a white woman that understands Country work, with a child upwards of two years old. . . . Mulatto Fellow very much pitted with small pox, honest and sober. . . . White lad fit to serve. . . . Wanted a servant able to drive a carriage, white or black. . . . Sober and prudent woman who. . . . Likely wench, white, 29 years with child. . . . Healthy Deutsch woman for rent. . . . Hardy female, Christianized and capable in all matters domestic available for exchange of goods or specie. (61)

Clearly, although America was a society with slaves, for most of the seventeenth century it was not a slave society. The transition from one to the other,[5] for Morrison's purposes, began with the 1676 Virginia uprising known as Bacon's Rebellion, after Nathaniel Bacon, an English planter. Phase one of the rebellion, from September 1675 to April 1676, according to the historian Theodore Allen, was an "anti-Indian" campaign during which Bacon, other planters, and bonded laborers attacked friendly and nonfriendly tribes in an effort to drive native people from English-occupied territory. Twenty-nine year-old Bacon was riled by what he saw as the governor's ineffectiveness in preventing and punishing Indian attacks. And, more generally, Bacon and others objected to Governor Berkeley's profitable relations with friendly tribes, through which he obtained beaver and other furs in exchange for guns and goods. The governor granted licenses to whomever he wished, including Bacon, who, in 1675, along with another planter, William Byrd, was given an exclusive permit.[6] Despite this, the men's discontent with Berkeley's leadership and authority apparently continued. Bond laborers and freedmen joined Bacon, perhaps, with some interest in acquiring freedom and tribal land. But, like Bacon, they were also protesting against authority, even if not for the same reasons as Bacon.

Morrison imagines a populist version of the rebellion in which "an army of blacks, natives, whites, mulattoes—freedmen, slaves and indentured—had waged war against local gentry led by members of that very class" (11). Allen calls this second phase of the rebellion, from April 1676 to January 1677, civil war. If bond laborers were allied with landowners in the early months, that circumstance changed in the second period, which focused on equitable tax apportionment and redistribution of land. Bacon and Bird, cousins of the governor by marriage, wanted privilege; freedmen and bond laborers fought for equality. Bacon died unexpectedly a few months into the conflict, and the rebel cause ended in defeat. Twenty-three persons were hanged and others pardoned. But the uprising upset the social hierarchy and led to new and more repressive laws. Allen offers a helpful analysis of the rebellion and its aftermath in the context of anxious planters and the new race laws:

> In their solidarity with the African-American bond-laborers in Bacon's Rebellion, the laboring-class European-American bond-laborers had demonstrated their understanding of their interests, and bond-laborers had had the sympathy of the laboring poor and propertyless free population.
>
> What was to be done? . . . How was laboring-class solidarity to be undone? . . . The solution was to establish a new birthright not only for Anglos but for every Euro-American, the "white" identity that [was separate] from laboring-class African-Americans, and enlisted [whites] as active, or at least passive, supporters of lifetime bondage of African-Americans.
>
> The exclusion of free African-Americans from the intermediate stratum was a corollary of the establishment of "white" identity as a mark of social status. If the mere presumption of liberty was to serve as a mark of social status for masses of European-Americans without real prospects of upward social mobility, and yet induce them to abandon their opposition to the plantocracy and enlist them actively, or at least passively, in keeping down the Negro bond-laborer with whom they had made common cause in the course of Bacon's Rebellion, the presumption of liberty had to be denied to free African-Americans.[7]

The result, according to Jacob Vaark, was "a thicket of new laws authorizing chaos in defense of order. By eliminating manumission, gatherings, travel and bearing arms for black people only; by granting license to any white to kill any black for any reason; by compensating owners for a slave's maiming or death, they separated and protected all whites from all others forever" (11–12). Vaark opposes codification of racial hierarchy as impractical and immoral. "Any social ease between gentry and laborers, forged before and during that rebellion, crumbled beneath a hammer wielded in the interests of the gentry's profits. . . . These were lawless laws encouraging cruelty in exchange for common cause, if not common virtue" (12).

Invention of the white race, Morrison suggests, gives the lie to the idea of America's founding society as distinctly free and democratic. Indeed, one could argue that *A Mercy* is an examination of American exceptionalism— the idea that American values are unique and admirable, that, in the vision of John Winthrop's much-touted 1630 sermon on or near the Massachusetts Bay, America is "as a city upon the hill," destined to build a church and a society that would uphold righteousness in every place.[8] That is the most popular use of exceptionalist ideology, but, as the late sociologist Seymour Martin Lipset pointed out in a 2000 review of a book by Deborah Madsen, a British professor of English, on the topic, the term is used in at least two other contexts. Stalin used the phrase in the 1920s in an effort to explain why America lacked a major socialist movement, and the third use is the postrevolutionary Tocquevillian formulation in which America is exceptional because democratic and wholly different from European, aristocratic societies.[9] In *Democracy in America,* Tocqueville writes that "The position of the American is therefore quite exceptional, and it may be believed that no democratic people will ever be placed in a similar one."[10] He is observing here that Americans are too pragmatic (Puritanical and commercial) to pursue interests in science, literature, and the arts but that their unique character is not the universal measure of democratic society. Tocqueville's use of the term in this specific context notwithstanding, most readers of *Democracy* find a broader application of exceptionalism implied. As Lipset explains it, exceptionalist ideology "in the Tocquevillian tradition looks at the ways America has differed in practice from other countries, both positively and negatively. It sees the country as sociologically unique, pointing to its ideological national identity, its religious institutions (the only Protestant sectarian country), its political structure and tradition (a constitutionally established weak state), its class structure (socially egalitarian, economically hierarchical), and a myriad of other traits and institutions that make it an outlier."[11] But this popular conception is an America of myth that the Maryland colony—as Morrison conceives it—seems to deconstruct. Europeans in the new world instituted elements of feudalism from the old; egalitarianism was too qualified to be a reality—either in the seventeenth century and or in Tocqueville's nineteenth century.

Vaark maliciously responds "Ah, England," when he is told that the D'Ortega children were born in Maryland, surreptitiously mocking any notion that Maryland and England were not part of the same society. Vaark is irritated by what he sees as the Catholic Church's abusive power: armed by the king and run by Papists, "sinister missions cropped up at the edge of villages . . . and overdressed women in raised heels rode in carts driven by ten-year-old Negroes" (15). The D'Ortegas, too, represent a similar overreaching in their gaudy garments, unearned authority, and predatory system of growing tobacco and slaves. In the social hierarchy, Vaark knows his disadvantage: a "trader" suing a "gentleman" for what the trader is owed, for example, would face "years in a lawsuit in a province ruled by the king's judges disinclined to favor a distant tradesman over a local Catholic gentleman" (26). Protestant reformers, too, perpetuated distinctions of rank and inequality. Denied religious tolerance and freedom at home, they, in turn, denied it to all but themselves in America. The new world is never free of the old. Its people are doomed to repeat the past. The garden is never free of a serpent. Class structure, subjugation, oppression, and violence, Morrison demonstrates, were America's founding inheritance and lasting legacy. Jacob and Rebekka—freethinking, independent, innocent—are its casualties. Jacob succumbs to the shadow of slave labor, after all, and Rebekka, once she is widowed and vulnerable, becomes like her bitter, sadistic, religious mother. Vaark's and Morrison's experiment in self-reliance fails. Certainly, he is motivated not by a wish to subjugate others, but by a desire to elevate himself. The difference is much more subtle than Vaark allows, however. In consequence, he, like D'Ortega, profits from slave labor, regardless of how little pleasure those profits bring him in the end. As Lina believes, "we never shape the world. . . . The world shapes us" (83). Even laborers like Scully and Willard, who aspire to neither wealth nor privilege, are destined to be reinvented as members of the white race. Indentured and partnered to each other, they are outsiders who cannot offer Sorrow, Lina, and Florens security or protection, but, for a time, they do give friendship. Yet, unlike Lina, Scully looks ahead and sees "dark matter out there, thick unknowable, aching to be made into a world" (183). Although bondmen, they are male, increasingly defined by law and custom as white, and they mistakenly "imagine a future" for them to shape (183).

Innocence, when lost, is replaced, for those who are left, by awful knowledge of the inevitability and solidity of class division, female oppression, and raced slavery. "Sad," Scully thinks. "They once thought they were a kind of family because together they had carved companionship out of isolation. But the family they imagined they had become was false. Whatever each one loved, sought or escaped, their futures were separate and anyone's guess. One thing was certain, courage alone would not be enough" (155). In Sorrow's estimation of the women, "[it] was as though . . . they were falling away from one another" (155), and Lina, like Scully, "had relished her place in this small, tight family, but now saw its folly. . . . As long as Sir was alive, it was easy to veil the truth: that they were not a family—not even a like-minded group. They were orphans, each and all" (68–69). Without common cause, expelled from the garden, they must learn, as Lina had following the coming of Europeans and what she calls "the death of the world," another way to be in that world.

Rebekka Vaark embraces religion as her way forward, and Morrison
examines that choice in a milieu of the female individual in society. As a
sixteen-year-old unattended girl, she came to the new world in retreat from
misery and barbarism. "The thought of what her life would have been had
she stayed crushed into those reeking streets, spat on by lords and prostitutes, curtseying, curtseying, curtseying still repelled her" (89). Growing
up, Rebekka experienced religion from her mother as "a flame fueled by a
wondrous hate" (86). In America she was lukewarm in faith, first because
churched women seemed out of touch with the vitality of real life and then
because the local church refused, following her accidental death, to baptize
her beloved firstborn, condemning the little girl, in Rebekka's thoughts,
to eternal hell. "Those [Baptist] women seemed flat to her, convinced they
were innocent and therefore free; safe because churched; tough because still
alive. A new people remade in vessels old as time. Children, in other words,
without the joy or curiosity of a child. They had even narrower definitions
of God's preferences than her parents. Other than themselves (and those of
their kind who agreed), no one was saved. The possibility was open to most,
however, except the children of Ham. In addition there were Papists and
the tribes of Judah to whom redemption was denied along with a variety of
others living willfully in error" (108). Rebekka at first refuses these views in
favor of her husband's free thinking; there is satisfaction and little risk in that
choice. As Lina puts it, Mistress runs to Sir because she has that privilege.
"They leaned on each other root and crown. Needing no one outside their
sufficiency" (102). That safe space closes with Vaark's death, and Rebekka
faces altered choices.

As a woman alone, accustomed to a man's direction and protection, she
contends with emerging doubts about the meaning and purpose of her experience: "Were the Anabaptists right? Was happiness Satan's allure, his tanta-
lizing deceit? . . . Her stubborn self-sufficiency outright blasphemy?" (114).
Lying feverish from smallpox, Rebekka entertains the possibility of a female
Job who might question her losses, only to be reminded by God of how weak
and ignorant she is. Imagined women come and go in her delirium. The seven
others assigned below deck in the *Angelus* had been her sisters in transport
to the New World; she and they had "become the kind of family sea journeys
create" (94). Prostitutes and thieves, the women liked themselves and encouraged Rebekka. In America, they "had got on with it. As she knew from
their [phantom] visits, whatever life threw up, whatever obstacles they faced,
they manipulated the circumstances to their advantage and trusted their own
imagination" (114). Lina is like these women in important ways—exiled
from family and tribe, made to suffer the cruelty of Anglos, strong enough

to reinvent herself. Once she risked her life to save Rebekka and her daughter from starvation. When the church refused to sanctify that daughter, Lina assured Rebekka that her deceased children were "stars," "yellow and green birds, playful foxes of the rose-tinted clouds collecting at the edge of the sky" (93). Yet, somewhere in the midst of fever, Rebekka withdraws from Lina and her sister immigrants. She has a near-death conversion to church and religion. She fears what all women know, that, "without the status or shoulder of a man, without the support of family or well-wishers, a widow was in practice illegal" (115). Piety, congregation, and clearly delineated class, racial, and gender boundaries solve much of that problem for Rebekka. Thereafter, she institutes a reign of disaffection and betrayal at home, relegating Lina to her position as slave, beating Sorrow, and putting Florens up for sale.

Morrison is never far from an interest in the historical and social evolution of female identity and relationships. In *A Mercy* she addresses the fragility of women's cohesive roles as sisters, daughters, and mothers in a period when all women were subject to "the promise and threat of men" (115). Morrison presents Rebekka's, Lina's, and Sorrow's development from this perspective, but Florens is her focus. Hers is the first-person voice. Her journey, both over land and into the interior self, captures the incubation and birth of the fierce female archetype in Morrison's fictional universe. Sula, Sethe, Celestial, and other outlaws might trace their historical and cultural beginning to Florens in seventeenth-century America. Florens is the youngest and the progenitor. She is "dangerous" and "wild," her mother tells her when she longs for shoes; even at age eight, she values the broken castoffs of Mrs. D'Ortega. Lina maintains that Florens's "feet are useless, will always be too tender for life and never have the strong soles, tougher than leather, that life requires" (4). Eight years later, Florens's feet "are hard as cypress" (189). She has walked from the blacksmith's on bare feet, but, more significant, she has moved past others' expectations into the fullness of her life. No longer the little girl or the adolescent wanting to please, she has earned independence. Her final declaration is "I am become wilderness but I am also Florens. In full. Unforgiven. Unforgiving. No ruth, my love. None. Here me?" she demands of the blacksmith. "Slave. Free. I last" (189). She claims the transgressive power that violates social boundaries: possibly murdering a man and injuring a child.

According to the blacksmith, "it is the withering inside that enslaves and opens the door for what is wild" (187). Florens believes her withering emerged in Widow Ealing's closet under the disinterested prodding of her naked body by religious strangers. Their callousness is a violation that sparks the dormant wildness that later informs Florens's painful liberation. Her mother named that wildness earlier as a fearlessness and hunger for life; Florens herself signifies it when she reveals that "I never cry" (81). And Lina's bedtime stories have shaped it. Perhaps it is this potential for willed power that Daughter Jane acknowledges with the kiss to Florens's forehead at their parting. Jane already exhibits such agency in her certainty about religious hypocrisy and the resolve to help Florens escape. Although her wayward eye is not the marking of a demon, independence of thought is in her world. Thus, when Florens asks, "Are you a demon," Jane's response is, "Yes. . . . Oh, yes" (135). Contemptuous of Old World fear-based perceptions, Jane is fearless and free. Florens later aligns her with untamed power in nature—a "she-lion" who "risks all to save the slave" (188).

The resting wildness that Jane senses and that Florens sometimes fears— as when she engages the great stag climbing a rock wall and is "loose" in the world to do what she chooses—comes fully to life in Florens during the flash of crisis when the blacksmith shelters Maliah and expels her. In that moment, Florens relives her mother's abandonment. The blacksmith had been, she relates, "my security from harm, from any who look closely at me only to throw me away" (184). A child with her mother before, this time, at age sixteen, she is a woman with resources. She is like the eaglet survivor in Lina's stories whose sharpened talons and lifted feathers mark a fierce self-defense. Linda Krumholtz calls this dynamic in Morrison's novels "repetition with a difference."[12] Morrison employs this narrative trope, she says, "to create multiple versions of stories, to revise dominant history, and to represent processes of healing, transformation, and insight"[13] for character and reader. The process of transformation begins for Florens with the repeating feeling of abandonment, but with the important difference that this time she resists. In Scully's characterization, after her encounter with the blacksmith, Florens changed from "have me always" to "don't touch me ever" (179).

Freedom and enslavement are multifaceted matters, Morrison indicates. Both are states of being quite apart from material conditions. As the blacksmith understands, slaves may be freer than free persons. It is a sovereignty of spirit, lost or gained, that marks the difference. Jacob Vaark loses to rum profits and slave labor and Rebekka to resentments and false piety. He becomes "meaner" and she "cold if not cruel" (179). In different ways, both lose their aptitude for free thinking and fall to convention. But what if the experiment in free thinking had succeeded? "Anything could have come out of this period" of early America, Morrison says. If not the Vaarks, then who? The answer is the enslaved women; it is they who triumph, they who gain self-dependence in the post-Edenic world.

Before the change, Lina had offered Rebekka friendship. After, she remains loyal, but, as Scully observes, not in the way of "submission [to authority]. . . ; it was a sign of her own self-worth—a sort of keeping one's word" (178). Under the new regime, Sorrow, too, liberates herself from others' valuation of her inadequacies. As a new mother, "she is impervious to . . . complaints. . . . 'My name is Complete,'" she declares (158). And Florens eschews obedience and discipleship. Unlike the biblical Ruth, she will not pledge loyalty, nor will she invite salvation or redemption. Her tone of defiance differs from Lina's and Sorrow's, suggesting youth but also, perhaps, as noted earlier, Morrison's recognition of the realities of unhealed wounds that persist. In her mother's words, "To be a female in this place is to be an open wound that cannot heal. Even if scars form, the festering is ever below" (191). Through Florens, Morrison advises that "this is now, but don't forget, don't forget."[14]

Beyond merely augmenting the historical record, Florens's story also suggests new possibilities, not for remaking the past but for opening up to the truth of that past and to a more thoughtful national narrative going forward. To borrow from a reading by Mina Karavanta, A Mercy is a "postnational"[15] accounting. The ash that Florens supposes will rise from Vaark's incinerated house—and that carries the words of her story inscribed on the walls and floor of what she calls this "talking room"—will change the landscape and the founding story of that landscape.

In American experience, natural landscapes figure prominently in the myth of the continent's special destiny that grew largely from the seventeenth-century Puritan mission. As Roderick Nash's extensive study illustrates, natural landscape most often translated to wilderness for Puritans. In Nash's view, Puritans "shared the long Western tradition of imagining wild country as a moral vacuum, a cursed and chaotic wasteland. As a consequence, frontiersmen acutely sensed that they battled wild country not only for personal survival but in the name of nation, race, and God. Civilizing the New World meant enlightening darkness, ordering chaos, and changing evil into good."[16] Ten years before John Winthrop charged his people with transforming wilderness into the shining city, William Bradford, also on a mission from God, settled his Mayflower group at Plymouth, Massachusetts. Writing about that enterprise, Bradford later recorded the difficulty of bringing about civil society: "What could they see but a hideous and desolate wilderness, full of wild beasts and wild men? And what multitudes there might be of them they knew not. Neither could they as it were, go up to the top of Pisgah, to view from

this wilderness a more goodly country to free their hopes; for which way
soever they turned their eyes (save upward to the heavens) they could have
little solace or content in respect of any outward objects. For summer being
done, all things stand upon them with a weather beaten force, and the whole
country, full of woods and thickets, represented a wild and savage hew."[17]
Nearly twenty-five years after its founding, Plymouth suffered the disunity
brought on by prosperity. Moves to larger and greener pastures occasioned
dissent among those who felt put upon to drive the long distance to the original church. Bradford, in a painful note, complained at the end of his history,
"And thus was this poor church left, like an ancient mother, grown old, and
forsaken of her children . . . in regard of their bodily presence and personal
helpfulness. . . . Thus she that had made many rich became herself poor."[18]

In 1692 Cotton Mather, in the midst of the Salem witch trials, looked
back at this period and cast these early settlers as warriors in a pitched battle
over wilderness:

> *The New Englanders* are a people of God settled in those, which were
> once the Devil's territories; and it may easily be supposed that the devil
> was exceedingly disturbed, when he perceived such a People there
> accomplishing the Promise of old made unto our Blessed Jesus. That he
> should have the Utmost parts of the Earth for His Possession . . . and so
> much of the church, as was *fled into this wilderness,* immediately found,
> *The Serpent cast out of his Mouth a Flood for the carrying of it away.* I
> believe, that never were more *Satanical Devices* used for the Unsettling of
> any People under the Sun, than what have been employ'd for the Extirpa-
> tion of the Vine which God has here *Planted, Casting out the Heather,*
> *and preparing a Room for it, and causing it to take deep Root and fill*
> *the Land, so that it sent its Boughs unto the Atlantic Sea Eastward, and*
> *its Branches unto the Connecticut River Westward, and the Hills were*
> *covered with the shadow thereof.*[19]

Morrison, then, examines two views of American wilderness and concludes
that neither tells an honest story of the American experience and character.
Jacob Vaark's story approximates the American Adam in his Eden—innocent, adventurous, creative. But more pervasive in 1682 is the Protestant
vision of unregenerate wilderness, tamed and redeemed by a Godly people.
Once cleansed, this America became the redeemer nation that survives in images of the city on the hill. Both myths promote the narrative of freedom and
opportunity and draw bold ideological and geographical contrasts—between
an old European world and the new America—that have shaped America's
sense of itself for nearly four centuries. As Morrison puts it, "The flight from

the Old World to the New is generally seen to be a flight from oppression and limitation to freedom and possibility. . . . In the New World there was the vision of a limitless future, made more gleaming by the constraint, dissatisfaction, and turmoil left behind. . . . With luck and endurance one could discover freedom, find a way to make God's law manifest; or end up rich as a prince."[20] Despite the potential to be otherwise, however, one person's freedom was contingent upon another's loss. The myth-busting reality of the American wilderness is that it was forever classed, gendered, and raced before the end of its first century.

That is the story that Florens tells. She writes first to the blacksmith, a man who cannot read the words, and then she commits it to the New World: "Perhaps those words need the air that is out in the world. Need to fly up then fall, fall like ash over acres of primrose and mallow. Over turquoise lake, beyond the eternal hemlocks, through clouds cut by rainbow and flavor the soil of the earth" (188). Consumed by fire, the house and the words, both trophies of lost virtue, naiveté, and innocence, will overlay the mountain and valley below that have been surveyed and possessed by "a traveler," a foreigner. In Lina's telling, the traveler had claimed all he beheld. Not even the fierceness of a mother eagle protecting her young was a match for the man's aggression. Struck down, the eagle is "still falling" (73). But her legacy of "feathers quietly lift[ing]" lives in Florens. Hers is a third account of American wilderness—that of assault and survival. She will accomplish the alchemy of transforming the traveler's *property* back into "soil" and "earth" by liberating it from myth through truth-telling. Only then, from Morrison's perspective, is there generous potential.

A Mercy, one imagines, is intended to flavor the national narrative that emanates from place—earth and soil. In her opening monologue, Florens asks, "can you read?" And then she explains, "If a pea hen refuses to brood I read it quickly and, sure enough, that night I see. . . . Other signs need more time to understand. Often there are too many signs, or a bright omen clouds up too fast. I sort them and try to recall, yet I know I am missing much, like not reading the garden snake crawling up to the door saddle to die" (3–4). This kind of literacy signals a holder of knowledge and truth. Lina and the blacksmith read the world. Both love Florens, and, separately, both teach her the skill. Florens's knowledge is incomplete, however; she has not been able to read her mother's meaning. "I will keep one sadness," she pledges: "That all this time I cannot know what my mother is telling me" (189). Certainly, with maturity and the accumulated insults of slavery, she will understand her mother's decision. But, until that time, she can interpret the mother's choice only as rejection and not grace or mercy. But what her mother knows and longs to tell her is that "to be given dominion over another is a hard thing; to wrest dominion over another is a wrong thing; to give dominion of yourself to another is a wicked thing" (196). This gap in her learning leads Florens to conflate love and dominion. She does not know that love has a virtuous cost. Her mother suffered a daughter's loss to prevent a worse fate. Morrison says that "there was a temptation on my part to have her learn, know that. . . . She'll never know because that's what slavery is."[21]

Yet, Florens has the final word. She does not read the natural world with the blacksmith's skill, but, more significant, he does not read her life writing. Morrison is not choosing Florens over him. She paints him as upright and free, descended from generations of men who forged iron. But he cannot share Florens's destiny. Even as a black man, the smith enjoys a freedom unknown to Florens. "I don't know the feeling of or what it means, free and not free," she says (81). Even so, as with her progeny, Sethe, her calling is liberation. Mingled with the soil, her words dilute the heroic myth, uproot the narrative of European ownership, and transform the meaning of wilderness. Florens will flavor the American landscape with what Andree Nicola McLaughlin described in 1990 as "black feminist consciousness." McLaughlin's discussion of the intellectual and artistic productivity of "a vibrant African American feminist movement" of the period is applicable to Florens's achievement. McLaughlin noted, then, that black feminist consciousness "is the basis of an expanding challenge to the postulates of domination in all its forms. It protests and takes to task the economic and cultural superstructures that exploit earth's life by pollution, militarism, human oppression, and other means. This awareness, at its root, is anti-imperialist and antipatriarchal."[22] Florens mounts a resistance to the imperialist traveler who lays claim to the landscape, the Puritan divines who reshaped it, the patriarchal blacksmith, in particular, and to the hegemonic American experience, more generally. That is her legacy.

This is another story of the American response to race that needs to be passed on, Morrison suggests. "There is not a great deal in fiction . . ." she says, "on what this country was really like in the seventeenth century before it was the United States. Writing required extraordinary research."[23] *A Mercy* continues Morrison's project of illuminating the "house that racism built."[24] A priority in her work, she says, is determining how to "convert a racist house into a race-specific yet non-racist home."[25]

CHAPTER 10

A Lesson of Manhood
Home

Home, Morrison's 2012 novel, is a 1950s story. "I wanted to rip the scab off that period," Morrison says, indicating an era of unhealed wounds. "There's all this *Leave It to Beaver* nostalgia," Morrison continues. "That it was all comfortable and happy and everyone had jobs."[1] Morrison, however, recalls that decade as years of "violent racism. There was McCarthy. There was this horrible war we didn't call a war where 58,000 people died."[2] There was "a lot of medical apartheid, the license of preying on black women, the syphilis trials on Black men."[3] What the midcentury historian Henry Steele Commager and others celebrated as a progressive period of economic and social innovation[4] Morrison renders as vicious and repressive. Parallel societies, systematically unequal, fuel a palpable social tension and danger that define most aspects of fifties America for blacks.

Frank Money, a Korean War veteran suffering posttraumatic stress disorder, and his younger sister are Morrison's lightening rods for these period storms. Both search for the best of human life and are repeatedly thwarted. But more important, perhaps, is their eventual triumph—a happy ending that Morrison acknowledged while responding to a question from an incredulous interviewer who suggested that *Home* goes against the grain. Morrison's characters often gain from their troubles, but not cheerfully or happily. Yet *Home* concludes on a buoyant note, and Frank and Cee emerge scarred but optimistic: they have acquired new, liberating knowledge, a loving, transformative relationship, and a place in community. At story's end, 1960s societal reforms are within view, and the narrative leans toward mostly bright changes to come for its characters. Morrison leaves them in the process of regeneration, but at peace in their place and time.

Lotus, Georgia, in 1952 or 1953[5] closes a circle whose making began about fourteen years earlier on the day Ycidra, called Cee, facilitated her brother's coming of age. Frank, age ten, and Cee, age six, crawled[6] into a field of tall grass and swarming gnats to stand in awe of fighting stallions. "Right in front of us," in Frank's telling, "about fifty yards off, they stood like men. Their raised hooves crushing and striking. Their manes tossing back from wild white eyes. They bit each other like dogs but when they stood, reared up on their hind legs, their forelegs around the withers of the other, we held our breath in wonder."[7] In that space, Frank felt the strong inkling of manhood, captured, as he was, by the horses' beauty and strength, which he associated with masculinity. Immediately after, in that forbidden place, he and Cee were forced to hide from white men in the act of burying a black man, victim of their sadism. They watched, Cee trembled, and Frank held her shoulders, trying to relieve and absorb her fear. Fourteen years later, he fully realizes, perhaps for the first time, how the experience shaped him and confesses that "Down deep inside her lived my secret picture of myself— a strong good me tied to the memory of those horses and the burial of a stranger. Guarding her, finding a way through tall grass and out of that place, not being afraid of anything—snakes or wild old men" (104).

Frank's heroism, clarified by that event, manifested in childhood as chivalry—protecting Cee at home from their grandfather's hateful wife and safeguarding her abroad from lecherous strangers up to no good. Years later, in trouble, Cee recalls times when her brother "would . . . touch the top of her head with four fingers, or stroke her nape with his thumb. Don't cry, said the fingers; the welts will disappear. Don't cry; mama is tired; she didn't mean it. Don't cry, don't cry girl; I'm right here" (53). It is not a surprise that twelve-year-old Jackie, seeing Frank when he returns to Lotus, remembers him as the boy who years earlier had made a collar for her rescued puppy. But, by age eighteen, Frank sought to demonstrate greater valor than aiding little girls and pet dogs. Justifying his decision to join the army, he was critical of his parents, who settled for "mindless work in fields." He understands, he says, that "Having been run out of one town, any other that offered safety and the peace of sleeping through the night and not waking up with a rifle in your face was more than enough" for them (84). Frank wanted more.

But when chivalry and war collided, Frank was their casualty. Despite valiant efforts, he lost two friends. Mike died thrashing, jerking, and urine soaked in his arms. Frank had dragged him to shelter, but, in the end, all that was left to Frank was to beat back the aggressive black birds intent on having his friend's body. Before Stuff died, Frank had stopped the bleeding and located an arm some distance away in case it could be reattached. These losses "gave a grotesque life to his childhood" (98). They had been boys and then men together—"Lotus boys [who] . . . argued, fought, laughed, mocked, and loved one another without ever having to say so" (98). With Cee in tow, they had been a foursome. Recalling those bonds in the face of such carnage is a gross absurdity that distorts the meaning of all experience for Frank.

Morrison does not draw a line from Mike's and Stuff's death to the Korean child's murder. Their deaths came later. Temporary insanity precipitated by grief is not Frank's defense. On the contrary, the child's daily appearance at the trash heap was a comfort. For Frank "each time she came it was as welcome as watching a bird feed her young or a hen scratching . . . for the worm she knew for sure was buried there" (94–95). Instead, Morrison implicates Frank's past. Her killing proceeded from horses, old men, and a heroic ideal of self. The girl threatened that self. "Better she should die" than cause Frank to doubt his ideal. "How could I let her live after she took me down to a place I didn't know was in me," he later asks with painful knowing. "How could I let her live after she took me down to a place where I unzip my fly and let her taste me right then and there? And again the next day as long as she came scavenging. What type of man is that?" (134). The dramatic irony of these events, of course, is that he kills a little girl the same age as the sister whose innocence had inspired his heroic manhood. He had been prepared to kill old men then. Fourteen years later, he killed a child to safeguard the "pictures . . . of a strong good me," he says (104). Protecting Cee is "the buried seed of all the rest" (104).

It is not clear that Frank's punishment matches his crime. As Morrison writes his story, he and the girl are part of a complex dynamic of human wrong that began for Frank in the American South and for the girl in South Korea, where she was taught to barter with sex. And Morrison, it must be said, is never as interested in the crime as she is in the response—how and whether her characters survive. Frank does overcome. He effectively deconstructs the troublesome heroic stereotype and remakes the old self into someone new and authentic. The process begins in Seattle. Discharged there, homeless, and psychically fragile, Frank meets Lily as a man whose constructed masculinity is shattered. The old Frank had assumed a composite power and responsibility in his relations with women. He admits, "I like the small breakable thing inside each one. Whatever their personality, smarts, or looks, something soft lay inside each. Like a bird's breastbone, shaped and chosen to wish on. A little V, thinner than bone and lightly hinged, that I could break with a forefinger if I wanted to, but never did. Want to, I mean. Knowing it was there

hiding from me, was enough" (68). That self-described exercise of control
and care died in Korea. With nothing to replace it, Frank exists in a kind
of stasis with Lily, who requires of him partnering and not protection. One
is his future; the other is his past, and neither is within Frank's reach. Their
separation, then, is a relief for both. Morrison can push Frank forward, and
Lily can heed her father's advice to "find your talent and drive it" (80).

Leaving Lily to find his sister opens Frank to reflection and insight. He
refuses, for example, the characterization of "enthusiastic hero" for heeding
Sarah's alarm. The moral seriousness of war has taught him to know better.
Later, after he rescues Cee from a racist doctor's experiments, he accepts that
he cannot end her pain or restore her loss; Cee must achieve that for herself
and, in the process, relieve Frank of an impossible obligation. In their new
roles, "She neither missed nor wanted his fingers at the nape of her neck
telling her not to cry, that everything would be all right" (131). Thus, when
Frank approaches the new Cee, she pushes him away. "You don't need to try
and make it go away," she tells him. "It shouldn't go away. It's just as sad
as it ought to be and I'm not going to hide from what's true just because it
hurts" (131). Here a reader might be reminded of Morrison's nearly exact
response to the loss of her son Slade, who died while she was writing *Home*.
Morrison tells an interviewer, "Somebody tries to say, 'I'm sorry, I'm so
sorry.' People say that to me. There's no language for it. Sorry doesn't do it."[8]
And neither does the word "closure." "It's such an American thing. I want
what I got," she insists.[9] Morrison stopped work for a while but returned to
writing (and to *Home*) as a life-affirming space for her. Similarly, Cee "was
gutted, infertile, but not beaten. She could know the truth, accept it and keep
on quilting," keep creating (132).

Free of paternal power, Frank is also free to follow Cee's example. He
will look ahead. He killed a child; that fact will persist. "Meantime there
were worthwhile things that needed doing" (135). He and Cee are finally
able to make a home for each other. Theirs is a partnership that Morrison
privileges throughout. Morrison was trying to think, she says, of when "a
man would love a woman without the baggage. Who is the female that he
would love selflessly? Not a mother, not a lover, not a wife—only a sister."[10]
Their final rehabilitation involves reburying the man Frank learns had chosen his son's life over his own. Sporting men had forced a father and son to
fight to the death. The son saved himself by killing his father as that father
commanded. And Lotus's men and women saved Jerome, the son, whose life
they "doubted was worth much after that" (120). In that summer, crouching
in the grass with his sister, Frank had stood on the threshold of manhood,

heroism, and violence. Now, again with Cee, Frank is a different man—with new understanding. The jerking foot from the past had belonged to a bona fide hero; Frank honors his achievement by placing his recovered bones under the sweet bay tree with its welcoming shade and "branches spread like arms" (118). Long ago Frank had been prepared to kill. That instinct had put him on the path to war, murder, and death. Now he honors life and survival— his, Cee's, and Jerome's. This time, Cee does not tremble, and Frank stands in observance of "the glow of a fat cherry-red sun" (145). A father died to save his son, and Frank's memorial to him reads, "Here Stands A Man." To witness brutish horses that stood like men was the boy's awakening joy; to contemplate a father's impossible choice is the man's final fulfillment. Sister and brother come home to themselves and to each other.

Morrison renders Frank's travel across the country to Cee as a black man's perilous journey home in real and symbolic terms. Arriving at Fort Lawton and afraid to face his life and his buddies' parents back in Georgia, Frank succumbs to alcohol, nightmares, and delusions. Called south by Sarah's telegram, he reverses a century of exodus in the other direction as blacks escaped slavery and its oppressive aftermath. Danger resides in both directions, and each phase of Frank's trip engenders risk. Although a ticketed passenger on a bus from Seattle to Portland, Frank is nevertheless contraband, directed by a midcentury underground rail of AME Zion and Baptist churches that ferry their passengers to new locations. The first church leader Frank encounters is Reverend John Locke, a satirical annotation of America's failure to implement the Enlightenment principles of life and liberty inspired by the seventeenth-century philosopher John Locke and written into the Declaration of Independence. The Reverend, like his predecessor, is a philosopher who tells Frank, before sending him east toward an illuminated life, that "an integrated army is integrated misery. You all go fight, come back, they treat you like dogs. Change that. They treat dogs better" (18).

Frank stops for a night in Chicago, where arbitrary street searches, theft, and random shootings by white policemen are routine. Still, black community thrives. An hour after arriving in the city, Frank "was scooping up navy beans and corn bread. . . . Bookers was not only a good and cheap place to eat, but its company—diners, counter help, waitresses, and a loud argumentative cook—was welcoming and high-spirited. Laborers and the idle, mothers and street women, all ate and drank with the ease of family in their own kitchens" (27). Billy Watson, a striking steel worker, and his attractive wife, Arlene, who works night shift at a metal factory, suggest progress and a rising generation. Their son is the future that places Frank's past in stark relief. Both have suffered race violence. Frank chose the heroic path and Thomas the pragmatic—math, scholarship, education. At eleven years of age, Thomas is already centered in a way that eludes Frank. "You shouldn't drink," he tells the older man, perhaps observing its residual effect. It is good that Frank admits to feeling bad about killing, Thomas asserts. "It means . . . [Frank's] not a liar." And when Frank asks what the boy will be in adulthood, Thomas can respond, with some assurance, "[a] man" (32–33).

Frank learns about Booker's Diner from the train waiter, who also, knowingly and surreptitiously, offers his passenger a cup, saucer, napkin, and shot of Johnny Walker Red. Waiters and porters, an extension of the underground, eased travel for blacks in that period. "Transportation was a major problem for African Americans," Morrison says. "What is redemptive about [Frank's] journey was those porters. It made the segregation almost irrelevant with that care."[11] As Larry Tye makes clear in *Rising from the Rails: Pullman Porters and the Making of the Black Middle Class*, for more than a century these men played an important and intricate role in American's cross-country train travel and in black community. According to Tye, "In his earliest years the Pullman porter was seen in the black world as a figure whose very presence captured the romance of the railroad, a traveling man with cosmopolitan sensibilities and money in his pocket."[12] Morrison conveys something of that romance in Frank's admiration. Traveling by bus is cheaper, but, as he tells Billy Watson, "long as there're porters, that's the way I want to travel" (19). Billy understands. "They sure make good money" is his response. "Four hundred five a month. Plus tip" (19). Morrison describes them as the "praetorian guard." She felt safe "traveling through the South on trains" because of porters, she says.[13]

Frank rides from Portland to Atlanta, with the stopover in Chicago— about three thousand miles and a journey of expanding perception. His first sobriety brings unexpected peace: "Sitting on the train . . . Frank suddenly realized that those memories [of war, the past], powerful as they were, did not crush him anymore or throw him into paralyzing despair. He could recall every detail, every sorrow, without needing alcohol to steady him" (100). Then, beating up a pimp at an unscheduled train stop in Tennessee triggers the old adolescent defiance that was personal and justifiable, "unlike the rage that had accompanied killing in Korea" (102). Not two days later, he takes Cee from the doctor, once more without rage, and this time without violence. Frank feels a "deep satisfaction that the rescue brought, not only because it was successful but also how markedly nonviolent it had been. . . . [Not] having to beat up the enemy to get what he wanted was somehow superior—sort of well, smart" (114). As a child, Frank was prepared to kill the old men if they "touched her." Now he was "smart[er]," a different man from the one the boy seemed destined to become. "Quiet" and "serene," Frank could be determined in the presence of such a pathetic "small white haired man" (110).

Returning to Lotus with a sister saved from death completes Frank's journey, if not his transformation. He is home, a place of "safety and goodwill," where no one "want[s] to degrade or destroy you" (118).[14] The emotion is a revelation to Frank, who is accustomed to images of Lotus as backward and its people as ignorant. Earlier, he claimed that "In Lotus . . . there was no future, just long stretches of killing time. There was no goal other than breathing, nothing to win and, save for somebody else's quiet death, nothing to survive or worth surviving for" (83). Frank had left the community, chasing his version of manhood inscribed from the narrative of fighting horses. "My family," he believed "was content or maybe just hopeless living that way" (84). But, in the aftermath of war and loss, nature and community open to him with a new narrative: "he could not believe how much he had once hated this place. Now it seemed both fresh and ancient, safe and demanding" (131). In his worst PTSD episodes, Frank had lost the capacity for color—"trees, sky, a boy on a scooter, grass, hedges. All color disappeared and the world became a black-and-white movie screen" (23). He had faced a frightening and "colorless landscape" (4). Back in Lotus, he sees color: the "deep, deep green" of trees; crimson, pink, and china-blue dahlias; "yellow butterflies"; "scarlet rosebushes"; "color . . . enveloped him" (118).

Frank's change of mind and feeling is a nod to black ambivalence about the South, a much-examined theme in Morrison's novels. As Lucille Fultz aptly puts it in a collection of essays related to this topic, "For many African Americans the South remains a place of comfort and contradictions—a place to turn toward and a place to turn from."[15] It is the house that race built, but it is also the ancestral home. Those, like Milkman, who would be spiritually and culturally coherent must reconnect with that home. This is the point that Catherine Jones makes in her comments on the dual nature of southern place in Morrison's work: "Ultimately . . . Morrison does not want to suggest that [southern] landscape is marked only by struggle, sorrow, and by disjunction. It is marked, too, by joy and reunion."[16]

Home also expands the South's story to accommodate Morrison's modernist perspective. While the South is home, Morrison's "struggle . . . is to keep it from being just the old place" (14). She explains that

> what Black people did in this country was brand new. Even if they did it a long time ago. These people were very inventive, very creative, and that was a very modern situation. It was, philosophically, probably the

earliest 19th century modernist existence. And out of thrown things they
invented everything: a music that is the world's music, a style, a manner
of speaking, a relationship with each other, and more importantly, psychological ways to deal with it. And no one gives us credit for the intelligence it takes to be forced into another culture, be oppressed, and make
a third thing. Other cultures who got moved like that die or integrate; or
because they're White, they don't even integrate, they disappear into the
dominate culture. That never happened to us.[17]

That is not to say that *Home* invalidates agency in northern cities, but it does
continue Morrison's investigation of the South's role in the black experience.
Booker's in Chicago surges with life. Still, its "down-home friendliness" signals a small transplanted southern community. The repartee among diners
about the hard times they faced in the South before they fled to the North,
along with the southern food, in effect gives the new community its identity.
Outside the café, patrons like Billy Watson live in distant apartments and
work around the clock in shifts. "You give up a lot," Morrison says, "to take
advantage of benefits of urban or working life elsewhere. . . . The problem
is trying to balance those two environments,"[18] the North and the South,
urban and rural. One is vital to economic survival; the other is the site of
cultural integrity.

Ethel Fordham advises Cee to stay in place. "Now you back home"; she
shouldn't allow anyone to chase her off again. And she tells the children's
story—a tutorial on freedom, slavery, and home—that not only inverts the
tale's moral meaning but revises definitions of those concepts that are rooted
in the meaning of place. "Remember that story about the goose and the
golden eggs?" she asks Cee. "How the farmer took the eggs and how greed
made him stupid enough to kill the goose? I always thought a dead goose
could make at least one good meal. But gold? Shoot. . . . Why didn't he plow
his land, seed it, and grow something to eat?" (125). Ethel's reinterpretation
argues that wisdom liberates, but fear, "that's slavery," she says. Home is
where you "seed your own land" and where one does "good in the world"—
especially in the South, as the farming metaphor suggests. Understanding
Ethel's meaning, Cee promises, "I ain't going nowhere, Miss Ethel. This is
where I belong" (126).

Lotus women are the ancestors in *Home*—those arbiters of useful knowledge: of good and evil, the ways of family and community, generosity and
kindness, pragmatism and tenacity. Ethel embodies them all. Cee observes
her after she delivers the hard news that Cee will not have children:

the older woman went into the backyard and stirred coffee grounds and
eggshells into the soil around her plants. . . . An aggressive gardener,
Miss Ethel blocked or destroyed enemies and nurtured plants. Slugs
curled and died under vinegar-seasoned water. Bold, confident raccoons
cried and ran away when their tender feet touched crushed newspaper
or chicken wire placed around plants. Cornstalks safe from skunks
slept in peace under paper bags. Under her care pole beans curved, then
straightened to advertise their readiness. Strawberry tendrils wandered,
their royal-scarlet berries shinning in morning rain. Honeybees gathered
to salute *Illicium* and drink the juice. Her garden was not Eden; it was so
much more than that. For her the whole predatory world threatened her
garden, competing with its nourishment, its beauty, its benefits, and its
demands. And she loved it. (130)

Ethel and the other Lotus women are the strong women of Eloe, Florida, that
Son Green remembers, and they are the neighbors whose primal song saves
Sethe and returns her to a community. In *Home* "they sang, too," including
Cee in their quilting circle, educating her mind and spirit. What Cee learns
from them, she models for Frank: to be "so strong / so beautiful. / Hurt right
down the middle / But alive and well" (147). Morrison gives Cee the final
line of the text: "Come on brother. Let's go home" (147). In that moment,
Cee evokes community, collaboration, and shared opportunities. There is
optimism in such a view of the flowering of human consciousness.

Morrison offers Lily as the necessary and troubling antithesis to Cee. One
wonders whether Ethel's parable on the limitations of gold is a commentary
on women like Lily. An amalgam of the shamed, pretentious Helen in *The
Bluest Eye* and Jadine, the modern woman with ambition in *Tar Baby*, Lily
is Cee's opposite in her cultural isolation and urban imprinting. Both women
acquire agency; Cee's is hard won under the tutelage of women and within
the bounds of community, whereas Lily's independence emerges in the glare
of a white gaze, causing her worry about perfect "straightened hair" (73) and
about impressing "well-to-do customer[s]" (78) with her sewing skills. Lily
heeds her father's advice to "let no insult or slight knock her off her ground"
(80). For her that means entrepreneurial enterprise, "her own house,"
"choosing the wall she wanted to break through," and putting away distrac-
tions, such as the dog tags Frank left behind, which she "hid . . . away in a
drawer [significantly]next to her bank book" (79). The final view of Lily with
the "found" coins predicts, she thinks, a shining economic future: "spread
out on the bed where Frank had slept, the coins, cold and bright, seemed a

perfectly fair trade. In Frank Money's empty space real money glittered. Who could mistake a sign that clear?" (81). Morrison does judge Lily, but she also respects her circumstance—a woman alone with courage and a plan. Unlike Lenore, who "loved [money], and thought it put her above everybody else," Lily escapes that particular pathology. She is not to be dismissed. Morrison explains that "I just like for women to do interesting stuff. I think the trajectory of Black women has been very different from the freed White women. . . . But more important than those differences, are the similarities and I like it although I know the risks; I know they're going to be very lonely."[19] "Interesting stuff" might be in Lily's future, but her prize will likely be owning the neat, perfect house she purchases with "cold and bright" coin, not the home (and the transcendent values it represents) that Cee creates in Lotus.

Meaning in *Home* also derives from its structure.[20] According to Morrison, plot is information about *what* happened. The structure, what lies underneath plot activity, manifests the writer's intention and shapes readers' experience of the text. Morrison "work[s] very hard" at this "sort of deep structure."[21] In *Home*, Frank's dual-voiced narrative structure signals the psychological effects of war and racial violence on masculine self-identity in 1950s America. Speaking retrospectively, in the first person, Frank continually queries and contradicts the third-person center-of-consciousness account of his experiences. Since a first-person retrospective view of one's life is not different from a third-person center-of-consciousness perspective of the same life, his is in effect a voice divided. "In both," Shlomith Rimmon-Kenan points out, "the focalization is a character within the represented world. The only difference between the two is the identity of the narrator."[22] That the voices are not in accord suggests Frank's unresolved psychic conflict. His autobiographical vignettes painfully unearth secrets that forestall his emergence from adolescence into manhood, while a third-person rendering of his consciousness looks forward to the immediate and distant future. One view is to the past, the other is to the future, but the novel moves toward integrating this bifurcated vision and reconciling its competing narratives.

Complex, fragmented, and a major source of cues to the novel's themes and motifs, Frank's "I" occupies very little text space and is a fraction of the novel's multilayered narrative in which Frank recounts the major episodes of his life to Morrison, in her role as *Home*'s author. As Morrison phrases it, "I let the character sit on my shoulder and talk to me."[23] (Morrison called the book *Frank Money* while she was writing it. It was her editor, she says, who suggested the title change.) That approach, she notes, was "my great discovery! I didn't want to take on the 'I' persona, so he and I are in this relationship."[24] Such an arrangement begs the question of how, in critical language, one might characterize Morrison's role in the text. Morrison clearly authors *Home*, a fully envisioned work of fiction, including its narrative strategy, which involves Frank telling Morrison his story that she is creating. A fictional writer inside the story to whom Frank might speak would be familiar literary ground. It would be light work, indeed, to distinguish between Frank and a fictional writer within *Morrison's* plot frame. *Home*, however, demands a more interesting critical discussion. And, given Morrison's emphasis, both inside and outside the text, on her collaborative writerly relationship to Frank, it seems appropriate, if a little awkward in the age of literary studies that insists on the distinction between author and narrator, to speak of *Frank's* first-person narrative in the one instance and *Morrison's*, not Frank's, third-person focalization in the other. Both are Frank's point of view, but in *Home's* narrative supposition, one voice is autonomous; the other is authorial.

Italicized passages suggest Frank's spoken monologue and distinguish his first-person retrospective voice from Morrison's focalization. As Frank looks backward to, in Morrison's words, "learn about what he does . . . learn about himself, and learn . . . with the aid of community,"[25] Morrison's focalization keeps the novel's temporal pace, what Susan Stanford Friedman refers to as a text's horizontal dimension, which "involves the linear movement of characters through . . . space and time."[26] It begins with Frank's escape from the Seattle mental ward and ends days later in Lotus. Through Frank's focalized point of view, Morrison also constructs Friedman's "vertical narrative axis," which generally constitutes a text's "literary, social, and historical intertexts."[27] Thus, Frank's journey by bus and train across the northwest to Atlanta with a stop in Chicago captures, especially, the precariousness and danger of blacks' encounters with white society in the 1950s and the black community's organized and ad hoc responses. While plot renders these elements of meaning, Frank's is the metanarrative that raises and answers *Home's* animating question about what it means to be a man, perhaps especially a black man, at midcentury.[28] That, according to Morrison, is Frank's dilemma, and the alternating conviction and doubt about the quality of his manhood shape Frank's narrative identity. Frank's telling is not continuous or consistent. Each of his eight chapters concerns a different memory or reflection, and each is Frank's attempt to reconcile his self-defining master narrative with contradicting experience. This narrative dissonance between what he believes and what he experiences resolves by the novel's end and is the reflection of internal coherence, at last. *Home*, then, is the story of

Frank's maturation, rendered as a process of narrative integration. Tension between the two voices relaxes in Frank's deepening willingness to see all the parts of himself over the course of the novel's lean plot.

These first-person and third-person focalized points of view, which may also be understood as the "I" and the "Me," facilitate Frank's storytelling about the past and allow him to achieve purpose and wholeness in the present. This narrative model of human development is the interdisciplinary work of the psychologist Dan McAdams and others who position narrative identity within a broadly integrated (rather than fragmented) framework for conceptualizing human selfhood.[29] As McAdams explains it, integrated narrative identity is essential to a generative life, and, in Morrison's words, "Word-work is sublime . . . because it is generative."[30] McAdams presents the narrative self in terms of the I-and-Me paradigm articulated by the psychologist William James, who saw personal identity as an integrated self, composed of the "empirical person" or "Me" and the "judging Thought" or "I."[31] Here, I am positioning Morrison's center of consciousness as the empirical, observing voice and Frank's as the judging I. In McAdams's comprehensive outline,

> Over the life course, the I develops increasingly sophisticated and nuanced understandings of the Me as it develops from an actor to an agent to an author. Reflecting our evolutionary heritage as social animals, human infants begin life as . . . social *actors*. Around one's second birthday, an initial actor-self begins to form, as the I begins reflexively to take note of the basic traits and proclivities that make it (the Me) up. With its collection of fixed traits and essential features, the actor-Me is similar to what Chandler (2001) describes as an *essentialist* rendering of selfhood. With the development of theory of mind (Wellman, 1993) in the fourth and fifth years of life and with the establishment of goals and motives in later childhood, human beings begin to see themselves from the standpoint of . . . motivated *agents,* as well, whose goals, plans, desires, programs, and long-term aims take up residency in the newly expanded Me. In adolescence and young adulthood, the I becomes . . . an *author* too, seeking to fashion the Me into a self-defining story, consistent with what Chandler (2001) describes as a *narrative* rendering of selfhood. That story, or narrative identity, explains what the social actor does, what the motivated agent wants, and what it all means in the context of one's narrative understanding of the self. By providing a story regarding how the Me came to be over time, as well as what the Me may become in the future, the self-as-author extends the Me back into one's personal history and

forward into the imagined distant future. Narrative identity, then, is that feature of human selfhood that begins to emerge when the adolescent or young-adult I assumes the guise of a storyteller.[32]

Frank's developing narrative identity reliably hits McAdams's markers and invites useful cognitive comparisons. At age four—the earliest period he chooses to recall—Frank knew the workings of his world, in which he experienced himself as part of a vulnerable family and community. When he was forced to leave Texas by vigilantes, his community and life broke open. At four these events were hypersensory: the discomfort of a flapping shoe, the searing heat that defied description, the piercing hunger, the sweetness of a newborn sister whose name was like music. Frank relates these details as a kind of coming out, a personal story of opening to new worlds—the birth; his namesake, Uncle Frank; crossing the geographical border from Texas to Louisiana; awakening to the sensate effects of racial hatred.

At age ten, as mapped on McAdams's continuum, Frank acquired agency. His defining beliefs about manliness grew from the seminal childhood encounter with horses and bad men. Years later, Frank's strongest memory of the afternoon is the way the horses reared up to a standing position. He insists that in the time since, he has not remembered the grave or the body. *"I really forgot about the burial,"* he declares to Morrison. *"I only remembered the horses. They were so beautiful. So brutal. And they stood like men"* (5).

Frank is wrong, of course. Both scenes have haunted his thoughts and shaped his sensibilities and ambitions; the trip south unmasks this dynamic and gives Frank perspective. He had come of age in Lotus, Georgia, as a restless adolescent—brave and stifled. After discharge, he had refused to return to Lotus in defeat and resents the current inevitability of going back, refuting not only the idea that he is the "enthusiastic hero" but insisting, defensively and perhaps disingenuously, that Lotus is not a place to live. *"Nobody in Lotus knew anything or wanted to learn anything,"* he claims. As if Morrison might doubt his story, Frank warns, *"you never lived there so you don't know what it was like"* (83–84). Likely, Frank also sees Lotus as he believes others saw it, such as the taxi driver who drops him at Ethel Fordham's and then, in Morrison's characterization, gets "as fast and as far away as he could from Lotus and its dangerous bed-bug-crazy country folk" (115). Frank's anger conceals what would otherwise be enervating feelings of inadequacy and guilt. He had survived; Mike and Stuff had not. How could he face their parents? What would he say to them? Can he save Cee? He had been wrong to leave his sister to manage a difficult life on her own. The decision had largely been the result of teenage angst: *"marbles, fishing, baseball, and shooting rabbits* [were not] *reason enough to get out of bed in the morning*" (84). But the consequences of leaving have been disastrous, and condemnation of the community disguises his disappointment in himself.

As the third-person focalization unfolds, Frank finds refuge for Cee and himself in Lotus, now seen as a verdant haven of safety. Before, in the first person, an angry Frank had substituted complacency for the community's steadfastness and ignorance for an ancient reliance on nature. He had marked every Lotus resident with meanness and indifference. But two months in place, tended by exceptional women, strengthen Cee and reinvent Frank. He can hold himself accountable for large failings and continue to evolve: "he had covered his guilt and shame with big time mourning for his dead buddies. Day and night he held on to that suffering because it let him off the hook, kept the Korean child hidden. Now the hook was deep inside his chest and nothing would dislodge it. The best he could hope for was time to work it loose" (138).

Toward the end of *Home,* Frank's narrative voice is no longer at war with itself—not intratextually, among the first-person passages, nor intertextually, between the first- and third-person accounts. This latter interplay is especially significant. By refuting, goading, and deceiving Morrison as she executes the focalized portion of his narrative, Frank struggles to justify old versions of himself as the watchful brother and good friend. In the opening chapter he warns, "*Since you're set on telling my story, whatever you write down, know this*" (5). In his next encounter with Morrison, he issues a challenge: "*Write about that, why don't you? . . . Describe that if you know how*" (40–41), suggesting, perhaps, that only he is equipped to recount a four-year-old's experience of hunger and privation. Later, he accuses the author of misrepresenting his thoughts and charges, "*I don't think you know much about love. Or me*" (69). Setting the record straight after lying about his crime, Frank is unapologetic: "*You can keep on writing, but I think you need to know what's true,*" he tells Morrison (134). These attempts at discursive authority do not work. Morrison's focalized response to Frank's assertions is to effect a gradual narrative shift—about Lotus, the meaning of home, and manhood. Lotus is not the worst place; it is vibrant, communal, and resilient. Home is where one feels alive, and manhood is not heroism but self-possession. While the first person tells its restrictive stories of past life, the third person embraces a healing truth in the present. This response pattern continues until there is integration of the narrative selves, the first and the third, I and Me. Once Frank admits his crime in chapter 14, the next time he speaks is in chapter 17, the novel's conclusion, and at that point he

seems to have achieved emotional clarity. After chapter 14, he issues no more
challenges to Morrison's knowledge or authority. The two are in sync.

Chapters 15 and 16, then, pivot the narrative dynamic. There the burial,
Korea, Lotus, and Frank's understanding of their lessons for him align.
Frank's metanarrative I, as McAdams would see it, joins with "the Me into
a self-defining story . . . [the] *narrative* rendering of selfhood." In chapter
15 Frank acknowledges that he can never be redeemed for taking a child's
life. The reburial in chapter 16 moves him and the text toward resolution.
Encouraged by the prospect of a home and future, he rights a wrong from
his and the community's past and eases tension in his disjunctive experiences
of beauty, violence, and heroic manhood—the awesome beauty of fighting
stallions, the violence implicit in a black man's quivering foot, the heroic
stance of brotherly vigilance. Excavating the bones, placing them in the
quilted shroud, removing them to the base of the sweet bay, honoring the
dead father's sacrifice—these acts discharge some of the obligation he feels to
the past.

In the novel's final scene, past and present glide into a future, as indicated
by the last appearance of the man in the zoot suit. His is the transformative energy of tomorrow and the new sort of manhood. When a little man
appeared, somber and distant, days earlier at the beginning of the journey,
Frank dismissed both man and suit as impotent. "If they [zoot suits] were
the signal of manhood, he would have preferred a loincloth and some white
paint artfully smeared on forehead and checks. Holding a spear, of course"
(34). This cavalier attitude barely hides the irony that it is Frank's romantic
narrative of manhood that is, in fact, as irrelevant as his mocking tribesman
reference. Frank does not perceive that the man's dress, starkly different from
his own ragged castoffs, is not a costume but a way of being in the world, a
manner of assertiveness, a kind of political resistance. Robin Kelley makes
this case in "The Riddle of the Zoot Suit": "The zoot suiters and hipsters
who sought alternatives to wage work and found pleasure in the new music,
clothes, and dance styles of the period were 'race rebels' of sorts, challenging middle-class ethics and expectations, carving out a distinct generational
and ethnic identity and refusing to be good proletarians."[33] Here Kelley is
examining the sociopolitical context of Malcolm Little's zoot-suit days as
portrayed in his autobiography.[34] Little was fifteen at the time and a long
way, psychologically and intellectually, from Malcolm X's 1960s activism.
But "the *little* man in the pale blue zoot suit" (33; emphasis added) suggests
metamorphosis. The man's changed demeanor in the final scene, "swinging
a watch chain. And grinning" (144), is confident and prophetic. Perhaps he

signifies the changes to come—that, in Morrison's words, "there was some-thing [about the forties and fifties] that became the seeds of the Civil Rights struggle" in the sixties and seventies.[35] *Home* is Morrison's latest novel. She says "there is one more" and that "it's sort of now-ish." She is looking to write about 2008, 2009. The new work, she continues, is "not really histori-cal the way the others have been."[36]

CHAPTER 11

Literary and Social Criticism
Playing in the Dark

Since 1974 Morrison's essays and interviews have comprised a reservoir of ideas about American culture. Over the years she has spoken and written about issues of race, class, and gender and how they shape perception and identity in American society. Of course, in the broadest sense these are also the subjects of her novels. And because this connection exists between her fiction and her nonfiction, it is possible, even desirable, to read one as a clarifying vision of the other. Indeed, in some cases Morrison's comments are extensive tutorials on meaning in her novels. But even when the relationship between her fiction and nonfiction is not absolute, a consistent thread of philosophical, literary, political, and cultural thought connects her writing.

Playing in the Dark, a work of nonfiction concerned with the way race and gender have defined American literature and life, illustrates this consistency. It is Morrison's most thorough treatment of these matters. It is a culmination of academic inquiry and scholarship that grew out of a course that Morrison taught in American literature at Princeton, and it explores ideas discussed in the three William E. Massey Sr. lectures she gave at Harvard. The result of her endeavors has been, according to Morrison, the emergence of a keen interest "in the way black people ignite critical moments of discovery or change or emphasis in literature not written by them."[1] Morrison has kept a file on such moments, which she believes deserve examination. In the preface to *Playing in the Dark,* Morrison recalls making an addition to her file of critical moments after reading Marie Cardinal's account of her descent into insanity in *The Words to Say It.* Morrison is intrigued by

Cardinal's description of her anxiety attack at age nineteen or twenty during a Louis Armstrong concert. Cardinal recalls that "my heart began to accelerate, becoming more important than the music, shaking the bars of my rib cage, compressing my lungs so the air could no longer enter them. Gripped by panic at the idea of dying there in the middle of spasms, stomping feet, and the crowd howling, I ran into the street like someone possessed" (vii). Morrison finds the "clarity" of Cardinal's recollection noteworthy. But she also asks, with eyebrows raised, "What on earth was Louie playing that night?" (vii). And then, more to her point, she wonders whether some other music—an Edith Piaf concert or an Antonin Dvorak composition—would have affected Cardinal with such force or whether the "cultural associations of Jazz" with blackness were the active ingredients responsible for precipitating Cardinal's anxiety. Morrison speculates that although "either [Piaf's or Dvorak's music] *could* have" (viii; emphasis added), it is significant that Armstrong's did. For a Frenchwoman born in Algeria, not surprisingly simultaneously repulsed and attracted by Arab (nonwhite) images, the exotic figurations of jazz perhaps possessed the power to unlock her subconscious and unleash its force.

Morrison believes that a writer's cultural and personal history undoubtedly shapes her work. This process is obvious in Cardinal's case: her narrative is an imaginative rendering of her life, her history. Fiction writers too are subject to historical influence, and, according to Morrison, in no context is that influence more demonstrable than in nineteenth- and twentieth-century American literature, where literary character and themes mirror life in America. Morrison is particularly concerned with the way literature reflects a racialized society—not in the recognizable way blacks are marginalized in texts (as they are in society) to provide local color or "a needed moral gesture, humor, or bit of pathos" (15) but in a more systemic, pathological way. "The major and championed characteristics of our national literature—individualism, masculinity, social engagement versus historical isolation; acute and ambiguous moral problematics; the thematics of innocence coupled with an obsession with figurations of death and hell," are, Morrison suggests, responses to a black presence (5). More than four hundred years of black suffusion (first African and later African American) in all aspects of life in the United States has a corresponding infusion of black images in literature. Morrison calls the presence of these images "American Africanism." It is the white writer's self-conscious and unconscious use of blackness that results from life in a society where racial identity dominates thinking and pervades the literary imagination as well. Any nonblack writer who perpetuates the ideology of "racial hierarchy, racial exclusion, and racial vulnerability and availability" (11) most likely makes use of Africanism.

Morrison traces Africanism from its early appearance in eighteenth-century personal narrative to its use in contemporary fictional narrative—from William Dunbar, an educated Scottish émigré to the American colonies, to Poe, Twain, and Cather, and finally to Hemingway. Dunbar's letters and diary, sketching in his life as a Mississippi planter and slaveholder, reveal much about the psychological use white European settlers made of black slaves in their sojourn toward power, authority, and authenticity. Absolute control over others' lives was exalting and empowering, and the result was the emergence of Dunbar (and slaveholders like him) as a "distinctive new man, a borderland gentleman, a man of property in a raw, half-savage world."[2] Blacks provided the contrast that made this identity of a new American possible, Morrison thinks. Their abjectness heightened the fulfillment derived from dominating them in the way that any desirable condition is made more so by fear of its opposite. Morrison proposes that the white population convinced itself that the slave population had offered itself up as surrogate selves for meditation on problems of freedom, failure, aggression, evil, sin, and greed. Americans did not have a "predatory" (47) noble class to struggle against and to counter its view of itself as morally good. (Only such a counterpoint could unify national character, by giving Americans a point of resistance.) Without a corrupt nobility, they turned for a counterpoint to the black population, which offered an ideological and visible basis for contrast. "For in that construction of blackness *and* enslavement," says Morrison, "could be found not only the not-free but also, with the dramatic polarity created by skin color, the projection of the not-me. The result was a playground for the imagination" (38). (Presumably, Morrison views the American fight with Britain as having no significant bearing on this argument. That war may be seen as a generic struggle for the rights of white men that informs the national spirit of independence, but it does not inform the aspect of national character—aristocratic privilege and license—that emanates from a sense of moral goodness; a black presence provided that identity.)

In consequence, a black presence is inextricably and uncomfortably bound to the American character, and Morrison sees this amalgam sharply reflected in the literature from its origins to its present. As in society historically, blacks in literature are not accorded full stature as agents of their own fictional destinies. Instead, the black character is reliably one dimensional, and the black experience created by the white imagination is reduced to Africanism: stereotypical personae, symbols of otherness (immorality, ignorance,

cowardice, enslavement, servility, savagery), objects of humor, or, in the
absence of black character and experience, a "deep abiding" darkness that
pervades the narrative.

Morrison illustrates her meaning in abbreviated analyses of Twain's
Huckleberry Finn, Cather's *Sapphira and the Slave Girl,* Poe's *Narrative of
Arthur Gordon Pym,* and Hemingway's *To Have and Have Not.* In review-
ing the much-discussed final chapters of *Huckleberry Finn,* Morrison declares
Jim's failed bid for freedom, his (re)enslavement, to be a perfect complement
to Huck's liberty. The latter cannot be comprehended without the former.
She supplements the prevailing and opposing views that explain the novel's
ending (when Tom's romantic machinations reemerge to overshadow Huck's
moral growth and Jim's integrity) as either evidence of Twain's deterioration
as an artist or as a lesson in real life. In addition to these interpretations, Morrison proposes that the ending be seen as Twain's unconscious adaptation of
the meaning of a black presence. The ending is "the elaborate deferment of
a necessary and necessarily unfree Africanist character's escape because freedom has no meaning to Huck or to the text without the specter of enslavement, the anodyne to individualism; the yard-stick of absolute power over
the life of another; the signed, marked, informing, and mutating presence of
a black slave" (56). Morrison makes in essence the same point about each
writer whose work she discusses. Each is subject, for the most part, to unex-
amined ideas about race that taint the imagination and sabotage the writer's
text.

Morrison approaches this study of America's literary imagination from
a writer's perspective and not from an academic critic's. She is, not unfairly,
accused of handling the language and work of criticism clumsily here,[3] but
she says early in *Playing in the Dark* that she does "not bring to these matters
solely or even principally the tools of a literary critic" (3). Rather, as a writer,
she is interested in the way writers develop their subjects and the conscious
but especially the unconscious literary strategies they employ. Experience
determines these strategies, and in a racialized society racial symbols are a
convenient literary shorthand. "The presence of black people is inherent . . .
in the earliest lesson every child is taught regarding his or her distinctive-
ness," Morrison asserts. "Africanism is inextricable from the definition of
Americanness" (65), she continues, and from the metaphorical (re)presenta-
tion of national character.

Morrison has never been tempted to the metaphorical and metaphysical
use of race in her fiction. Obviously, she is not inclined to embrace a literary tradition that may promote "racial superiority, cultural hegemony, and
dismissive 'othering' of people" (x). Resisting temptation, Morrison wishes

to "free up the language from its sometimes sinister, frequently lazy, almost always predictable employment of racially informed and determined chains" (xv).

"Recitatif," the only short story Morrison has written, is an experiment in communicating without using racial codes as a shortcut. The narrative, which Morrison describes (in the preface to *Playing in the Dark*) as a story "about two characters of different races for whom racial identity is crucial" (xi), deftly avoids racial stereotyping. In the story, eight-year-old girls develop bonds of friendship and trust during four months that both are placed temporarily at St. Bonaventure, an orphanage. Initially divided by their differences—Twyla, the first-person speaker, protests being "stuck in a strange place with a girl from a whole other race"[4]—the girls quickly find an ally in each other. Mutual need neutralizes race hatred and makes their similarities much more important than their differences. Unlike the other children at St. Bonaventure, the girls are not "real orphans with beautiful dead parents in the sky" (244). In place of these, Twyla and Roberta have dysfunctional living mothers: one is neglectful, and the other suffers from mental illness. For this and for being poor students, they are ostracized and so have only each other as companions. Together they endure intimidation by older girls on the second floor and by other girls at the orphanage, who taunt them with the names "salt" and "pepper." Together they spy on the big girls and occasionally watch helplessly when they harass Maggie, a mute woman who works in the kitchen at the orphanage.

Morrison does not reveal which of the girls is black and which is white, and yet, as she says, racial identity is crucial. It not only defines her characters' relationship to each other but locates that relationship within America's successive and changing epochs of racial disharmony from the late 1950s through the early 1980s. In the 1950s the petty prejudices at the orphanage prove to be innocuous, and the girls easily transcend these in their girlhood need for companionship. Even when Roberta's mother insults Twyla's by refusing to greet her on visitor's day (and Twyla's mother responds with name calling), the girls are able to dissociate the women's behavior from the affection of their own relationship. When Roberta leaves the orphanage to go back to her mother, the girls promise to keep in touch, but time fades memories. Many years later, during a chance meeting at a Howard Johnson's, where Twyla waits tables and Roberta is passing through, the girls, now women, are essentially strangers swept up in the strife of the 1960s. This time it is Twyla who is naive and Roberta who is wise to the ways of the world. With her "big and wild hair," "earrings the size of bracelets" (253), and heavy makeup, Roberta has traveled too far from the orphanage to acknowledge a past that included an unhip uniformed waitress who does not know who Jimi Hendrix is. In the present they are just "a black girl and a white girl meeting in a Howard Johnson's on the road and nothing to say" (253).

Twelve years later, the women, since married, meet again at a supermarket in an affluent suburb where Roberta lives with her wealthy husband and where Twyla occasionally shops even though on the salary of her husband, a fireman, she cannot afford the fancy groceries marketed there. Over coffee, they are reconciled, "behaving like sisters separated for much too long" (253). Time has no rational meaning for them. Just as a few moments had veiled them from each other in the Howard Johnson's years earlier, now "in just a pulse beat, twenty years disappeared and all of it came rushing back" (253)—until, in the act of recall, Roberta encourages Twyla to remember the day the big girls at the orphanage pushed Maggie, the woman from the kitchen, and tore her clothes as the two younger girls watched. Twyla is disturbed because her memory's version of the event is less malevolent: Maggie fell and the other girls laughed. The conflicting narratives produce a rupture that each feels but that neither acknowledges. The rupture deepens into an impassable divide a few years later when the two face each other from opposite sides of a school busing issue. Twyla accuses Roberta of bigotry for opposing busing, and Roberta hurls a more astonishing accusation: Maggie was black, and Twyla, Roberta asserts, had kicked her when the other girls pushed her to the ground. In a confrontation at the picket line, Roberta charges Twyla with being "the same little state kid who kicked a poor old black lady when she was down on the ground. You kicked a black lady," Roberta continues, "and you have the nerve to call me a bigot" (257). Twyla rejects both counts: that Maggie was black and that she assaulted her.

This exchange is typical of the racial dystopia Morrison devises for her characters and for her readers. The orphanage offers an unlikely cover of protection for the unfettered intimacy each girl feels with the other. Later, in adulthood, where new alliances are possible—husband, friends, children—the hothouse intimacy of the orphanage is impossible between a black woman and a white woman. The utopian past becomes the dystopic present of shattered memories.

Morrison's readers experience a kind of dystopia as well, if one may view Morrison's deliberate and clever misappropriation of racial stereotype as a dystopic condition for readers accustomed to stereotypes. In "Recitatif" racial identities are shifting and elusive. The reader cannot draw easy conclusions. Some readers may be tempted, for example, to deduce that Twyla is echoing white stereotypes of blacks when she says that they (and Roberta) never wash their hair and that they smell funny and to deduce that Roberta's big hairstyle at the Howard Johnson's is an Afro and that Roberta must therefore be black. Other readers, however, may believe that only as a white woman could Roberta outpace Twyla socially and financially. Only a white woman could plausibly live so well, with an affluent husband who affords a driver and servants. Only a white woman could demonstrate on the street against school busing, since most blacks saw it as Twyla does—as an opportunity for children of both races to be better educated. And yet, why would Twyla, if she is black, kick Maggie, who is one of her own? Questions beget questions in Morrison's text, and all require strenuous consideration. Despite most readers' wish to assess, settle, draw conclusions, Morrison is resolute in requiring readers to participate in creating meaning. She will offer no convenient stereotypes as shortcuts. (In speaking of the one unidentified white girl in *Paradise,* Morrison wonders what difference not knowing makes to a reader. She wants to encourage examination of "racial baggage." Moreover, she says, "not signaling race frees me up to talk about the characters in all sorts of ways—to not have race be the only way in which they are understood."[5]

Morrison does not resolve the dilemma of Maggie's racial identity, but in the final exchange between her characters—another chance meeting in a coffee shop on Christmas Eve many years after the busing conflict—whether Maggie is black or white is irrelevant. For Twyla and Roberta, Maggie is a symbol of defeat, a reminder of their own helplessness. Her being deaf, mute, and a victim is what they both remember about Maggie and what they both hated about her. Neither had kicked the old woman, but both had wanted to. The burden of their young lives was bearable when their pain, transformed to anger, was shifted to Maggie. Without realizing it, however, in hating Maggie, they hated themselves and each other. Now, after many years, they face the guilt over that anger and, having done so, can forgive each other and review the past truthfully, remembering Maggie not defensively but empathically, as Roberta urgently wonders, "What the hell happened to Maggie?" (261).

By the time this question is asked, the storm over race has passed. Morrison has momentarily raised the familiar specter of race prejudice, and, just as the reader took a relaxing breath, grateful finally for the sure footing of predictable stereotype, Morrison changes direction. She is interested not in bigotry but in humanity, lost and found. Maggie is not the Africanist set piece that Morrison decries.

Morrison shuns Africanism, but too many authors have not. *Playing in the Dark* puts the spotlight on some of those who have not and delineates what Morrison believes is the underexamined and overlooked subtext of race that imprints the literary canon of America.[6] Despite gaps in her discourse (she does not account for Indians as a dark presence in the literature of early America, and her examination of text is too brief and too arbitrary to allow her to make anything but speculative conclusions), Morrison's review is preliminary to the kind of penetrating exploration of the canon that she invites.

Conclusion

Language as a symbol of culture is especially Morrison's concern. She is keenly interested in the authentic and authenticating language of public narrative (in literature, politics, society), a point that she makes eloquently in her Nobel Prize lecture to the Swedish Academy. The lecture is an ode to language, the essential conduit of knowledge between individuals and generations. Language is the building block of narrative with which the artist inexplicably, illuminatingly weaves together the past, present, and future experiences of life. Narrative bequeaths continuity. Narrative language is continually threatened, however, by narrow thinking that reduces rather than creates, that excludes rather than includes, that shrouds rather that illuminates. Morrison's work opposes these threats as it elevates narrative language to heights of truth and understanding. To use Morrison's own words spoken in praise of another, her "word-work is sublime . . . because it is generative" and not reductive.[1]

In the narrative of her Nobel Prize lecture, Morrison chronicles the dangers of language abuse and misuse and celebrates the language of hope and possibility. Beginning with the standard narrative opening "once upon a time," which may be, according to Morrison, "the oldest sentence in the world and the earliest one we remember from childhood" (7), she recalls a fable familiar to her in many cultural variations. Choosing a version that reflects her cultural background, Morrison relates that a wise old woman, the daughter of African slaves, is asked by a gathering of young people to demonstrate her wisdom by saying whether the bird they hold is alive or dead. After considerable reflection the woman answers, "I don't know whether the bird you are holding is dead or alive, but what I do know is that it is in your hands" (11). Fascinated by the significance of the children's question and the woman's response, Morrison (again reflecting her own interests and work) "choose[s] to read the bird as language and the woman as a practiced writer" (12). In that context the old woman's response acknowledges the responsibility that all users of language have for its death and for its survival. Language that does not ask questions "cannot form or tolerate new ideas . . . [cannot] tell another story" (14) and is dead. Language that "reach[es] toward the ineffable . . . [and that] surges toward knowledge, lives" (21). The children hear the old woman and ask more questions, but this second time their questions are less arrogant than pleading. This time they do not brandish their own limited knowledge as a weapon to defeat her wisdom. Understanding more about the transforming force of narrative, they say,

> Tell us what it is to be a woman so that we may know what it is to be a man. What moves at the margin. What it is to have no home in this place. To be set adrift from the one you knew. What it is to live at the edge of towns that cannot bear your company. Tell us about ships turned away from shorelines at Easter, placenta in a field. Tell us about a wagonload of slaves, how they sang so softly their breath was indistinguishable from the falling snow. How they knew from the hunch of the nearest shoulder that the next stop would be their last. How, with hands prayered in their sex, they thought of heat, then sun. Lifting their faces as though it was there for the taking. They stop at an inn. The driver and his mate go in with the lamp, leaving them humming in the dark. The horse's void stems into the snow beneath its hooves and the hiss and melt are the envy of the freezing slaves.
>
> The inn door opens: a girl and a boy step away from its light. They climb into the wagon bed. The boy will have a gun in three years, but now he carries a lamp and a jug of warm cider. They pass it from mouth to mouth.
>
> The girl offers bread, pieces of meat and something more: a glance into the eyes of the one she serves. One helping for each man, two for each woman. And a look. They look back. The next stop will be their last. But not this one. This one is warmed. (28–30)

Narrative, stories, links the past with the present and with a future. In weaving a narrative of cultural history, the old woman, whom Morrison envisions as a practiced writer, gives the young people in her audience a knowledge of the past on which to construct their future experiences. Like the old woman, Morrison, herself a practiced writer, also weaves stories that bridge eras and generations. In her hands the language lives as extraordinary narratives of the humanity of her people.

NOTES

Preface

1. T. S. Eliot, "Tradition and Individual Talent," *Modernism: An Anthology* (Malden, Mass.: Blackwell, 2005), 153.

2. Hackney, Sheldon, "I Come from People Who Sang All the Time: A Conversation with Toni Morrison," *Humanities* 4, no.1 (March/April 1990): 4–9, 48. Rpt. In *Toni Morrison: Conversations*, ed. Carolyn C. Denard (Jackson: University of Mississippi Press, 2008), 137.

Chapter 1 — Understanding Toni Morrison

1. I am using this term as defined by the late Columbia University literary critic Edward Said, who wrote that "the intellectual belongs on the same side with the weak and underrepresented. . . . At bottom, the intellectual . . . is neither a pacifier nor a consensus-builder, but someone whose whole being is staked on a critical sense, a sense of being unwilling to accept easy formulas, or ready-made clichés, or the smooth, ever-so accommodating confirmation of what the powerful or conventional have to say, and what they do. Not just passively unwilling, but actively willing to say so in public." See Edward W. Said, *Representations of the Intellectual: The 1993 Reith Lectures* (New York: Vantage Books, 1996), 22–23.

2. Toni Morrison, *The Dancing Mind: Speech upon Acceptance of the National Book Foundation Metal for Distinguished Contribution to American Letters* (New York: Random House, 1996). Rpt. in *What Moves at the Margins*, ed. Carolyn C. Denard (Jackson: University Press of Mississippi, 2008), 187.

3. Morrison, *The Dancing Mind*, 189.

4. Morrison, *The Dancing Mind*, 190.

5. John Duvall offers an interesting context for understanding Morrison's acquisition of the name Toni. See John Duvall, *The Identifying Fictions of Toni Morrison: Modernist Authenticity and Postmodern Blackness* (New York: Palgrave Macmillan, 2000).

6. Jian Ghomeshi, "Toni Morrison on Her Two Selves," *Q*, CBC News (May 24, 2012).

7. Ghomeshi, "Toni Morrison."

8. Lorain's population in 1940, as the Depression came to an end, was 44,512. Ten years later, in 1950, postwar Lorain had increased in population by 16 percent, to 51,202, and was fueled by an economy dependent upon shipbuilding and steel. Morrison describes herself as having grown up "in a little industrial town in Ohio where everybody came for work—Mexicans, East Europeans, Greeks, and first generation

Italian—and I never lived in a black neighborhood, we were all just poor. One high school to which we all went. I didn't know the Southern thing; I didn't know the big city or eastern thing, so I am aware of how easy it is to share common aspirations." See *Toni Morrison: Conversations*, ed. Carolyn C. Denard (Jackson: University Press of Mississippi, 2008), 249–50.

9. Morrison's son Slade, with whom she coauthored nine children's books, died in 2010 of pancreatic cancer.

10. Toni Morrison, "Lecture and Speech of Acceptance, upon the Award of the Nobel Prize for Literature," *The Nobel Lecture in Literature* (New York: Knopf, 1994), 5.

11. This partial list of Morrison's lectureships is exemplary but certainly not comprehensive.

12. See, for example, Stanley Crouch's "Review of *Beloved*," *New Republic* 19 (October 1987): 38–43. See also Edna O'Brien's review of *Jazz* in "The Clearest Eye," *New York Times* (April 5, 1992); and James Wood's critique of *Paradise* in "The Color Purple," *The New Republic* (March 2, 1998): 29–31.

13. Nellie Y. McKay, "An Interview with Toni Morrison," *Contemporary Literature* 24 (Winter 1983): 413–29. Rpt. in *Toni Morrison: Critical Perspectives Past and Present*, ed. Henry Louis Gates Jr. and K. A. Appiah (New York: Amistad, 1993), 407.

14. Toni Morrison, "Rootedness: The Ancestor as Foundation," in *Black Women Writers (1950–1980): A Critical Evaluation*, ed. Mari Evans (New York: Doubleday, 1984), 344.

15. Morrison, "Rootedness," 345.

16. Morrison, "Rootedness," 345.

17. Morrison, "Rootedness," 345.

18. Morrison, "Rootedness," 340.

19. Thomas LeClair, "'The Language Must Not Sweat': A Conversation with Toni Morrison," *New Republic* 184 (March 21, 1981): 26.

20. Trudier Harris, *Fiction and Folklore: The Novels of Toni Morrison* (Knoxville: University of Tennessee Press, 1991), 11.

21. Morrison, "Rootedness," 343.

22. Christina Davis, "Interview with Toni Morrison," *Presence Africaine* (First Quarterly, 1988). Rpt. in *Toni Morrison: Critical Perspectives Past and Present*, ed. Henry Louis Gates Jr. and K. A. Appiah (New York: Amistad, 1993), 418–19.

23. Morrison, "Rootedness," 341.

24. Morrison, "Rootedness," 341.

25. Terry Otten, *The Crime of Innocence in the Fiction of Toni Morrison* (Columbia: University of Missouri Press, 1989), 5.

26. Toni Morrison, *Beloved* (New York: Knopf, 1987), 70.

27. Otten, *The Crime of Innocence*, 96.

28. Deborah E. McDowell, "'The Self, and the Other': Reading Toni Morrison's *Sula* and the Black Female Text," in *Critical Essays on Toni Morrison*, ed. Nellie Y. McKay (Boston: G. K. Hall, 1988), 80.

29. McDowell, "'The Self and the Other,'" 79.

30. This phrase is borrowed from Robert Grant in "Absence into Presence: The Thematics of Memory and 'Missing' Subjects in Toni Morrison's *Sula*," in *Critical Essays on Toni Morrison*, ed. Nellie Y. McKay (Boston: G. K. Hall, 1988), 100.

31. Sandi Russell, "It's OK to Say OK," in *Critical Essays on Toni Morrison*, ed. Nellie Y. McKay (Boston: G. K. Hall, 1988), 46.

32. Davis, "Interview with Toni Morrison," 418.

33. Russell, "It's OK to Say OK," 46.

34. Russell, "It's OK to Say OK," 45.

35. Rosemarie K. Lester, "An Interview with Toni Morrison, Hessian Radio Network, Frankfurt, West Germany," in *Critical Essays on Toni Morrison*, ed. Nellie Y. McKay (Boston: G. K. Hall, 1988), 49.

36. Robert B. Stepto, "'Intimate Things in Place': A Conversation with Toni Morrison," *Massachusetts Review* 18 (Autumn 1977): 473–89. Rpt. in *Toni Morrison: Critical Perspectives Past and Present*, ed. Henry Louis Gates Jr. and K. A. Appiah (New York: Amistad, 1993), 386.

37. Stepto, "Intimate Things in Place," 180.

38. McKay, "An Interview with Toni Morrison," 406.

39. Toni Morrison, *Song of Solomon* (New York: Knopf, 1977), 311.

40. Russell, "It's OK to Say OK," 43.

41. Morrison, *Song of Solomon* 311.

42. Morrison, "Rootedness," 344.

43. LeClair, "Language," 26.

44. Karla F. C. Holloway and Stephanie A. Demetrakopoulos, *New Dimensions of Spirituality: A Biracial and Bicultural Reading of the Novels of Toni Morrison* (Westport, Conn.: Greenwood Press, 1987), 15–16.

Chapter 2—Black Girlhood and Black Womanhood

1. I am using the term "sequentially" broadly to suggest that there is a continuity of theme from one book to the other, rather than a continuation of plot and identifiable characters. The novels reflect Morrison's desire to follow up her exploration of female friendships in childhood and adulthood.

2. Nellie Y. McKay, "An Interview with Toni Morrison," *Contemporary Literature* 24 (Winter 1983): 413–29. Rpt. in *Toni Morrison: Critical Perspectives Past and Present*, ed. Henry Louis Gates Jr. and K. A. Appiah (New York: Amistad, 1993), 399.

3. Robert B. Stepto, "'Intimate Things in Place': A Conversation with Toni Morrison," *Massachusetts Review* 18 (Autumn 1977): 473–89. Rpt. in *Toni Morrison: Critical Perspectives Past and Present*, ed. Henry Louis Gates Jr. and K. A. Appiah (New York: Amistad, 1993), 386.

4. Toni Morrison, *The Bluest Eye* (New York: Holt, Rinehart and Winston, 1970), 3. Subsequent references will appear in parentheses in the text.

5. Toni Morrison, "Unspeakable Things Unspoken: The Afro-American Presence in American Literature," *Michigan Quarterly Review* 28 (Winter 1989): 20.

6. Morrison, "Unspeakable Things Unspoken," 21.

7. Morrison, "Unspeakable Things Unspoken," 22.

8. Michael Awkward, "'The Evil of Fulfillment': Scapegoating and Narration in *The Bluest Eye*," in Awkward, *Inspiriting Influences, Tradition, Revision, and Afro-American Women's Novels* (New York: Columbia University Press, 1989), 75. See also Chikwenye Ogunyerni's "Order and Disorder in Toni Morrison's *The Bluest Eye*," *Critique: Studies in Modern Fiction* 19 (1977): 112–20.

9. Stepto, "Intimate Things in Place," 386.

10. Stepto, "Intimate Things in Place," 384.

11. Morrison, "Unspeakable Things Unspoken," 23.

12. See, for example, Stanley Crouch's "Review of *Beloved*," *New Republic* 19 (October 1987): 38–43. See also Edna O'Brien's review of *Jazz* in "The Clearest Eye," *New York Times* (April 5, 1992); and James Wood's critique of *Paradise* in "The Color Purple," *The New Republic* (March 2, 1998): 29–31. Morrison, "Unspeakable Things Unspoken," 23.

13. Timothy B. Powell, "Toni Morrison: The Struggle to Depict the Black Figure on the White Page," *Black American Literature Forum* 24 (Winter 1990): 752. For other clever readings of the Dick-and-Jane story in *The Bluest Eye*, see Shelly Wong, "Transgression as Poesis in *The Bluest Eye*," *Callaloo* 13 (Summer 1990): 471–81; Phyllis Klotman, "Dick-and-Jane and the Shirley Temple Sensibility in *The Bluest Eye*," *Black American Literature Forum* 13 (Winter 1979): 123–25, among others.

14. Stepto, "Intimate Things in Place," 389.

15. Stepto, "Intimate Things in Place," 388.

16. Toni Morrison, *Sula* (New York: Knopf, 1973), 44. Subsequent references will appear in parentheses in the text.

17. Maureen T. Reddy ("The Tripled Plot and Center of *Sula*," *Black American Literature Forum* 22 [Spring 1988]: 29–45) enlarges this view of Sula's deficiencies. Reddy, surprisingly, labels Sula a woman with "no true inner core of self [who] tries to appropriate Nel's by doing what Nel does, including having sex with Jude" (37). According to Reddy, "In spite of her deathbed claim that she 'sure did live in this world' and her insistence that she owns herself, Sula never reaches real self under-standing because she has no abiding self to understand nor any way of creating a self" (37). Reddy's interpretation does not negate the view that Sula inspires Nel to act imaginatively. What Sula does not have and what Nel offers her is definition and order. Each has something that the other needs.

18. Stepto, "Intimate Things in Place," 381.

19. Stepto, "Intimate Things in Place," 382.

20. Claudia Tate, "Conversation with Toni Morrison," *Black Women Writers at Work*, ed. Claudia Tate (New York: Continuum, 1983), 125–26.

21. Tate, "Conversation with Toni Morrison," 343.

22. All of Morrison's novels have an extraordinary sense of place, but in *Sula* the author says she felt place "very strongly, not in terms of the country or the state, but in terms of the details, the feeling, the mood of the community, of the town." See Stepto, "Intimate Things in Place," 378.

23. Stepto, "Intimate Things in Place," 379.

24. Stepto, "Intimate Things in Place," 379.

25. Stepto, "Intimate Things in Place," 380.

Chapter 3 — Male Consciousness

1. Nellie Y. McKay, "An Interview with Toni Morrison," *Contemporary Litera-ture* 24 (Winter 1983): 413–29. Rpt. in *Toni Morrison: Critical Perspectives Past and Present*, ed. Henry Louis Gates Jr. and K. A. Appiah (New York: Amistad, 1993), 399.

2. Rosemarie K. Lester, "An Interview with Toni Morrison, Hessian Radio Net-work, Frankfurt, West Germany," in *Critical Essays on Toni Morrison*, ed. Nellie Y. McKay (Boston: G. K. Hall, 1988), 48.

3. Lester, "An Interview," 47–48.

4. Toni Morrison, *Song of Solomon* (New York: Knopf, 1977), 163. Subsequent references will appear in parentheses in the text.

5. Toni Morrison, "Unspeakable Things Unspoken: The Afro-American Presence in American Literature," *Michigan Quarterly Review* 28 (Winter 1989): 29.

6. Morrison, "Unspeakable Things Unspoken," 29.

7. For a discussion of Morrison's inversion of the male monomyth, see Gerry Brenner, "*Song of Solomon*: Morrison's Rejection of Rank's Monomyth and Feminism," *Studies in American Fiction* 15 (Spring 1987): 13–24. For a discussion of Morrison's use of female narrative to counteract male narrative, see Michael Awkward, "'Unruly and Let Loose': Myth, Ideology, and Gender in *Song of Solomon*," *Callaloo* 13 (Summer 1990): 482–98.

8. McKay, "An Interview," 403.

9. McKay, "An Interview," 406.

10. Morrison, "Unspeakable Things Unspoken," 29.

11. Morrison, "Unspeakable Things Unspoken," 29.

12. McKay, "An Interview," 402.

13. McKay, "An Interview," 402.

14. Although Morrison finds the comparison unflattering, some see parallels between Milkman's quest and the quests in the works of William Faulkner and between images of flying in *Song of Solomon* and in James Joyce's *A Portrait of the Artist as a Young Man*. David Cowart discusses these similarities in "Faulkner and Joyce in Morrison's *Song of Solomon*," *American Literature* 62 (March 1990): 87–100.

15. Thomas LeClair, "'The Language Must Not Sweat': A Conversation with Toni Morrison," *New Republic* 184 (March 21, 1981): 26–27.

Chapter 4—Community and Cultural Identity

1. Robert G. O'Meally, "Review of *Tar Baby*," *Callaloo* (February–October 1981): 193.

2. Gloria Naylor and Toni Morrison, "A Conversation," *Southern Review* 21 (1985): 581.

3. Toni Morrison, *Tar Baby* (New York: Knopf, 1981), 7. Subsequent references will appear in parentheses in the text.

4. Terry Otten, *The Crime of Innocence in the Fiction of Toni Morrison* (Columbia: University of Missouri, 1989), 4–5.

5. Nellie Y. McKay, "An Interview with Toni Morrison," *Contemporary Literature* 24 (Winter 1983): 413–29. Rpt. in *Toni Morrison: Critical Perspectives Past and Present*, ed. Henry Louis Gates Jr. and K. A. Appiah (New York: Amistad, 1993), 405.

6. Toni Morrison, "Unspeakable Things Unspoken: The Afro-American Presence in American Literature," *Michigan Quarterly Review* 28 (Winter 1989): 30.

7. Naylor and Morrison, "A Conversation," 573.

8. Barbara Christian, "The Concept of Class in the Novels of Toni Morrison," *Black Feminist Criticism: Perspectives on Black Women Writers* (New York: Pergamon Press, 1985), 79.

9. Naylor and Morrison, "A Conversation," 575.

10. Toni Morrison, "Rootedness: The Ancestor as Foundation," *Black Women Writers 1950–1980*, ed. Marie Evans (New York: Doubleday, 1984), 340.

11. Morrison, "Rootedness," 340.

Chapter 5—Remembering the "Disremembered"

1. Gloria Naylor and Toni Morrison, "A Conversation," *Southern Review* 21 (1985): 588. Morrison says that she was compelled to do what she thought others had not because she was "ill-taught"; she did not know the work of black women writers like Zora Neale Hurston or Paule Marshall.

2. Naylor and Morrison, "A Conversation," 588.

3. Naylor and Morrison, "A Conversation," 583.

4. Naylor and Morrison, "A Conversation," 583–84.

5. Naylor and Morrison, "A Conversation," 585.

6. Toni Morrison, *Beloved* (New York: Knopf, 1987), 163. Subsequent references will appear in parentheses in the text.

7. Naylor and Morrison, "A Conversation," 584.

8. Angels Carabi, "Toni Morrison," *Belles Lettres* (Winter 1994): 89.

9. Morrison is expressing the African principle of death as transition and liberation. According to this eschatology, "death is not a destruction of the individual. Life goes on beyond the grave," a view that effectively undermines the slaveholder's power over his slave by dissolving the fear of death. See John S. Mibiti, *African Religions and Philosophy* (Garden City, N.Y.: Doubleday, 1970), 113.

10. Alice Walker's womanist theory, which is concerned with the survival of an entire people, male and female, seems appropriate here. See Alice Walker, *In Search of Our Mothers' Gardens* (San Diego: Harcourt Brace, 1984).

11. Narratives of slaves' experiences in slavery and in freedom flourished before and after the Civil War. For an examination of slave narrative and the African American literary tradition, see, among others, Deborah E. McDowell and Arnold Rampersad, eds., *Slavery and the Literary Imagination* (Baltimore: Johns Hopkins University Press, 1989); William Andrews, *To Tell a Free Story: The First Century of Afro-American Autobiography, 1760–1865* (Champaign: University of Illinois Press, 1988).

12. Toni Morrison, "The Site of Memory," in *Inventing the Truth: The Art and Craft of Memoir*, ed. William Zinsser (Boston: Houghton Mifflin, 1987), 106.

13. Morrison, "Site of Memory," 110–11.

14. Morrison, "Site of Memory," 112.

15. Morrison, "Site of Memory," 115.

16. Morrison, "Site of Memory," 118.

17. Morrison, "Site of Memory," 118.

18. Naylor and Morrison, "A Conversation," 585.

19. Carabi, "Toni Morrison," 88.

20. Carabi, "Toni Morrison," 88.

21. Morrison acknowledges that "it may be a little too romantic to think about Africa as a kind of Eden, before corruption, the cradle of humanity." With Sethe's image she intended to communicate "a picture of community" that was unconquered. See Carabi, "Toni Morrison," 86.

22. Carabi, "Toni Morrison," 88.

23. Karla F. C. Holloway, "*Beloved*: A Spiritual," *Callaloo* 13 (1990): 522.

24. Morrison, "Site of Memory," 122.

25. Carabi, "Toni Morrison," 90.

26. Naylor and Morrison, "A Conversation," 586.

27. Naylor and Morrison, "A Conversation," 586.

28. Morrison, "Site of Memory," 112.

29. Morrison, "Site of Memory," 112–13.

30. Christina Davis, "Interview with Toni Morrison," *Presence Africaine* (First Quarterly 1988). Rpt. in *Toni Morrison: Critical Perspectives Past and Present*, ed. Henry Louis Gates Jr. and K. A. Appiah (New York: Amistad 1993), 4 4.

31. The exception to this critical view of Morrison's achievement is Stanley Crouch's review of *Beloved* in which he asserts that Morrison stereotypes and simplifies complex human motivations. See Stanley Crouch, "Review of *Beloved*, by Toni Morrison," *New Republic* 19 (October 1987): 38–43.

32. Naylor and Morrison, "A Conversation," 585.

Chapter 6 — City Blues

1. Morrison has written that she is committed to in medias res openings in her novels because she is interested in how things happen, who did what, and why. She therefore puts the significant details up front to entice the reader into wanting to know the rest of the story. See Morrison, "Unspeakable Things Unspoken: The Afro-American Presence in American Literature," *Michigan Quarterly Review* 28 (Winter 1989): 1–34; and Elissa Schappell and Claudia Brodsky Lacour, "Toni Morrison: The Art of Fiction," *Paris Review* 134 (Fall 1993): 83–125.

2. Nellie Y. McKay, "Interview with Toni Morrison," *Contemporary Literature* 24 (Winter 1983): 413–29. Rpt. in *Toni Morrison: Critical Perspectives Past and Present*, ed. Henry Louis Gates Jr. and K. A. Appiah (New York: Amistad, 1993), 405.

3. Toni Morrison, *Jazz* (New York: Knopf, 1992), 73. Subsequent references will appear in parentheses in the text.

4. Mark Twain, *Pudd'nhead Wilson*, ed. with an introduction by Malcolm Bradbury (New York: Penguin, 1969), 230–31.

5. Per Seyersted, *Kate Chopin: A Critical Biography* (Baton Rouge: Louisiana State University Press), 176.

6. Schappell and Lacour, "The Art of Fiction," 106.

7. In her interview with Schappell and Lacour, Morrison talks about the visual images that control the structure of each novel's focus as she writes.

8. Schappell and Lacour, "The Art of Fiction," 116.

9. Schappell and Lacour, "The Art of Fiction," 117.

Chapter 7 — Utopia and Moral Hazard

1. Boris Kachka, "Who Is the Author of Toni Morrison?," *New York Magazine* (April 29, 2012), http://nymag.com/news/features/toni-morrison-2012-5/.

2. Anna Mulrine, "This Side of 'Paradise,'" *U.S. News and World Report* (January 19, 1998): 71.

3. Elizabeth Farnsworth, "Interview with Toni Morrison," *PBS NewsHour* (March 9, 1998).

4. A. J. Verdelle, "Loose Magic: Interview with Toni Morrison," *Double Take* 4, no. 3 (Summer 1998): 121–28. Rpt. in *Toni Morrison: Conversations*, ed. Carolyn C. Denard (Jackson: University of Mississippi Press, 2008), 164.

5. A. J. Verdelle, "Paradise Found: A Talk with Toni Morrison about Her New Novel," *Essence Magazine* (February 1998): 78.

6. Toni Morrison, *Paradise* (New York: Knopf, 1998), 165. Subsequent references will appear in parentheses in the text.

7. Toni Morrison, "Chat," *Time Online* (January 21, 1998).

8. Verdelle, "Loose Magic," 164.

9. Toni Morrison, "Lecture and Speech of Acceptance, upon the Award of the Nobel Prize for Literature," *The Nobel Lecture in Literature* (New York: Knopf, 1994), 33.

10. Carolyn C. Denard, "Blacks, Modernism, and the American South: An Interview with Toni Morrison," *Studies in the Literary Imagination* 31, no. 2 (Fall 1998): 1–16. Rpt. in *Toni Morrison: Conversations*, ed. Carolyn C. Denard (Jackson: University of Mississippi Press, 2008), 191.

11. Dinitia Smith, "Toni Morrison's Mix of Tragedy, Domesticity and Folklore," *New York Times* (January 8, 1998), http://www.nytimes.com/1998/01/08/books/toni-morrison-s-mix-of-tragedy-domesticity-and-folklore.html?pagewanted=allandsrc=pm. Accessed January 25, 2012.

12. Smith, "Toni Morrison's Mix of Tragedy."

13. Zia Jaffery, "Interview with Toni Morrison," *Salon* (February 2, 1998), http://www.salon.com/1998/02/02/cov_si_02int/. Accessed January 25, 2012.

14. Toni Morrison, "Chat."

15. Michael Silverblatt, "Interview with Toni Morrison on *Beloved*," *Bookworm*, KCRW Radio (October 22, 1998).

16. Toni Morrison, *Beloved* (New York: Knopf, 1987), 88. Subsequent references will appear in parentheses in the text.

17. In this collection of essays, Nussbaum, a philosopher, makes a case for philosophy's relevance to literature and vice versa. See Martha C. Nussbaum, *Love's Knowledge: Essays on Philosophy and Literature* (New York: Oxford University Press, 1992).

18. Silverblatt, "Interview on *Beloved*."

19. Harry Frankfurt, *The Reasons of Love* (Princeton, N.J.: Princeton University Press, 2004).

20. Silverblatt, "Interview on *Beloved*."

21. Silverblatt, "Interview on *Beloved*."

22. Toni Morrison, *Jazz* (New York: Knopf, 1992), 220. Subsequent references will appear in parenthesis in the text.

23. Martha C. Nussbaum, "Capabilities as Fundamental Entitlements: Sen and Social Justice," *Feminist Economics* 9 (2003), 41.

24. Silverblatt, "Interview on *Beloved*."

25. Silverblatt, "Interview on *Beloved*."

26. Toni Morrison, *Paradise* (New York: Knopf, 1998), 159. Subsequent references will appear in parentheses in the text.

27. Morrison, *Beloved*.

28. Elissa Schappell and Claudia Brodsky, "The Art of Fiction," *Paris Review* 134 (Fall 1993): 128–34.

29. Silverblatt, "Interview on *Beloved*."

30. Silverblatt, "Interview on *Beloved*."

31. In addition to the novel's historiography, Justine Tally foregrounds matters of narratology in her reading of the trilogy. See Justine Tally, "The Morrison Trilogy,"

The Cambridge Companion to Toni Morrison, ed. Justine Tally (Cambridge: Cambridge University Press, 1997).

32. Noel Carroll, "The Wheel of Virtue: Art, Literature, and Moral Knowledge," *Journal of Aesthetics and Art Criticism* 60, no. 1 (2002): 3.

33. Ann Hostetler, "The Art of Teaching: An Interview with Toni Morrison," Princeton University, April 17, 2002. Rpt. in *Toni Morrison: Conversations*, ed. Carolyn C. Denard (Jackson: University Press of Mississippi, 2008), 196.

34. Toni Morrison, "How Can Values Be Taught in the University?" *Michigan Quarterly Review* 40:2 (Spring 2001): 273–78.

35. Morrison, "How Can Values Be Taught?"

36. Silverblatt, "Interview on *Beloved*."

Chapter 8 — The Language of Love

1. Michael Silverblatt, "Interview with Toni Morrison on *Love*," *Bookworm*, KCRW Radio (February 12, 2004).

2. Toni Morrison, *Love* (New York: Knopf, 2003), 199. Subsequent references appear in parentheses in the text.

3. Silverblatt, "Interview on Love."

4. I am using narration in the sense of Dorrit Cohn's definition of "narrated monologue" as an aspect of dramatized consciousness, a feature of which is recalling the past. See Dorrit Cohn, "Narrated Monologue: Definition of a Fictional Style," *Comparative Literature* 18, no. 2 (Spring 1966): 97–112.

5. Pam Houston, "Interview with Toni Morrison," *Other Voices* 18, no. 42 (Fall/Winter 2005): 209.

6. Michael Saur, "I Want to Write like a Good Jazz Musician: Interview with Toni Morrison," in *Toni Morrison: Conversations*, ed. Carolyn C. Denard (Jackson: University Press of Mississippi, 2008), 225.

7. Silverblatt, "Interview on Love."

8. Saur, "I Want to Write," 225.

9. Saur, "I Want to Write," 225.

10. Silverblatt, "Interview on Love."

11. Silverblatt, "Interview on Love."

12. Silverblatt, "Interview on Love."

13. Silverblatt, "Interview on Love."

14. 1 Cor. 12: 4–7, RSV.

15. Houston, "Interview with Toni Morrison," 212.

16. Houston, "Interview with Toni Morrison," 211.

17. Houston, "Interview with Toni Morrison," 210.

18. Houston, "Interview with Toni Morrison," 210.

19. St. Clair Drake and Horace R. Cayton. *Black Metropolis: A Study of Negro Life in a Northern City* (Chicago: University of Chicago Press, 1945).

20. Victor Green, *The Negro Motorist Green Book: An International Travel Guide* (New York: Victor H. Green, 1949).

21. Everett L. Fly and La Barbara Wigfall Fly, *Black Settlements in America* (Austin: Entourage Incorporated, 1980).

22. Houston, "Interview," 214.

23. Houston, "Interview," 214.

24. Sheryll Cashin, *The Failures of Integration: How Race and Class Are Undermining the American Dream* (New York: Perseus Books Group, 2004), xii–xiii.

25. Houston, "Interview," 227.

26. Houston, "Interview," 212.

Chapter 9—The Race[ing] of Slavery

1. Charlie Rose, "A Conversation with Author Toni Morrison," *Charlie Rose* (November 10, 2008), http://www.charlierose.com/guest/view/1690.

2. Toni Morrison, *A Mercy* (New York: Knopf, 2008), 14. Subsequent references will appear in parentheses in the text.

3. J. Hector St. John Crevecœur, *Letters from an American Farmer* (rpt., New York: Fox, Duffield, 1904).

4. Lynn Neary, "Interview with Toni Morrison," NPR Webcast (October 29, 2008), http://www.npr.org/player/v2/mediaPlayer.html?action=1&t=1&islist=false&id=95961382&m=96097293.

5. See Ira Berlin, *Generations of Captivity: A History of African-American Slaves* (Cambridge, Mass.: Harvard University Press, 2003). Berlin's history tracks the evolution of slavery from its institutionalization in the seventeenth century.

6. Theodore Allen, *The Invention of the White Race: The Origin of Racial Oppression in Anglo-America* (New York: Verso, 1997), 2: 209.

7. Allen, *Invention* 248–49.

8. John Winthrop, "A Model of Christian Charity," in *Collections of the Massachusetts Historical Society*, ser. 3, vol. 7 (Boston: Little Brown, 1838), 44.

9. Seymour Martin Lipset, "Book Review," *Journal of American History* 87, no. 3 (December 2000): 1019.

10. Alexis de Tocqueville, *Democracy in America*, 3rd ed., vol. 2, ed. Francis Bowen, trans. Henry Reeve (Cambridge: Sever and Francis, 1863), 2: ix.

11. Lipset, "Book Review," 2000.

12. Linda Krumholz, "Reading and Insight in Toni Morrison's *Paradise.*" *African American Review* 36, no. 1 (Spring 2002): 21–34. Krumholz traces this critical use of the term from Freud to contemporary feminist, music, and African American literary scholarship.

13. Krumholz, "Reading," 21.

14. Pam Houston, "Interview with Toni Morrison," *Other Voices* 18, no. 42 (Fall/Winter 2005): 227.

15. See Mina Karavanta, "Toni Morrison's *A Mercy* and the Counterwriting of Negative Communities," *Modern Fiction Studies* 58, no. 4 (Winter 2012): 723–46.

16. Roderick Nash, *Wilderness and the American Mind*, 3rd ed. (New Haven and London: Yale University Press, 1982), 24.

17. William Bradford, *Original Narrative of Early American History: Bradford's History of Plymouth Plantation. 1606–1646*, ed. William T. Davis (New York: Charles Scribner's Sons, 1908), 96.

18. Bradford, *Original Narrative* 391.

19. Cotton Mather, "The Wonders of the Invisible World," in *The Puritans in America: A Narrative Anthology*, ed. Andrew Delbanco and Alan Heimert (Cambridge, Mass.: Harvard University Press, 2001), 339.

20. Toni Morrison, *Playing in the Dark: Whiteness and the Literary Imagination* (Cambridge, Mass.: Harvard University Press, 1992), 34.

21. Rose, "Conversation."

22. Andree Nicola McLaughlin, "A Renaissance of Spirit: Black Women Remaking the Universe," in *Wild Women in the Whirlwind: Afra-American Culture and the Contemporary Literary Renaissance*, ed. Joanne M. Braxton and Andree Nicola McLaughlin (New Brunswick, N.J.: Rutgers University Press, 1990) xiv.

23. Toni Morrison, "Toni Morrison Talking about Her Book *A Mercy*," StartUp Media (November 7, 2008).

24. This phrase is borrowed from Wahneema Lubiano's *The House That Race Built: Black Americans, U.S. Terrain* (New York: Pantheon, 1997).

25. Toni Morrison, "Home," in *The House That Race Built: Black Americans, U.S. Terrain*, ed. Wahneema Lubiano (New York: Pantheon, 1997), 5.

Chapter 10—A Lesson of Manhood

1. Bob Minzesheimer, "New Novel *Home* Brings Toni Morrison Back to Ohio," *USA Today* (May 7, 2012), http://usatoday30.usatoday.com/life/books/news/story/2012–05–07/toni-morrison-home-books/54814002/1.

2. Minzesheimer, "New Novel."

3. Lisa Shea, "Toni Morrison on *Home*," *Elle* (June 15, 2012), http://www.elle.com/pop- culture/reviews/toni-morrison-on-home-655249.

4. Commager, an activist scholar and midcentury liberal, was certainly not blind to the failing of democratic society; he did not hesitate to speak out against McCarthyism, for example. But, despite what he referred to as the considerable "discrepancy between democratic pretensions and practices," including in "race relations," Commager promoted, sometimes glibly, in his writings and work an America of optimism and happy potential. See Henry Steele Commager, "The Twentieth-Century American," in *The American Mind: An Interpretation of American Thought and Character since the 1980's* (New Haven: Yale University Press, 1950), 406–44.

5. Morrison, in speaking about *Home*, dates the setting as "nineteen fifty-two or fifty-three"; the text is not more specific, nor would a more precise year change the meaning.

6. Frank is twenty-four when the novel opens. He left home four years earlier (assuming he spent three years in the war and one in Seattle before returning to Lotus). Cee, we are told, was fourteen when Frank left. Frank, who is four years older (he was four when Cee was born), would have been between eighteen and twenty (allowing for graduated time periods—years plus months; Cee, for example, could have been fourteen years and nine months old when her brother joined the army). Additionally Salem, Frank's grandfather, remembers that the murdered man's son had been spirited out of town ten or fifteen years earlier. Ten is unlikely, since Frank would have been fourteen and no longer the little boy he remembers. Given other references, fourteen or fifteen is more likely. That would make Frank nine or ten and his sister five or six at the time of the incident.

7. Toni Morrison, *Home* (New York: Knopf, 2012), 34. Subsequent references will appear in parentheses in the text.

8. Emma Brockes, "I Want to Feel What I Feel. Even If It's Not Happiness," *The Guardian* (April 13, 2012), http://www.guardian.co.uk/books/2012/apr/13/toni-morrison-home-son-love.

9. Brockes, "I Want to Feel."

10. Shea, "Toni Morrison on *Home*."

11. Toni Morrison, "On Point with Tom Ashbrook," *On Point*, WBUR (May 11, 2012).

12. Larry Tye, *Rising from the Rails: Pullman Porters and the Making of the Black Middle Class* (New York: Henry Holt, Owl Books, 2004), 13.

13. Carolyn C. Denard, "Blacks, Modernism, and the American South: An Interview with Toni Morrison," *Studies in the Literary Imagination* 31, no. 2 (Fall 1998): 2. Rpt. in *Toni Morrison: Conversations*, ed. Carolyn C. Denard (Jackson: University Press of Mississippi, 2008), 178–95.

14. Catherine Jones, "Southern Landscape as Psychic Landscape in Morrison's Fiction," *Studies in the Literary Imagination* 31, no. 2 (Fall 1998): 46.

15. Lucille Fultz, "Southern Ethos/Black Ethics in Morrison's Fiction," *Studies in the Literary Imagination* 31, no. 2 (Fall 1998), 85.

16. Jones, "Southern Landscape as Psychic Landscape."

17. Denard, "Blacks," 15.

18. Denard, "Blacks," 3.

19. Denard, "Blacks," 11.

20. This discussion of narrative strategy in the novel is part of a longer analysis in my essay "Telling Stories: Evolving Narrative Identity in Toni Morrison's *Home*," forthcoming.

21. Michael Silverblatt, "Interview with Toni Morrison on *Love*," *Bookworm*, KCRW Radio (February 12, 2004).

22. Shlomith Rimmon-Kenan, *Narrative Fiction: Contemporary Poetics* (Florence, N.Y.: Routledge, 1983), 73.

23. Jian Ghomeshi, "Toni Morrison on Her Two Selves," *Q*, CBC News (May 24, 2012).

24. Shea, "Toni Morrison on *Home*."

25. Shea, "Toni Morrison on *Home*."

26. Susan Stanford Friedman, "Spatialization: A Strategy for Reading Narrative," *Narrative* 1, no. 1 (1993): 14.

27. Friedman, "Spatialization," 14.

28. Christopher Bollen, *Interview Magazine* (June 15, 2012).

29. Dan P. McAdams, "Narrative Identity," in *Handbook of Identity and Research*, ed. Seth J. Schwartz, Koen Luyckx, and Vivian L. Vignoles (New York: Springer, 2011), 1: 103.

30. Toni Morrison, "Lecture and Speech of Acceptance, upon the Award of the Nobel Prize for Literature," *The Nobel Lecture in Literature* (New York: Knopf, 1994), 22.

31. William James, *The Principles of Psychology* (New York: Henry Holt, 1890), 371.

32. McAdams, "Narrative Identity," 103.

33. Robin D. G. Kelley, "The Riddle of the Zoot: Malcolm Little and Black Cultural Politics during World War II," in *Generations of Youth: Youth Cultures and History in Twentieth- Century America*, ed. Joe Austin and Michael Nevin Willard (New York: New York University Press, 1998), 137–38.

34. See Malcolm X and Alex Haley, *The Autobiography of Malcolm X* (New York: Grove Press, 1965).

35. Toni Morrison, "Interview with Jeffrey Brown," *PBS NewsHour* (May 29, 2012).

36. Toni Morrison, "Interview with Charlie Rose," CBS (May 28, 2012).

Chapter 11—Literary and Social Criticism

1. Toni Morrison, *Playing in the Dark: Whiteness and the Literary Imagination* (Cambridge, Mass.: Harvard University Press, 1992) viii. Subsequent references will appear in parentheses in the text.

2. Morrison is quoting Bernard Bailyn, *Voyagers to the West: A Passage in the Peopling of America on the Eve of the Revolution* (New York: Knopf, 1986), 488–92.

3. See Mark Edmundson, "Literature in Living Color," *Book World* (June 7, 1992).

4. Toni Morrison, "Recitatif," in *Confirmation: An Anthology of African American Women,* ed. Amiri Baraka and Amina Baraka (New York: William Morrow, 1983), xi.

5. A. J. Verdelle, "Loose Magic: Interview with Toni Morrison," *Double Take* 4, no. 3 (Summer 1998): 121–28. Rpt. in *Toni Morrison: Conversations,* ed. Carolyn C. Denard (Jackson: University of Mississippi Press, 2008), 165.

6. Morrison is also interested in the way race perverts the American character and the American mind. In her introduction to *Race[ing] Justice, [En]gender[ing] Power: Essays on Anita Hill, Clarence Thomas, and the Construction of Social Reality* (New York : Pantheon, 1992), she gives an unflinching analysis of the consequences of cultural hegemony on the body politic. In discussing the Clarence Thomas confirmation hearings, Morrison discerns in the entire episode—from nomination to confirmation—patterns of dysfunction related to race, gender, and class. The spectacle of the hearings was tolerated only because the agents were black, says Morrison, and because the charges by Hill and the countercharges by Thomas evoked two black stereotypes with which the country is familiar, even comfortable: the sexually aggressive black male and the sexually easy black female. These and other stereotypes, Morrison believes, provided an unofficial narrative, a subtext, to the official narrative of the proceedings; for the observant, this subtext of racial stereotype effectively undermined and wholly invalidated the official narrative.

Conclusion

1. Toni Morrison, "Lecture and Speech of Acceptance, upon the Award of the Nobel Prize for Literature," *The Nobel Lecture in Literature* (New York: Knopf, 1994), 22. Subsequent references appear in parentheses in the text.

SELECTED BIBLIOGRAPHY

Novels

The Bluest Eye. New York: Hold, Rinehart and Winston, 1970. London: Chatto and Windus, 1979.

Sula. New York: Knopf, 1973. London: Allen Lane, 1974.

Song of Solomon. New York: Knopf, 1977. London: Chatto and Windus, 1978.

Tar Baby. New York: Knopf, 1981. London: Chatto and Windus, 1981.

Beloved. New York: Knopf, 1987. London: Chatto and Windus, 1987.

Jazz. New York: Knopf, 1992. London: Chatto and Windus, 1992

Paradise. New York: Knopf, 1998. London: Chatto and Windus, 1998.

Love. New York: Knopf, 2003. London: Chatto and Windus, 2003.

A Mercy. New York: Knopf, 2008. London: Chatto and Windus, 2008.

Home. New York: Knopf, 2012. London: Chatto and Windus, 2012.

Short Story

"Recitatif." *Confirmation: An Anthology of African American Women.* Ed. Amiri Baraka and Amina Baraka. New York: William Morrow, 1983. 243–62.

Theatrical Works

"Dreaming Emmett." Premiere at Market Place Theatre, Albany, New York. January 4, 1986.

Margaret Garner: A New American Opera in Two Acts. Libretto by Toni Morrison, music by Richard Danielpour (2005). http://www.operaCarolina.org/content/operas/libretto/207.pdf. Accessed January 1, 2013.

Desdemona, with lyrics by Rokia Traore and foreword by Peter Sellers. London: Oberon Books, 2012.

Literary Criticism

Playing in the Dark: Whiteness and the Literary Imagination. Cambridge, Mass.: Harvard University Press, 1992.

Edited Volumes

Race[ing] Justice, [En]gender[ing] Power: Essays on Anita Hill, Clarence Thomas, and the Construction of Social Reality. New York: Pantheon, 1992.

Birth of a Nation'hood: Gaze, Script, and Spectacle in the O.J. Simpson Case, ed. Toni Morrison and Claudia Brodsky Lacour. New York: Pantheon, 1997.

Essays

"Behind the Making of *The Black Book.*" *Black World* 23 (February 1974): 86–90.

"A Slow Walk of Trees." *New York Times Magazine* (July 4, 1976): 104–5, 150–64.

"Rootedness: The Ancestor as Foundation." In *Black Women Writers (1950–1980): A Critical Evaluation,* ed. Marie Evans. New York: Doubleday, 1984. 339–45.

"The Site of Memory." In *Inventing the Truth: The Art and Craft of Memoir,* ed. William Zinser. Boston: Houghton Mifflin, 1987. 101–24.

"Unspeakable Things Unspoken: The Afro-American Presence in American Literature." *Michigan Quarterly Review* 28 (Winter 1989): 1–34.

"Lecture and Speech of Acceptance, upon the Award of the Nobel Prize for Literature." In *The Nobel Lecture in Literature.* New York: Knopf, 1994.

Introduction. *Adventures of Huckleberry Finn.* New York: Oxford University Press, 1996.

"Home." In *The House That Race Built: Black Americans, U.S. Terrain,* ed. Wahneema Lubiano. New York: Pantheon Books, 1996. 3–12.

The Dancing Mind: Speech upon Acceptance of the National Book Foundation Medal for Distinguished Contribution to American Letters. New York: Knopf, 1996.

"How Can Values Be Taught in the University?" *Michigan Quarterly Review* 40, no. 2 (Spring 2001): 273–78.

Toni Morrison: What Moves at the Margins, Selected Nonfiction, ed. Carolyn C. Denard. Jackson: University Press of Mississippi, 2008.

Interviews

Ashbrook, Tom. "On Point with Tom Ashbrook." *On Point.* WBUR (11 May 2012). http://onpoint.wbur.org/2012/05/11/toni-morrison. Accessed May 12, 2012.

Bollen, Christopher. *Interview Magazine* (June 15, 2012). http://www.interviewmagazine.com/culture/toni-morrison#_. Accessed January 3, 2013.

Brockes, Emma. "I Want to Feel What I Feel. Even if It's Not Happiness." *The Guardian* (April 13, 2012). http://www.guardian.co.uk/books/2012/apr/13/toni-morrison-home-son-love. Accessed August 5, 2012.

Brown, Jeffrey. "In Toni Morrison's *Home,* Soldier Fights War Abroad, Racism at Home." *PBS NewsHour* (May 21, 2012). http://www.pbs.org/newshour/bb/entertainment/jan-june12/tonimorrison_05-29.html. Accessed May 22, 2012.

Carabi, Angels. "Toni Morrison." *Belle Lettres* (Winter 1994): 38–39, 86–90.

Davis, Christina. "Interview with Toni Morrison." *Presence Africaine* (First Quarterly, 1988). Rpt. in *Toni Morrison: Critical Perspectives Past and Present,* ed. Henry Louis Gates Jr. and K. A. Appiah. New York: Amistad, l993.

Denard, Carolyn C. "Blacks, Modernism, and the American South: An Interview with Toni Morrison." *Studies in the Literary Imagination* 31, no. 2 (Fall 1998): 1–16. Rpt. in *Toni Morrison: Conversations,* ed. Carolyn C. Denard. Jackson: University Press of Mississippi, 2008. 178–95.

Farnsworth, Elizabeth. "Interview with Toni Morrison." *PBS NewsHour* (March 9, 1998). http://www.pbs.org/newshour/bb/entertainment/jan-june98/morrison_3-9.html. Accessed March 10, 1998.

Ghomeshi, Jian. "Toni Morrison on Her Two Selves." *Q*. CBC News (May 24, 2012). http://www.cbc.ca/q/blog/2012/05/24/toni-morrison-on-her-two-selves/. Accessed October 29, 2012.

Gray, Paul. "Paradise Found." *Time* 151, no. 2 (January 19, 1998): 62–68.

Hostetler, Ann. "The Art of Teaching: An Interview with Toni Morrison." Princeton University. April 17, 2002. Rpt. in *Toni Morrison: Conversations*, ed. Carolyn C. Denard. Jackson: University Press of Mississippi, 2008. 196–205.

Houston, Pam. "Interview with Toni Morrison." *Other Voices* 18, no. 42 (Fall/Winter 2005). Rpt. in *Toni Morrison: Conversations*, ed. Carolyn C. Denard. Jackson: University Press of Mississippi, 2008.

Jeffery, Zia. "Interview with Toni Morrison." *Salon* (February 2, 1998). http://www .salon.com/1998/02/02/cov_si_02int/. Accessed December 12, 2012.

Jones, Bessie W. "An Interview with Toni Morrison." *The World of Toni Morrison*, ed. Bessie W. Jones and Audrey L. Vinson. Dubuque, Iowa: Kendall/Hunt, 1985.

Kachka, Boris. "Who Is the Author of Toni Morrison?" *New York Magazine* (April 29, 2012). http://nymag.com/news/features/toni-morrison-2012-5/. Accessed November 29, 2012.

LeClair, Thomas. "'The Language Must Not Sweat': A Conversation with Toni Morrison." *New Republic* 184 (March 21, 1981): 25–30.

Lester, Rosemarie K. "An Interview with Toni Morrison, Hessian Radio Network, Frankfurt, West Germany." In *Critical Essays on Toni Morrison*, ed. Nellie Y. McKay. Boston: G. K. Hall, 1988. 47–54.

McKay, Nellie. "An Interview with Toni Morrison." *Contemporary Literature* 24 (Winter 1983): 413–29. Rpt. in *Toni Morrison: Critical Perspectives Past and Present*, ed. Henry Louis Gates Jr. and K. A. Appiah. New York: Amistad, 1993.

Minzesheimer, Bob. "New Novel *Home* Brings Toni Morrison Back to Ohio." *USA Today* (May 7, 2012).

Mulrine, Anna. "This Side of 'Paradise.'" *U.S. News and World Report* (January 19, 1998): 71.

Naylor, Gloria, and Toni Morrison. "A Conversation." *Southern Review* 21 (1985): 567–93.

Neary, Lynn. "Toni Morrison Discusses *A Mercy*." NPR Webcast (October 29, 2008). http://www.npr.org/player/v2/mediaPlayer.html?action=1andt=1andislist=falseandi d=95961382andm=96097293. Accessed January 10, 2009.

Rose, Charlie. "Conversation with Author Toni Morrison." *Charlie Rose* (November 10, 2008). http://www.charlierose.com/guest/view/1690. Accessed August 5, 2012.

Rose, Charlie. "Toni Morrison Talks Writing, New Book." *CBS This Morning* (May 28, 2012). http://www.cbsnews.com/8301-505263_162-57442460/toni-morrison -talks-writing-process-new-book/. Accessed June 1, 2012.

Saur, Michael. "I Want to Write like a Good Jazz Musician: Interview with Toni Morrison." In *Toni Morrison: Conversations*, ed. Carolyn C. Denard. Jackson: University Press of Mississippi, 2008. 224–27.

Schappell, Elissa, and Claudia Brodsky Lacour. "Toni Morrison: The Art of Fiction." *Paris Review* 134 (Fall 1993): 83–125.

Shea, Lisa. "Toni Morrison on *Home*." *Elle* (June 15, 2012). http://www.elle.com/ pop-culture/reviews/toni-morrison-on-home-655249. Accessed January 3, 2013.

Silverblatt, Michael. "Interview with Toni Morrison on *Beloved*." *Bookworm*. KCRW Radio (February 12, 2004). http://www.kcrw.com/etc/programs/bw/bw040 212toni_morrison. Accessed July 12, 2012.

Silverblatt, Michael. "Interview with Toni Morrison on *Love*." *Bookworm*. KCRW Radio (October 22, 1998). http://www.kcrw.com/etc/programs/bw/bw981022toni _morrison. Accessed July 12, 2012.

Stepto, Robert B. "Intimate Things in Place: A Conversation with Toni Morrison." *Massachusetts Review* 18 (Autumn 1977): 473–89. Rpt. in *Toni Morrison: Critical Perspectives Past and Present*, ed. Henry Louis Gates Jr. and K. A. Appiah. New York: Amistad, l993.

Tate, Claudia. "Conversation with Toni Morrison." In *Black Women Writers at Work*, ed. Claudia Tate. New York: Continuum, 1983. 117–31.

Verdelle, A. J. "Loose Magic: Interview with Toni Morrison." *Double Take* 4, no. 3 (Summer 1998): 121–28. Rpt. in *Toni Morrison: Conversations*, ed. Carolyn C. Denard. Jackson: University Press of Mississippi, 2008. 159–70.

Verdelle, A. J. "Paradise Found: A Talk with Toni Morrison about Her New Novel." *Essence Magazine* (February 1998): 78–79.

Critical Books, Essay Collections, and Special Journal Editions

Duvall, John N. *The Identifying Fictions of Toni Morrison: Modernist Authenticity and Postmodern Blackness*. New York: Palgrave Macmillan, 2000. Reads Morrison's novels as reflecting and informing her developing identity as writer—that in writing fiction, Morrison is also writing herself.

————, John N., and Nancy J. Peterson. Special Toni Morrison Issue. *Modern Fiction Studies*. 52.2 (Summer 2006). Eleven essays examine *The Bluest Eye, Sula, Beloved, Tar Baby*, and *Paradise*.

Furman, Jan. *Toni Morrison's Song of Solomon: A Casebook*. New York: Oxford University Press, 2003. Documents and essays locate the novel within its historical context and reception.

Gates, Henry Louis, Jr., and K. A. Appiah, eds. *Toni Morrison: Critical Perspectives Past and Present*. New York: Amistad Press, 1993. Reviews, interviews, and critical essays on Morrison's first six novels. Extensive, although not recent, bibliography of critical books and essays.

Harris, Trudier. *Fiction and Folklore: The Novels of Toni Morrison*. Knoxville: University of Tennessee Press, 1991. Examines the folk traditions in Morrison's novels and proposes that Morrison goes beyond the casual use of folklore to a replication of the culture that gives rise to folk traditions. Devotes a chapter to each of Morrison's first five novels.

Heinz, Denise. *The Dilemma of "Double-Consciousness": Toni Morrison's Novels*. Athens: University of Georgia Press, 1993. Describes an ever-enlarging artistic perspective in Morrison's work that expands from the individual, to the family, community, and then to society.

Holloway, Karla F. C., and Stephanie A. Demetrakopoulous. *New Dimensions of Spirituality: A Biracial and Bicultural Reading of the Novels of Toni Morrison*. Westport, Conn.: Greenwood Press, 1987. A subjective approach to a scholarly reading of Morrison's texts. Each author takes a turn interpreting the novels in terms of her academic and cultural background.

Jennings, La Vinia Delois. *Toni Morrison and the Idea of Africa*. Cambridge: Cambridge University Press, 2008. Argues that Morrison writes out of American, creolized West and Central African cultures.

King, Lovalerie, and Lynn Orilla Scott. *James Baldwin and Toni Morrison: Comparative, Critical and Theoretical Essays*. Gordonville, Va.: Palgrave Macmillan, 2008. Thirteen essays examine the thematic and structural intersections in the authors' fiction and nonfiction.

Mbalia, Doreatha Drummond. *Toni Morrison's Developing Class Consciousness*. 2nd Edition. Cranbury, N.J.: Susquehanna University Press, 2004. Devotes a chapter to each of Morrison's first seven novels. Treats each novel as a solution to some aspect of "oppression afflicting African people" and defines each novel as a reflection of Morrison's growing social consciousness.

McKay, Nellie, ed. *Critical Essays on Toni Morrison*. Boston: G. K. Hall, 1988. Interviews with Morrison, essays on her fiction, and selected reviews of her first four novels.

Nicol, Kathryn, and Jennifer Terry. *Toni Morrison: New Directions*. MELUS 36, no. 2 (Summer 2011). Essays in this special issue focus on Morrison's novels, short fiction, and children's books.

O'Reilly, Andrea. *Toni Morrison and Motherhood: A Politics of the Heart*. Albany: SUNY Press, 2004. Interesting study of Morrison as a "maternal theorist" who defines black motherhood as empowering and essentially different from notions of motherhood in the dominant culture.

Otten, Terry. *The Crime of Innocence in the Fiction of Toni Morrison*. Columbia: University of Missouri Press, 1989. Compact and thoughtful examination of Morrison's evolving moral vision in the early novels.

Solomon, Barbara, ed. *Critical Essays on Toni Morrison's Beloved*. New York: G. K. Hall, 1998.

Schreiber, Evelyn Jaffe. *Race Trauma, and Home in the Novels of Toni Morrison*. Baton Rouge: Louisiana State University Press, 2010. Examines the generational effect of slavery's trauma from psychological, social, and biological perspectives in nine novels.

Smith, Valerie. *Toni Morrison: Writing the Moral Imagination*. Malden, Mass.: Wiley-Blackwell, 2012.

Stave, Holly, Ed. *Toni Morrison and the Bible: Contested Intertextualities*. New York: Peter Lang, 2006. Essays explore the Bible as source material for six of Morrison's novels.

Tally, Justine. *The Cambridge Companion to Toni Morrison*. Cambridge: Cambridge University Press, 2007. Extensive collection of essays on Morrison's fiction and criticism.

Critical Articles

Alexandre, Sandy. "From the Same Tree: Gender and Iconography in Representations of Violence in *Beloved*." *Signs* 36, no. 4 (2011): 915–40. Posits "that in *Beloved* Morrison piggybacks on the power and currency of lynching iconography—particularly tree imagery—as a way to demonstrate continuity between violence committed against black men and violence committed against black women and as a way to interpolate black women's sexually violated bodies into the publicity that black men have mostly benefited from through antilynching efforts organized as legislative campaigns and even art exhibitions."

Awkward, Michael. "'Unruly and Let Loose': Myth, Ideology, and Gender in *Song of Solomon*." *Callaloo* 13 (Summer 1990): 482–98. Discusses Morrison's revision of African and Western myths in *Song of Solomon*, which is seen to reflect, to an extent, feminist ideology.

———. "'The Evil of Fulfillment': Scapegoating and Narration in *The Bluest Eye*." In *Inspiring Influences, Tradition, Revision, and Afro-American Women's Novels*, ed. Michael Awkward. New York: Columbia University Press, 1989. 57–95. Thoughtful discussion of Morrison's placement within the African American literary tradition.

Blake, Susan L. "Folklore and Community in *Song of Solomon*." *MELUS* 7 (1981): 77–82. Sees Milkman's journey in *Song of Solomon* as not only a discovery of individual and family identity, but as an essential discovery of community.

Bryant, Cedric Gael. "The Orderliness of Disorder: Madness and Evil in Toni Morrison's *Sula*." *Black American Literature Forum* 24 (Winter 1990): 731–45. Discussion of the balanced tension between unsocialized individuals—those who are crazy, mentally deficient, evil—and the communities that keep them.

Cowart, David. "Faulkner and Joyce in Morrison's *Song of Solomon*." *American Literature* 62 (March 1990): 8–100. Locates Morrison's accomplishment within a larger literary tradition.

Capuamo, Peter J. "Truth in Timbre: Morrison's Extension of Slave Narrative Song in *Beloved*." *African American Review* 37, no. 1 (Spring 2003): 95–103. Proposes that in *Beloved* Morrison responds directly to Frederick Douglass's description of slave song in the narrative by incorporating song to signal the emotional turmoil of postemancipation community.

Carruth, Allison. "'The Chocolate Eater': Food Traffic and Environmental Justice in Toni Morrison's *Tar Baby*." *Modern Fiction Studies* 55, no. 3 (2009): 596–619. Explores Morrison's "environmental imagination," which foregrounds *Tar Baby*'s African Caribbean characters caught in the intersection of hunger, consumption, and food trafficking. Sees Morrison as speaking directly to the environmental justice movement.

Christian, Barbara. "The Concept of Class in the Novels of Toni Morrison." In *Black Feminist Criticism: Perspectives on Black Women Writers*. New York: Pergamon Press, 1985. 71–80. Brief discussion of the relationship among class, race, and gender, in *The Bluest Eye, Sula, Song of Solomon*, and *Tar Baby*.

Coleman, James W. "The Quest for Wholeness in Toni Morrison's *Tar Baby*." *Black American literature Forum* 20 (Spring/Summer 1986): 63–73. General discussion of the quest for identity in *Sula, The Bluest Eye, Song of Solomon*, and *Tar Baby*.

Davidson, Rob. "Racial Stock and 8-Rocks: Communal Historiography in Toni Morrison's *Paradise*." *Twentieth Century Literature* 47, no. 3 (Fall 2001): 355–73. Locates the novel within the trilogy books, which are all concerned with storytelling as the process by which the individual reconstitutes the self. In *Paradise* that self is communal, and storytelling serves the aim of undermining patriarchal historiography.

Flint, Holly. "Toni Morrison's *Paradise*: Black Cultural Citizenship in the American Empire." *American Literature* 78, no. 3 (September 2008): 585–612. Asks two questions: "What form of cultural citizenship does *Paradise* imagine when it retells the story of American settler colonialism from a Black perspective? And what happens when we read *Paradise* as a text that envisions an American landscape in which an individual's cultural citizenship is tied to his or her ability to recognize the effects of U.S. imperialism?"

Guerrero, Edward. "Tracking 'the Look' in the Novels of Toni Morrison." *Black American Literature Forum* 24 (Winter 1990): 761–73. Explores Morrison's delineation of white male standards of beauty in her first five novels.

Holloway, Karla F. C. "*Beloved*: A Spiritual." *Callaloo* 13 (1990): 516–25. Sees *Beloved* as a revision of the historical record of black women's experiences. Examines the literary devices Morrison uses to transform one woman's history into cultural myth.

Harris, A. Leslie. "Myth and Structure in Toni Morrison's *Song of Solomon*." *MELUS* 7 (Fall 1980): 69–76. Finds myth in *Song of Solomon* to be a universalizing force, which broadens the novel's appeal.

Jones, Carolyn M. "Southern Landscape as Psychic Landscape in Morrison's Fiction." *Studies in the Literary Imagination* 31, no. 2 (Fall 1998): 37–48. Examines landscape in *Beloved* and *Song of Solomon* as both alienating and healing. Discusses a black, southern, rural cosmology in Morrison's fiction that insists upon knowledge of a past that engendered an ethos of "intra-racial and universal respect."

Karavanta, Mina. "Toni Morrison's *A Mercy* and the Counterwriting of Negative Communities." *Modern Fiction Studies* 58, no. 4 (Winter 2012): 723–46. Sees marginalized communities in *A Mercy's* "prenational" period as offering a counter narrative to the dominant story of American modernity and exceptionalism.

Krumholz, Linda. "Reading and Insight in Toni Morrison's *Paradise*." *African American Review* 36, no. 1 (Spring 2002): 21–34. Engaging analysis of Morrison's employment of the "repetition with a difference" trope in *Beloved*, *Jazz*, and *Paradise*, the trilogy novels.

Lee, Dorothy H. "The Quest for Self: Triumph and Failure In the Works of Toni Morrison." In *Black Women Writers (1950–1980): A Critical Evaluation*, ed. Mari Evans. Garden City, N.Y.: Anchor-Doubleday, 1984. 346–60. Approaches each of Morrison's first four novels as a variation on Morrison's singular concern with the relationship between community and the individual quest for identity; sees the quest as an organizing principle in Morrison's work.

Mellard, James M. "'Families Make the Best Enemies': Paradox of Narcissistic Identification in Toni Morrison's *Love*." *African American Review* 43, no. 4 (Winter 2009): 699–712. Psychoanalytical reading of Heed and Christine's "marriage" as narcissistic identification, a dynamic also present in character pairings in earlier novels.

Montgomery, Maxin Lavon. "A Pilgrimage to the Origins: The Apocalypse as Structure and Theme in Toni Morrison's *Sula*." *Black American Literature Forum* 23 (Spring 1989): 127–37. Proposes that, although catastrophe abounds in *Sula*, it is not a signal of defeat as it is in the Western apocalyptic vision but is an opportunity for self-definition and rebirth.

Moore, Geneva Cobb. "A Demonic Parody: Toni Morrison's *A Mercy*." *Southern Literary Journal* 44 (2011): 1–18. Sees Morrison as deconstructing and refuting the early American master narrative in *A Mercy*. Demonic parody recreates the "hell on earth" Native Americans, black Africans, and African Americans suffered in the colonial experience.

Munro, C. Lynn. "The Tattooed Heart and the Serpentine Eye: Morrison's Choice of an Epigraph for *Sula.*" *Black American Literature Forum* 18 (Winter 1984): 150–54. Treats Tennessee Williams's play *The Rose Tattoo* as an analog to *Sula.*

Paquet-Deyris, Anne Marie. "Toni Morrison's *Jazz* and the City." *African American Review* 25, no. 2 (2001): 219–31. Presents the "City" as a cultural and historical repository of both unrealized dreams and glittering potential as expressed in the music and narrative voice.

Paquet, Sandra Pouchet. "The Ancestor as Foundation in *Their Eyes Were Watching God* and *Tar Baby.*" *Callaloo* 13 (1990): 499–515. Discusses Hurston's and Morrison's novels as evidence of the authors' belief in the restorative significance of folk myth and knowledge of ancestry.

Powell, Timothy B. "Toni Morrison: The Struggle to Depict the Black Figure on the White Page." *Black American Literature Forum* 24 (Winter 1990): 747–60. Working with her first three novels, defines Morrison's success in resurrecting the black self, black culture, and the black text, which have, since slavery, been systematically repressed.

Reddy, Maureen T. "The Tripled Plot and Center of *Sula.*" *Black American Literature Forum* 22 (Spring 1988): 29–45. Proposes that *Sula* has not one but three protagonists: Sula/Nel, Shadrack, and the black community. Each of their stories contributes to a central antiwar theme in the novel.

Rosenburg, Ruth. "Seeds in Hard Ground: Black Girlhood in *the Bluest Eye.*" *Black American Literature Forum* 21 (Winter 1987): 435–45. General discussion of *The Bluest Eye* as a long-delayed chronicle of black girlhood.

Schmudde, Carol E. "Knowing When to Stop: A Reading of Toni Morrison's *Beloved.*" *CLA Journal* 37 (December 1993): 121–35. Discusses the novel's treatment of cultural significance in defining the limits of human suffering.

Schur, Richard L. "Locating *Paradise* in the Post–Civil Rights Era: Toni Morrison and Critical Race Theory." *Contemporary Literature* 45, no. 2 (Summer 2004): 452–504. Sees *Paradise* as part of a conversation about the possibility of social, cultural, and legal reform in a post–civil rights America where racialized power is implicit and embedded.

Stein, Karen F. "Toni Morrison's *Sula*: A Black Woman's Epic." *Black American Literature Forum* 18 (Winter 1984): 146–50. Summary reading of *Sula* as a heroic tale about the black woman's experience.

Turner, Darwin T. "Theme, Characterization and Style in the Works of Toni Morrison." In *Black Women Writers (1950–1980): A Critical Evaluation,* ed. Mari Evans. Garden City, N.Y.: Anchor-Doubleday, 1984. 361–69.

Wallace, Maurice. "Print, Prosthesis, (Im)Personation: Morrison's *Jazz* and the Limits of Literary History." *American Literary History* 20, no. 4 (Winter 2008): 794–806. Inventive discussion of *Jazz* as a text with agency writing itself and, as such, nearly able to overcome the limitations of passive print texts in generating and encouraging new critical thought and theory.

Wardi, Anissa Janine. "A Laying on of Hands: Toni Morrison and the Materiality of 'Love.'" *MELUS* 30, no. 3 (Fall 2005): 201–18. The focus here is "love as verb, not as noun." The laying on of hands ritual in Morrison's work is a vehicle for healing and a performance of love.

Wong, Shelley. "Transgression as Poesis in *The Bluest Eye*." *Callaloo* 13 (Summer 1990): 471–81. Traces the technical strategies Morrison uses in *The Bluest Eye* to deconstruct European American cultural values that are hostile to blackness and examines the textual strategies used to combat that hostility.

INDEX

CPSIA information can be obtained at www.ICGtesting.com
Printed in the USA
LVOW06s0306200514

386337LV00007B/10/P